convert. The results
survey are combined
published testimonies
icant traits that distinguish converts to
Islam.

About the Author

Larry Poston is Chairman of the Department of Missiology at Nyack College in Nyack, New York. He holds a Ph.D. in the History and Literature of Religions from Northwestern University and has taught in Sweden and in Indonesia.

Islamic Da'wah in the West

Islamic Da'wah in the West

Muslim Missionary Activity
and the Dynamics of
Conversion to Islam

LARRY POSTON

New York   Oxford
OXFORD UNIVERSITY PRESS
1992

Oxford University Press

Oxford   New York   Toronto
Delhi   Bombay   Calcutta   Madras   Karachi
Kuala Lumpur   Singapore   Hong Kong   Tokyo
Nairobi   Dar es Salaam   Cape Town
Melbourne   Auckland

and associated companies in
Berlin   Ibadan

Copyright © 1992 by Larry Poston

Published by Oxford University Press, Inc.
200 Madison Avenue, New York, NY 10016

Library of Congress Cataloging-in-Publication Data
Poston, Larry
Islamic da'wah in the West : Muslim missionary activity and the
dynamics of conversion to Islam / Larry Poston.
p. cm.   Includes bibliographical references and index.
ISBN 0-19-507227-8
1. Islam—Missions—United States.   2. Muslim converts—
United States.   I. Title.
BP170.3.P67   1992   297'.7—dc20   91-19400

1 3 5 7 9 8 6 4 2

Printed in the United States of America
on acid-free paper

To Linda and Helena,
whose patience and encouragement
have consistently exceeded
the call of duty

ACKNOWLEDGMENTS

I would like to acknowledge my indebtedness to several of the individuals who have been instrumental in this project. Many thanks to John Hunwick, who with his indisputable mastery of the academic disciplines associated with Islamic studies served as a continual inspiration; to Edmund Perry, who introduced me to the subject of religious conversion; to Carl Petry, whose knowledge of the Islamic Middle East formed a background and framework without which much of this work could not have been written; to Muhammad Eissa, for his consistent encouragement throughout my struggle to learn the Arabic language; and to Musa Qutub, who selflessly gave many hours to discussion concerning Islamic daʿwah in the United States. May each experience the satisfaction of being able to trace his own thinking in the pages that follow.

CONTENTS

Islamic Da'wah in the West

INTRODUCTION

In a lecture delivered at Westminster Abbey in December of 1873, Max Müller introduced a system of classification according to which the six major religions of the world could be divided into "missionary" and "nonmissionary." The former designation may be applied to any faith that has as an intrinsic part of its raison d'être the proclamation of its precepts to persons unfamiliar with them, in the hope that at least some—if not all—of those persons will adopt these tenets as their own. The orientation of such a religion is centrifugal; it is directed outward and seeks to expand its boundaries in both a quantitative and qualitative sense. A nonmissionary religion, on the other hand, is centripetally oriented; its focus is inward and its boundaries are extended only in the qualitative realm (i.e., adherents of such a faith are preoccupied with their own spiritual development in either an individual or a collective sense). This is not to say that quantitative expansion cannot take place within a nonmissionary faith, only that such expansion is not considered by the adherents to be a primary objective of the religion.

This paradigm has been used extensively since Müller's time, and Western writers have shown general agreement in placing Christianity, Buddhism, and Islam in the category of missionary faiths while consigning Judaism, Hinduism, and Zoroastrianism to a nonmissionary position. This study is concerned only with Islam, seeking to explicate those characteristics that enable it to be classified as a religion in which (to use Müller's terminology) "the spreading of the truth and the conversion of unbelievers are raised to the rank of a sacred duty by the founder or his immediate successors."

The concept of missionary activity in Islam is subsumed under the Arabic word "da'wah," a noun formed from a root composed of the radicals dāl–'ain–wāw. In its verbal form this word has as its basic meaning "to call," "to summon," "to invite." "Da'wah" thus becomes "a call" or "an invitation," and, in specialized usage, "missionary activity." In the Qur'ān the concept appears in such passages as Sura 16:125: "Call unto the way of thy Lord with wisdom and fair exhortation, and reason with them in the better way."[1] The use of the imperative form of the verb in conjunction with the ideas of "exhortation" and "reasoning" lends an activist tone to the verse, which finds favor with such writers as Muhammad Khurshid, who states that "Da'wah can work only as an active, dynamic, progressive force, or it is no Da'wah at all."[2] However, the precise form this "force" is to take in the modern world is currently a matter of serious debate. Isma'il al-Faruqi claimed that "the example of his own life, his commitment to the values he professes, [and] his engagement, constitute [the Muslim's] final argument."[3] Al-Faruqi was convinced that the lifestyle of the truly devout Muslim will exercise such a powerful attraction that members of the society in which he is immersed will be tantalized to the extent that they will take the initiative to inquire as to the basis of that lifestyle.

Other Muslims, such as Khurshid, advocate a much more direct approach: one must verbally communicate the message of Islam to specific individuals and/or groups. The Muslim is to invite, to call, to reason with, and to exhort others, with the objective that every individual eventually submit to the will of Allah. Advocates of the lifestyle approach, while admitting that every Muslim is indeed obligated to live in such a way as to attract others to the faith, nevertheless deny that every Muslim can or should be a proclaimer of the message in the activist meaning. Khurshid, however, rails against "so-called Muslims" who make "half-hearted attempts to absolve [Muslims] of this duty"; in present-day North America those who would side with him in the debate appear to be increasing in number. At the same time, even a casual acquaintance with indigenous Muslim communities is enough to convince the unbiased observer that no more than a tiny minority perceives an activist mission as being a religious duty for all.

Even among the activists there is disagreement as to the extent of da'wah activity. Some Muslims who desire to remain true to Quranic principles find themselves compelled to "call," to "invite," and to "exhort," but at the same time feel restricted by the injunctions that prohibit compelling others to enter the Islamic faith (i.e., Sura 2:256: "There is no compulsion in religion"). The activist may find himself caught in a philosophical tension generated by these seemingly contradictory statements. According to the convictions of some, "conversion" of others to Islam is prohibited as a conscious objective for Muslims. Ahmad Sakr, for instance, believes that "through the method of Da'wah one has to inform people about Allah, His Prophet and their teachings [but] Muslims are not to convert people to Islam as there is no compulsion in religion."[4] Robert Crane of the International Institute of Islamic Thought frames his objections even more strongly in this statement:

> Good Muslims do not even think of conversion ... because the task of Muslims [is] to implement the will of Allah in the world. We can never know what the will of Allah is for any individual human being ... the concept of conversion is associated with the belief that one has a monopoly of truth, whereas the Qur'ān repeatedly emphasizes that only on the Last Day will anybody know what truth is.[5]

Closely associated with this discussion is the matter of the Muslim's relation to Christians and Jews, whom the Qur'ān designates "People of the Book" (*'ahl al-kitāb*). This subject is particularly significant since North America is perceived by Muslims as being a Christian continent with a highly influential Jewish minority. Due to ambiguities existing in the Quranic text[6] and later traditions, Muslims have experienced difficulty in determining the exact status of these people with regard to the Islamic faith. Traditional Muslim missiology has not required the conversion of Jews or Christians to Islam, but has rather accorded them a somewhat nebulous position as *'ahl al-dhimma* ("protected persons"). As such they are—insofar as religious matters are concerned—to be left to themselves. Christians and Jews need not be invited to cross over religious boundaries. But other writers are not so isolationist in their outlook, allowing that Muslims have at least some responsibility to intervene in the affairs of the 'ahl al-kitāb. Sakr, for instance, believes that "as far as the People of the Book are concerned, Allah has advised the Muslims to call upon them for the universal concept of Tawheed, the living of a moral life and that all should cooperate on the common and mutual terms." Asghar Ali Engineer, in a statement made during a lecture presented at Northwestern University in November 1987, goes even further in claiming that although the Qur'ān requires that other religions are not to be condemned, "priests" (i.e., clergymen) have distorted the two religions in question and it is the Muslim's duty to correct these distortions. But for many such a position is tantamount to a condemnation of these religions (at least in their present forms), and it contains a covert intention to convert the adherents of these faiths to Islam. For if the "distortions" must be corrected to the point of satisfying Islamic theology, nothing would remain of the religions as separate and distinct entities. A paradox is presented here, for while seeking to remain open to and tolerant of alternative truth claims, the Muslim is simultaneously confronted with his responsibility to reshape the world around him.

The situation is further complicated by the fact that da'wah is almost never limited to the "calling" of non-Muslims exclusively. Isma'il al-Faruqi set forth the parameters of Muslim missionary work in his statement that

> all men stand under the obligation to actualize the divine pattern in space and time. This task is never complete for any individual ... hence da'wah is necessarily addressed to both [the Muslim and the non-Muslim]; to the Muslim to press forward to actualization and to the non-Muslim to join the ranks of those who make the pursuit of God's pattern supreme.[7]

The "actualization" which al-Faruqi speaks of is the implementation of Islamic principles in the individual Muslim's life. This idea implies that distinctions may be made between Muslims on a scale of "Islamicity" and that one aspect of da'wah is the extension of an "invitation" to Muslims to attain to the "higher" end of the scale. According to al-Faruqi, no Muslim can ever claim to have reached the uppermost limits, for "Islamicity is never a *fait accompli.* Islamicity is a process. It grows, and it is sometimes reduced. There is no time at which the Muslim may carry his title to Paradise, as it were, in his pocket." Such a concept is prone to subjectivity, however, for it fails to specify the authority that is to determine the standards by which Islamicity is to be measured and the aspects that characterize the "higher" reaches of the scale. For Muslims to engage in da'wah among other Muslims implies that those doing the calling believe that they have progressed further along the scale than those who are being called, and in extreme cases, Muslims are invited to actually convert to Islam (or at least to some particular form of the faith). But such an attitude is resented by many as a form of spiritual chauvinism and this gives rise to friction between groups.

In the following chapters these and other questions are delved into more deeply. The study begins with a brief examination of the expansion of Islam during the early centuries of its existence and seeks to explicate the concept of da'wah as it was understood by the earliest followers of Muhammad. The Western world and modern times are then discussed, and an attempt is made to ascertain how far, if at all, the original paradigm has been and is being used in North America. Part II contains a discussion of the missiological dynamics involved in the expansion of missionary religions in general, and these dynamics are applied to the Muslim faith, showing the necessity of developing a particular approach suited to the Western milieu. This is followed by an examination and analysis of the writings of three men who have innovated, interpreted, and applied such an approach.

Part III explores the institutionalization process that has occurred with regard to the missionary strategy delineated in Part II. An analysis is made of organizations and institutions established specifically for the propagation of the teachings of the Islamic faith. This study includes profiles of organizations at different levels of society and of differing Muslim sects, followed by an analysis of the philosophies, strategies, and techniques implemented by these organizations in their da'wah activity. Receiving special attention will be the literature used to convey the message of Islam.

The subject of Part IV is conversion to Islam, which, despite the tendency to downplay its importance, is occurring at an ever-increasing rate in North America. This study begins with a discussion of the research concerning religious conversion conducted during the last ninety years and attempts to draw from this a profile of the "typical" religious convert. The conversion experiences of seventy-two Western converts to Islam are then analyzed, and the conclusions of this examination are compared with the profile mentioned previously. The concluding chapter summarizes the predisposing conditions existing in contemporary American culture for conversion to Islam and seeks to discern the future potential for continued missionary activity.

The information contained in this study comes from a variety of sources. General works on Islamic da'wah formed a useful background for Part I, but at the present time there is no source available that gives a detailed analysis of Muslim missionary activity in North America. It was therefore necessary to examine the literature produced by Muslim organizations established for the purpose of communicating to Americans the message of Islam, and it is this literature which has yielded the bulk of the information contained in Part III.

As for Part II, the works of Hasan al-Bannā', Abul A'lā Mawdūdī, and Khurram Murad form the core of the thesis which is presented. Nearly all of their most significant books and tracts are available in English translation (with the notable exception of Mawdūdī's *Tadhkira du'ah al-islām*).

The research method employed for Part IV yielded disappointing results. A survey questionnaire was developed for the purpose of obtaining a profile of the North American convert to Islam, but this approach was met with such suspicion that for the most part, it had to be abandoned. Despite this handicap, sufficient material was obtained from the publications of a number of organizations to allow the construction of a very useful profile, and this material was supplemented by the few questionnaire interviews that were conducted.

The discerning reader may be struck by the absence of references to the American Islamic Mission, certainly one of the most "evangelical" of the Islamic sects in North America. It has been my desire to explore strictly nonindigenous Islamic movements operative in the North American context rather than native American groups, and so this subject has been left to historians concerned with an angle somewhat different from that pursued here.

I

DAʿWAH IN ISLAM:
FROM EAST TO WEST

1

Da'wah in the East: The Expansion of Islam from the First to the Twelfth Century, A.D.

The territory brought under Islamic suzerainty during the first century following the inception of the religion stretched from the shores of the Atlantic in the West to the Indian subcontinent in the East—a remarkable achievement given the relatively small forces that accomplished it. Among the many questions that could be asked with regard to this phenomenon is one having to do with the initiative that produced it: Was this expansion the intended result of tactical and strategic planning on the part of the founder of Islam or was it rather an accident resulting from a chance combination of historical circumstances? Was it in Muhammad's mind to produce a world religion or did his interests lie mainly within the confines of his homeland? Was he solely an Arabian nationalist—a political genius intent upon uniting the proliferation of tribal clans under the banner of a new religion—or was his vision a truly international one, encompassing a desire to produce a reformed humanity in the midst of a new world order? These questions are not without significance, for a number of the proponents of contemporary da'wah activity in the West trace their inspiration to the Prophet himself, claiming that he initiated a worldwide missionary program in which they are the most recent participants. Ahmad Sakr, the former director of the Muslim World League Office to the United Nations and North America and founder of the American Islamic College in Chicago, believes that "Allah commanded the Prophet Muhammad to start making Da'wa from the first day he was entrusted with the mission of Islam,"[1] and Muhammad Imran, a Pakistani writer and chronicler of Islamic missionary activity in

11

many parts of the world, contends that "Islam is ... a missionary religion from its very inception. The Muslims are ... missionaries of a world message and representatives of the greatest world movement yet known to history."[2] Ānwar al-Jindī, a professor of literature at Cairo University, adds that

> the expansion of Islam into these extensive areas on the face of the earth is attributable to many social, political and religious causes. But the most important of the factors which produced this exciting and admirable result is [seen] in the successive efforts of the Muslims which were kindled by the Prophet himself. For [these Muslims] strove in a way which brought people into the religion of Allah. The duty of "calling to Islam" was not a belated idea, but was rather a command determined upon the believers since the dawn of the call [of Muhammad].[3]

Despite the claims of these and other writers, it is difficult to prove that Muhammad intended to found a world-encompassing faith superseding the religions of Christianity and Judaism. His original aim appears to have rather been the establishment of a succinctly Arab brand of monotheism, as indicated by his many references to the Qurʾān as an *Arab* book[4] and by his accommodations to other monotheistic traditions. The original *qibla* (direction of prayer) was Jerusalem, not Mecca; the Fast of Ashura coincided with the Jewish Day of Atonement; Muslims could eat the food and marry the women of the People of the Book, and the prohibitions against the eating of blood, pork, and animals strangled or dying a natural death as well as animals offered to idols were reminiscent of the edicts of the Jerusalem Council as recorded in the Christian Scriptures (see Acts 15:29).

The fact that these accommodations were not reciprocated by the ʾahl al-kitāb may have led to the conviction that Islam was needed not only among the Arabs but among the Christians and Jews as well. The failure of these peoples to accept Muhammad's prophethood and teachings was interpreted as indicative of a backslidden condition, and the idea that religious reform was needed outside the peninsula may have gradually occurred to him. Certainly the Quranic text indicates a change in attitude with respect to Jews and Christians over the course of time,[5] and the military expedition to Tabuk (A.D. 630) together with the planning which took place regarding a raid in the Transjordan immediately prior to Muhammad's death are interpreted by some as the beginnings of international endeavors.[6]

But if Muhammad himself did not envision the expansion of Islam beyond the confines of Arabia, certainly his followers did so. With the renewed subjection of the apostatized tribes following the Riddah Wars, a base of operations was secured and military forays began.[7]

It was not a purely religious advance. It was not a "missionary movement" in which the chief objective of the Muslim warriors was the conversion of men and women to the Islamic faith. Some individuals may have joined in the conquests for altruistic purposes, but even in these cases it is difficult to know whether conversions were desired for religious reasons or were seen as a means to economic and political ends. Warfare conducted under a religious banner was certainly not new in the history of the world, but this phenomenon had perhaps never been elevated to the position which it attained in Islam: that of being an intrinsic part of the faith's doctrinal tenets. Battles had been fought for Yahweh by the Hebrews in Canaan, and Constantine allegedly was divinely commanded to conquer under the sign of the cross, but these incidents were not considered by the participants as anything analogous to the Muslim concept of *jihād*.

The term jihād evokes differing sentiments. For some Western observers it conveys the idea of the fanatical Arab horseman, galloping wildly into battle with robes billowing in the wind and unsheathed sword flashing in the sun, offering men and women the choice of accepting Muslim religious traditions or death. Students of Islamic history, on the other hand, have tended in recent years to follow the thinking of T. W. Arnold, who downplayed the militant ideas connected with the term and sought to portray the Muslims as political liberators who were welcomed with open arms by the oppressed masses of the Middle East and North Africa. Muslim writers display a similar ambivalence with regard to this concept, although recently there has been a tendency to accept military endeavors as necessary and therefore acceptable aspects of the Islamic faith. Ali Issa Othman, a Palestinian sociologist, states his conviction that "the spread of Islam was military. There is a tendency to apologize for this and we should not. It is one of the injunctions of the Qur'ān that you must fight for the spreading of Islam."[8]

But this is not considered political imperialism. There are definite religious objectives connected with the concept of jihād and it is the accomplishment of these objectives that allows the Muslim to justify his militant stance. According to the classical theory of jihād, Muslims must issue a summons (da'wah) to their enemies either to convert or submit to the *jizya* tax before attacking them. Bukharī records the hadīth "wa'l-da'wah qabla al-qatāl" ("the invitation to Islam is essential before declaring war"). According to Rudoph Peters, this doctrine is based upon Suras 17:15 and 16:125, and "the function of the summons is to inform the enemy that the Moslems do not fight them for worldly reasons, like subjecting them and taking their property, but that their motive is a religious one, the strengthening of Islam."[9]

In short, the entire program of Muslim expansion may be interpreted as a measure by means of which the world may be made safe for islamicity. Othman says that "Jihād ... may be a preparation, producing conditions in which people will be receptive." According to Islamic theory, political subjugation was not an end in itself but rather a means to a greater end, whatever the motivation of particular individuals may have been. The political conquests were designed to create a milieu, an environment in which the Muslim faith could be planted, tended, and harvested. Nehemia Levtzion notes that even modern Muslim historians stress "the role of temporal power in creating a total Islamic environment as a precondition of the fostering of the right attitude and state of mind in individuals."[10]

This is solidly pragmatic. Certainly one of the greatest threats to overt missionary activity is the danger of incurring the displeasure of governmental authorities. This is even more dangerous than incurring the wrath of the general populace, for the consequences of the latter can be forestalled by a sympathetic police force. But if such authorities are not disposed to allow nontraditional or nonconformist religious activity, the situation of the proselytizer becomes tenuous indeed. The capture of executive, judicial, and legislative control by those with an interest in missionary activity ensures that such activity can go forward unhindered.

Mervin Hiskett pointed out that "military conquest cannot, of

itself, force men to abandon their beliefs and ideas. But the Muslim
political authorities can set up the institutions which, given time,
will persuade them or pressure them into doing so."[11] The establishment of Muslim institutions, then, was an integral part of the process
of Islamization. Included among these were the *masjid* (mosque)
as a specifically religious agency, the *madrasa* as an educational
institution, a legislative system based on the Shari'a, a court system,
and an economic structure. As Islamic history developed, it became
apparent that Muslim control of these institutions (particularly the
legislative and judicial branches of government) contributed to the
progress of Islamization, even though these structures were not used
to impose Islam *directly* upon the people. Levtzion notes that "direct
intervention of the political authorities in exerting pressure or
bestowing favors was somewhat limited and sporadic. It certainly cannot explain the conversion of the majority of the people
in territories under Muslim rule."[12] Political conquest and the
establishment of Muslim institutions were thus only preludes to the
introduction of true missionary activity. How and when did this
occur?

Of supreme importance was the establishment of contact between the non-Muslim population and adherents of the Islamic
faith. This was retarded somewhat by the early tendency to isolate
the *mujāhidūn* (the Muslim participants in the jihāds) in specially
built towns such as Basra, Kūfa, Fustāt, and Qayrawān. These
garrison cities were built for the purpose of keeping the Muslim
warriors (a tiny minority in the midst of the conquered peoples)
from intermingling too quickly and too freely with the local populations, thus minimizing the risk that the new religion would be
absorbed by indigenous traditions. Hodgson adds another reason
for this tactic: "Centered on its mosque and kept in order by its
commander, each garrison town formed a self-sufficient Muslim
community, dominating and living from the district under its military
control; in the process *it molded its own people into an Islamic
pattern.*"[13]

Islam was, after all, still comparatively new to many of the
mujāhidūn and a large number must have been highly susceptible
to the temptations usually associated with conquest: pillage and rape
on the one hand, assimilation into the native culture on the other.
Neither of these would serve the purposes of a religious conquest. In

the first case the relational distance between the invaders and the invaded would be increased to the point where transmission of religious precepts would be impossible; in the second, necessary relational distance would be erased, yielding the same result.

After it was sufficiently demonstrated that Islam could be practiced and maintained in territories far removed from the environs of the Ka'ba and the tomb of the Prophet, the garrison towns were gradually opened up. Fustāt was disbanded and its inhabitants dispersed under 'Abd al-Azīz b. Marwan (ca. A.D. 700). Kūfa and Basra became flourishing trade centers. Intermingling began between Muslims and natives and the true process of conversion was begun. "The amsar [, which were] strongholds of Arab segregation." says Levtzion, "became centers of acculturation in which the indigenous population adopted the Arabic language and converted to Islam." What he calls an "Islamic ambience" was created; a surrounding, all-encompassing atmosphere of Muslim religiosity that eventually appeared in every institution and at every level of society.

This ambience gave to the Muslim proselytizer a distinct psychological advantage. In conquered lands the Muslim could always speak from a position of power. This is in stark contrast to the situation of Christian and Buddhist missionaries, who were often forced to testify in groveling submission before the authorities of China, Japan, and other countries. In certain geographical locations Muslims were considered superior because of their literacy, their powers of magic and healing, and their wealth. Here again is seen a contrast with Christian and Buddhist proselytizers, who were considered "running dogs" and "foreign devils"—in short, supremely *inferior* peoples.

Commerce was another factor in the early expansion of Islam. Non-Muslims often converted for quite mundane reasons: for instance, "a non-Muslim who desires to expand his trade beyond a certain limit must convert in order to be admitted to the credit system. A trader's credit is higher if he exhibits orthodoxy and strictly observes the precepts of Islam."[14] In these cases it was not the Muslim trader's theological convictions that won a convert but rather his conformity to a certain Islamic lifestyle orientation. Levtzion says that indigenous traditional accounts hardly mention traders as agents of Islamization ... it seems that traders were not themselves engaged in the propagation of Islam. They were accompanied or followed by Muslim divines, professional men of religion, who rendered religious services to the traders in the caravans or to the newly established commercial communities.[15]

But this does not imply that the traders played no role at all in Islamization; it means only that they were not itinerant preachers. Although the actual precepts of the religion may have been proclaimed by "Muslim divines," the indigenous populations were better able to identify with the lay-oriented lifestyles of the traders.

In the activity of "the professionals" who accompanied the traders, a new phase is seen in the expansion of Islam in which adaptation and contextualization of Islamic precepts took place in the course of proselytization efforts. The use of amulets and other such items involved adaptations of the Muslim faith to indigenous beliefs. Levtzion believes that such phenomena were concessions to pagan culture (and therefore violations of the original spirit of Islam) but were usually of a temporary nature. J. O. Hunwick, however, interprets them differently, noting that "the making of Qur'anic amulets and the use of Qur'anic verses in healing is approved by almost all Muslim authorities and is considered to have been sanctioned by the Prophet."[16] They represented neither concessions nor accommodations but rather absorptions of facets of alien cultures.

While trading associations played a part in advancing Islam outside of the conquered territories, this was a somewhat limited expansion. It was not until the advent of Sufism that Islam began to make significant incursions into non-Muslim territories. It would have been difficult to predict that this phenomenon, which traces its origins to the eighth century but which did not gather historical momentum until the tenth, would come to have such socially radical consequences, for its ethos was based upon a decidedly antisocial point of view. Those aspects of Muslim political, economic, and cultural authority which formed the framework for conversion to Islam were precisely the aspects to which the Sufis raised strong objections. A politicized Islam was for them not Islam at all, but rather represented a corruption of the founder's teachings.[17] Early Sufis such as al-Hasan al-Basrī, Mālik ibn Dīnār, and Muhammad ibn Wāsi began to disengage themselves from the political and social order in which they were immersed and sought instead to pursue God by esoteric and individualistic means. Such an emphasis would not seem to allow for social interaction, and this is borne out in the biographies of some of these early figures, who, in the tradition of Christian monks, withdrew from society. Sufis were not always as missionary-minded as they sometimes have been portrayed.

Despite the antisocial tendencies inherent in Sufism and the propensity of some authors to overrate the influence of the movement in certain geographical areas, it did play a vital role in the spread of Islam outside the Muslim world, particularly in northern and eastern Africa. Once the antisocial attitudes were overcome, ideas intrinsic to the Sufi ethos gave both motivation and impetus for outreach. One of the most important of these was the previously mentioned conviction that the political, social, and economic structures which Islam had produced had deviated from the precepts of the Qur'ān. Consequently, Muslims who were involved with these structures were flirting with "worldly matters." Sufis believed that this "worldliness' on the part of Muslims was certain to result eventually in the judgment of God upon the community. The experiences of the Israelites after the division of the Hebrew kingdom in 931 B. C. were interpreted as a solemn warning applicable to Muslims as well. Reynold Nicholson describes the somewhat paradoxical effect such views had upon Sufi activities:

> An overwhelming consciousness of sin, combined with a dread ... of Judgement Day and the torments of Hell-fire, so vividly painted in the Koran, drove them to seek salvation in flight from the world. On the other hand, the Koran warned them that salvation depended entirely on the inscrutable will of Allah. ... Their fate was inscribed on the eternal tables of His providence; nothing could alter it. Only this was sure, that if they were destined to be saved by fasting and praying and pious works—then they would be saved.[18]

Piety, then, was important. But neither the religious institutions nor the political, social, and economic structures were targeted by

Sufis for their efforts at reform. They traced the degradation of these structures to the corrupt thinking of individual theorists and practitioners of the Islamic faith and it was therefore upon the transformation of individuals that they concentrated. This emphasis on the human element is also attributed by Hodgson to the fact that the Sufis "had inherited the populist outlook of the Hadīth folk, with its tenacious sense of the dignity of common people and of their conceptions."[19] In addition, he sees as significant the movement's early growth in lands formerly occupied by the Manicheans, who, because of their minority status within a Zoroastrian population, had been forced to propagate their teachings at the individual level. Manichean strategy was used by the Sufis—who also occupied a minority position—as a model for outreach. Armed with a clear-cut objective (to spread a "pure" form of Islam in order to forestall the judgment of God upon worldly evil) and a workable strategy (reaching the masses), Sufis were able to propagate their teachings without benefit of an Islamic ambience and the protective cover of a Muslim political and judicial system.

Despite the conjunction of these factors, it was some time before missionary efforts were actually organized. This did not occur until the emergence of the tarīqas from the twelfth to the fourteenth century A.D. Prior to this the spread of Islam by Sufi divines was more accidental than intentional, since most of these were seeking to leave Muslim lands in order to escape persecution or simply from a desire to avoid worldly entanglements by leading a mendicant life. Even the early tarīqas were characterized not so much by a centrifugal as by a centripetal philosophy of mission; 'Abd al-Qādir al-Jīlānī, for instance, is reported to have converted many persons to Islam, but he did not take the message to them; they came to his seat in Baghdād. Few of the early tarīqas exhibited the truly centrifugal missiology that eventually characterized the neo-Sufi reformist orders of the eighteenth and nineteenth centuries.

Muslims experienced their first losses of the territory which had been acquired during the early jihāds as a result of the Christian Crusades. These incursions were minor, however, and relatively short-lived (except in the case of Spain). The Mongol invasions, on the other hand, represented a serious setback for the Muslim program of expansion. It does not appear that anyone has calculated the effects of this cultural disintegration upon the missionary motivation and momentum of the Muslims, for although the actual geographic expansion of the religion had, for the most part, ceased after the Battle of Tours in A.D. 732, the period following could be considered a time of consolidation of the gains made prior to that defeat. According to Richard Bulliet, the Muslims of the first era of Islamic history were following a plan of conquest and of consolidation which necessitated such a period of nonexpansion:

> What was required to make the society of the Middle East and North Africa as a whole a single Islamic society was, first, the completion of the conversion process at least to the point at which internal threats to the dominance of the Islamic religion became inconceivable and, second, the elaboration and spread of a more or less uniform set of social and religious institutions.[20]

According to this paradigm the entire classical period of Islamic history was an integral part, as well as a result, of the consolidation process. It is difficult to say whether expansionary plans still existed by the end of this period (ca. A.D. 1250), for such ideas are not found in the literature of that time. Saladin's military adventures were defensive in nature. The Almoravids and Almohads added to the traditional boundaries of Islam by small gains within the confines of the Mediterranean world, but in the main they were only recapturing lost territory. Fathi Osman believes that ideas of conquest did indeed remain within the minds of Muslim thinkers, though he sees in these ideas a defensive rather than offensive motivation: "The Muslims of that era believed that a continuous threat existed in some part of the world and it could be removed only when they could impose on the world a 'pax Islamica', which they thought to be possible and necessary."[21]

The process of consolidation, whether it is seen as an essential but temporary phase in an overall strategy of conquest or as representative of an inevitable abatement of the original expansionary energies, was rudely interrupted by the Mongols. The chaotic social conditions that accompanied the annihilation of entire populations were no more destructive to Islamic cultures than were the burnings of entire libraries and the death or forced emigration of a large number of scholars.

If the classical period had indeed been a time of consolidation for the purpose of preparing for further conquests, the process was now halted. Complete Islamization had never occurred, or, if it had, it was not followed by the next phase of expansion, as it should have been. Now such an expansion could not occur, for much of the consolidation that had been accomplished was undone by the invasions.

The advent of the Mongols was not entirely devoid of redeeming aspects, however, for two phases of expansion did actually occur as a consequence. First, the Turkic peoples who were driven westward by the advance of Ghengis Khan and the Golden Horde formed a new power base in the Anatolian peninsula, and from this base new territorial gains were made in eastern Europe and much territory from the original conquests was recaptured. Second, some of the Islamized descendants of the Khans made extensive incursions into India, forming the Mogul Empire. Nevertheless, there were distinct, qualitative differences between the expansionary programs of both the Ottomans and the Moguls and that of the original mujāhidūn. This does not refer to differences in warfare tactics and/or strategies but rather to the motivation and impetus which empowered these new Islamic forces and to the type of Islam that was spread. The very name by which these soldiers were characterized (ghāzīs, "raiders," as opposed to mujāhidūn) reveals something of the secularized nature of these military adventures. This is not to say that Islamic aspects were absent from Ottoman society during this period; on the contrary, "it was militantly Islamic. The pastoralists tended to be prejudiced against Christian villagers while they were more tolerant of Muslim ones ... and the wandering darvishes that pastoralists and ghāzīs alike revered commonly encouraged imposing Islam on the conquered by force."[22] But this "Islam" was not that which had originally been propagated by the early expansionists. Levtzion notes that

> the credal gap between the ill-instructed Christian and the ill-instructed Muslim became narrower and easier to cross, as the "Islam of the babas", already diluted by the tolerance of pagan Turkish beliefs and customs, became still further diluted by the adoption as popular cult-centers of the Christian ... sacred sites and the accretion of Christian feastdays, saints and even rituals.[23]

As the Empire was consolidated, this trend was mitigated by an "influx of cadres of more formal Islamicate culture, bearing the prestige of the lands of old Islam."[24] But the effects of Greek and Christian culture were never entirely erased, and Islam was thus altered ever so slightly in Anatolia by Western concepts. This adaptive tendency reached its full fruition in the secular orientation of the modern Turkish state.

In the case of India a similar and even more pronounced tendency toward syncretism is seen. The tone set by Akbar's government was one of openness and even universalism, an outgrowth of an atmosphere that had pervaded the subcontinent for centuries. The presence of Jacobite Christians, Jews, Zoroastrians, and Isma'ili Shi'ites had forced the inhabitants of the country to seek means of coexistence. It is said of Akbar that he was

> moved by the universalist appeal. ... Even in the first years of his reign, his reforms took a direction that reflected respect for other faiths; they were less purely Shari' ah-oriented than the typical reforms Muslim rulers commonly proclaimed in inaugurating a new reign, abolition of non-Shari'ah trade and market taxes, for instance.[25]

This eclectic spirit extended even to the point of abolishing the jizya tax, which according to Shari'a law was to be imposed upon all non-Muslims. Akbar apparently maintained a profound respect for all of the various religious communities residing in his realm.

Such a concept of tolerance can be seen as a liberal interpretation of the Quranic injunctions regarding treatment of the *dhimmis* ("protected persons") residing within the confines of Muslim-dominated territories. With respect to Christians and Jews this can perhaps be justified, but it is difficult to see how the polytheistic Hindus and dualistic Zoroastrians were subsumed under this category. Akbar's actions appear to represent a significant departure from the original expansionary strategies of the Muslims. Akbar went further than pragmatism would seem to require in abandoning certain aspects of Shari'a law; his power was certainly sufficient to have enforced Quranic regulations. But he was apparently not motivated to make Islam the overriding religion of the region. It enjoyed a special status by virtue of the fact that it was the religion of the ruling class, and this appears to have sufficed. This could be interpreted as a return to the missiological strategy of creating and maintaining an Islamic ambience were it not for Akbar's pronounced universalist leanings. Hodgson states that "the universalist sort of cultural and moral life which Akbar fostered ... was not in itself inconsistent with Islam. Indeed, it was cast in Islamicate terms," but he is forced to admit that this "presupposed an alternative interpretation of Islam ... which excluded the more particularist, communalistic, interpretation of the Islamic mission in the world."[26]

With Akbar the mission of Islam was interpreted in a new way. Perhaps this was a result of the humiliating defeats suffered at the hands of the Mongols three centuries earlier. Because of the success of these pagan barbarians a new view of history had been adopted which hesitated to consider military victories as indicative of the favor of God. History had proven that Islam was not the invincible force that it was believed to be during the first hundred years of its existence. Perhaps Akbar realized that to impose in the subcontinent the stricter interpretations of Shari'a law—which protected monotheists but which took a much more severe view of blatant polytheism—would have resulted in a holocaust of immense proportions. It has been estimated that upwards of 150 million persons inhabited Mogul India at the time of Akbar, and he must have quailed at the thought of imposing the death penalty upon so many.

One successor who was not so liberal-minded was Aurangzīb, a strong advocate of Shari'a law who eliminated many of the innovations introduced under Akbar and his immediate successor. He reimposed the jizya tax on non-Muslims and engaged in a widespread destruction of Hindu temples. He began to expand Muslim suzerainty, and it was during his reign that Islam realized its greatest territorial gains in the subcontinent. Aurangzīb's policies represented a return to the original jihadist philosophy in that he attempted to extend Muslim political and judicial control over non-Muslim populations. But in attempting to duplicate the early conquests he failed to take into account the profound differences between the North African and Middle Eastern territories of the seventh century and the India of the seventeenth. The early mujāhidūn had encountered disgruntled and often persecuted adherents of non-Muslim religious traditions, and these persons were not averse to submitting to a tolerant and protective ruling authority. Indian Hinduism, on the other hand, had not alienated its adherents, and they were not so receptive of a foreign religion, particularly one associated with an invading force. Thus in the long run Aurangzīb's military adventures actually had a deleterious effect on the Muslim control of the country, and by 1707 the Mogul Empire had begun its decline.

During the Ottoman and Mogul periods, Muslim missiology underwent significant transformations. At the beginning of Islamic history a program of conquest had been initiated which included in its theological underpinnings a clear distinction between the Muslim and non-Muslim faiths. Political, economic, and judicial control over various cultures was required in order to create an Islamic ambience that would in turn provide an ideological framework through which the precepts of Islam could be disseminated. This also served as a protective agency for the propagators of these teachings. The message—at least in its fundamental form—was concise, including the Five Pillars, such theological concepts as Tawhīd, and the more essential elements of Shari'a law. Within this Islamic ambience the Muslim faith was held to be superior to all other forms of religious belief; any syncretic tendencies were labeled as *bidā'* ("innovation") and summarily dismissed as heretical.

With the Ottomans and the Moguls these clear-cut distinctions became increasingly blurred. Perhaps this was inevitable due to the multiplicity of cultures which the Islamic empires spanned and to the increasing chronological distance from the time when the faith was established. The Ottomans tolerated the absorption of Greco-Christian thinking into their worldview and several of the Mogul rulers were openly universalist in their approach to religion. Both of these thought trends served to undercut the missionary ethos of the faith.

The eighteenth and nineteenth centuries saw the development of new historical situations, most notably that of the rapid development of Western Europe. The Ottoman Empire, which was already experiencing the consequences of internal dissension, was now faced with external threats as well. Far from being able to continue the world mission of Islam, Muslims were once again faced with the prospect of losing much of what they had acquired during the religion's original expansion. In eastern Europe, North Africa, the Middle East, and the Indian subcontinent, the orientation changed from offensive to defensive and has remained so in most Muslim countries until the present day.

While "official" Islam struggled to maintain the status quo, the Sufi orders were experiencing an awakening. Since their ethos was not intimately bound up with political and/or bureaucratic structures, their organizations were relatively undisturbed by international events. Though political expansion on the scale of the early jihāds was now clearly impossible, the neo-Sufi tarīqas spawned in Africa discovered that gains could still be made at the local level. The movements of al-Hajj 'Umar Tal, Usman dan Fodio, and others in ninetenth-century Africa, are considered to be jihadist, using as their model the pattern of the Prophet and his immediate followers and adding to this model various eschatological aspects. The thinking which surrounded and motivated these movements has had a continuing influence in this region of the world. Here da'wah activity has been closely connected with reformist ideologies. The aim has not so much been to gain new adherents to the faith from non-Muslim communities (although such persons are welcome) as it has been to revive or reform communities that had abandoned "true Islam."

This phenomenon represents yet another innovation in Muslim missionary activity, for the neo-Sufi groups combined externalist and internalist orientations in a unique way. The original jihāds were concerned to impose an external societal structure upon large groups of people, whereas the original Sufi movements bypassed such concerns and concentrated upon the inner life of individuals. The neo-Sufis were active at both levels, seeking to reform the inner life but at the same time to impose an Islamic structure at the level of the masses. The temporary nature of their successes demonstrates that such a synthesis is doomed to failure. Attempting to accomplish both objectives simultaneously divides the focus and the energies of the persons involved. The problem becomes one of prioritizing the one objective over the other. Should the external conditions be dealt with first, as was the philosophy of the early Islamic warriors? Or should internal matters be given priority, as the original Sufis believed? Such are the questions facing Muslim communities in the modern world.

2

Daʿwah in the West: The Arrival of Muslims in North America

The arrival of African slaves on the North American continent is considered to be the first event for which there is reliable documentation demonstrating the existence of Muslims in America. Beverlee Turner Mehdi indicates 1717 as the first year that names such as Omar ibn Said, Job Ben Solomon, Prince Omar, and Ben Ali begin to appear in the texts of slave documents.[1] One might expect that the slave trade, carried on by so-called Christian Europeans and Americans, would furnish an excellent apologetic for Muslims to use against their religious competitors. But in fact such a tactic appears to be of quite recent origin. As late as 1963 a remarkably uncritical account is given of Negro slavery in a booklet printed in Cairo:

> These dark Americans were among the first emigrants to America from the continent of Africa. They assisted the first European emigrants in reaping profits from the land of the vast America, especially in the southern states. ... Among them were some who traveled to the Northern states and settled there, working side by side with white Americans in various and sundry fields of commerce, industry and agriculture.[2]

The author of this statement was for a time the director of the Federation of Islamic Associations of the United States and Canada and served on the board of directors of the Islamic Center in Washington, D.C. He was perhaps desirous of fostering better relations between Americans and Egyptians and chose to interpret history somewhat benevolently for that reason. The late Temple University professor Ismaʿil al-Faruqi, however, handed down a much harsher judgment in an essay which appeared in 1983. He viewed the institution of slavery as particularly restrictive: "The climate of slavery was not one in which Muslims could perpetuate their religion or culture. Slave masters gave the slaves their own names, forced them into their own faith, and rejoiced in seeing in them the reflection of themselves."[3]

Al-Faruqi is correct in asserting that Muslim slaves were unable to propagate their religion. Any attempts to perform da'wah activity were immediately stifled, and the Muslim faith was thus absorbed into the American milieu and dissipated.

Voluntary migrations of Muslims to North America did not begin before the last quarter of the nineteenth century. According to Yvonne Haddad and Adair Lummis, the time span from 1875 to 1912 was the first of five major "waves" of immigration. The first wave consisted mainly of single individuals or nuclear families who were either fleeing from deteriorating political situations or seeking an improved economic environment. The majority were Arabs from rural sections of Syria, Jordan, Palestine, and Lebanon. Being for the most part unskilled and uneducated workers and hampered by the language barrier, these immigrants were forced to work in factories and mines or as peddlers. Some were successful and returned to the Middle East, but most remained and began to form Muslim communities in urban settings.

The second period was from 1918 to 1922. Immigration at this time was attributable to the chaotic conditions prevailing in eastern Europe and the Middle East following World War I. Muslims arriving in America during these years and during the third period (1930–1938) were in the main relatives and acquaintances of the earlier immigrants. Improved communications media facilitated contact between America and the various homelands, and reports of the economic promise of the United States proved to be as attractive to Muslims as they had been to Europeans. As al-Faruqi notes, "For two hundred years the image of America in the minds of Muslims was one of a haven where the persecuted could lead lives of religious freedom and piety and where they could earn from God's bounty to feed and clothe themselves and their families."[4]

The fourth wave followed World War II, another time of upheaval characterized by massive displacement of peoples. This period saw the entrance into American culture of not only persons from the Middle East but from India, Pakistan, eastern Europe, the Soviet

Union, and other countries of the Muslim world as well. And whereas nearly all earlier immigrants had come from rural environments and from the uneducated, lower classes of society,

> a growing number were the children of the ruling elites in various countries, mostly urban in background, educated, and Westernized prior to their arrival in the United States. They came to America as refugees or in quest of a better life, higher education, or advanced technical training and specialized work opportunities, as well as for ideological fulfillment.[5]

This is significant, for the new arrivals were able to approach life in the United States differently than previous individuals had been equipped to do. Whereas earlier immigrants were forced by circumstances to assimilate into American society in order to ensure their economic survival, later arrivals were not so dependent upon such considerations, having adequate financial resources of their own. The new immigrants had the luxury of more leisure time than previous Muslim immigrants had enjoyed and they more easily avoided excessive absorption into the culture.

The most recent wave of immigration is continuing today. It began in 1967 following President Lyndon Johnson's relaxation of immigration quotas as part of his "Great Society" project and consists of mostly wealthy or middle-class individuals and families. Many are highly educated professionals from Pakistan in particular and the Arab world in general: most of the remainder are semiskilled workers from Yemen, Lebanon, and Iran.

It is difficult to compose a profile of Muslims in contemporary North America. They are one of the least studied (and consequently least understood) of the minority populations. The first reason for this lack of information is that until 1967 they were actually so few in number that the interest of researchers was not aroused. Second, Muslim immigrants for the most part do not clump together in ghettolike enclaves. Although certain cities such as New York, Detroit, and Chicago have become widely known for their Muslim populations, the Muslims have tended to disperse themselves throughout an entire metropolitan area rather than confine themselves to a particular locale. Such demographics do not facilitate research efforts. Third, until quite recently the majority of Muslims in the United States were members of the "Black Muslim" sects, and Islam in America has therefore tended to be considered an aspect of Black sociology and history rather than an aspect of American sociology and history in general.

This situation is changing rapidly. The entanglement of the United States in Middle Eastern affairs has created a widespread interest in Islam among Americans of all social and educational backgrounds. The proliferation of television and radio programs as well as newspaper and magazine articles has served to inform the general populace concerning the most fundamental aspects of the Muslim faith. At the same time, Muslims residing in the United States have been emboldened by this rising interest and have exhibited a renewed pride in their ethnic and religious heritages. They have also become concerned with both the quality and accuracy of the media's presentation of Muslims and Islam and have become increasingly vocal in their attempts to correct what they perceive to be intentional or unintentional distortions in the reporting.

Haddad and Lummis note in their recent study that estimates with regard to the Muslim population of the United States range from under seven hundred thousand to nine million—a striking example of the lack of reliable information. They regard three million to be an accurate estimate, but demographic information presented at the Islamic Society of North America's September 1987 conference held in Peoria, Illinois, would indicate a figure of closer to five million.

Adherents of the Islamic faith in North America come from more than sixty countries. The Arab community presently numbers some two million persons, of whom more than half are "well-assimilated third and fourth generation descendants of immigrants who arrived between 1875 and 1940."[6] These are considered by Lois Gottesman to be the most devout of the Muslims.[7] The Turks, who number approximately one hundred thousand, are considered to be the most secularized of the immigrants.

The interest which Muslim countries display toward their expatriates residing in North America varies considerably. During the 1950s and 1960s Egypt occupied the most influential position, being deeply involved in the establishment of the Federation of Islamic Associations and the Islamic Cultural Center in Washington, D.C. This influence took the form of substantial contributions of both money and personnel. Following the Nasser regime, however, Egypt became preoccupied with other matters, and the place of preeminence with respect to influence in America has in recent years been shared by Saudi Arabia and Pakistan. The former, for example, announced grants in 1978 totaling over three million dollars for building projects in North America. This is in addition to the substantial backing which it has given to Rabita al-Alam al-Islamī (The Muslim World League), founded in Mecca in 1962 to function as a support and service organization for Islamic endeavors on a worldwide scale.

Nearly all North American Muslims live in large metropolitan areas. Many remained in New York City upon their arrival from the Middle East and Europe; most, however, eventually moved westward. The cities of Detroit, Dearborn, Toledo, and Chicago provided work for the unskilled and semiskilled, and populations of more than three hundred thousand are found in each of these cities today. Some moved south from New York to eastern Pennsylvania, northern Virginia, and North Carolina, and others concluded their journeys at the Pacific Ocean in the cities of Los Angeles and San Francisco. It appears that very few settled in the Deep South or in the Pacific Northwest.

An urban orientation has also been characteristic of Canadian Muslims, the majority of whom have chosen as their homes the cities of Toronto, Montreal, Edmonton, Calgary, Halifax, Ottawa, and Vancouver. These number perhaps one hundred thousand and distinguish themselves from their brethren in the United States by the fact that threefifths of them are foreign born. The ethnic proportions of Canadian Muslims parallel those noted previously as characteristic of Muslims in the United States.

Shiʿites are not numerous in North America. Worldwide they form some 10–12 percent of the Muslim population, but in the Western Hemisphere the proportion is smaller. Gottesman estimates that there are no more than three hundred thousand, and this would represent only about 6 percent of the total number of Muslims (using a figure of five million for the Muslim population of North America). It appears that they have confined themselves to the coasts; nearly all major organizations are located in Washington, D.C., northern Virginia, New England, and southern California.

In addition to the categorization of Muslims according to ethnic background and cultic adherence, other attempts have been made to classify North American adherents of the Islamic faith. Haddad and Lummis, for instance, believe that it is possible to distinguish between three kinds of Muslims:

> There are those who are liberal, generally secularized, and governed more by collective consensus than by any judicatory or ecclesiastical organization. ... Then there are members of the "born-again evangelical" independent groups, with a strong emphasis on personal piety and righteous living, which attempt to bring both backsliders and new members into the faith. Finally, there are those who are highly organized, with international connections and specific identification of what constitutes right practice. They are committed to an Islamic vision, striving to realize an Islamic order and an Islamic status where religious laws are implemented and where a just government rules equitably.[8]

These divisions are useful but unnecessarily complicated. A twofold distinction may instead be made between "defensive-pacifist" and "offensive-activist" Muslims. These terms reflect a missiological interpretation of the worldviews and lifestyle orientations of various Muslim communities existing in present day North America. The paradigm divides between Muslims who are introversionist in the sense that they are concerned primarily or solely with the retention and maintenance of their Islamicity, and not with the transmission of that Islamicity to the non-Muslim environment which surrounds them, and those who are desirous of transforming the non-Muslim society of which they are a part at both the individual and communal levels so that it will reflect Islamic values and beliefs.

Defensive-Pacifist Muslims

Sulayman Nyang and Mumtaz Ahmad observed that originally, Muslims did not voluntarily choose to make the West a permanent abode for two reasons. First, there was a theological sense of superiority, "which manifested itself in the Muslim's smug feeling that the West had nothing to teach him or to confer upon him." Second, there was a feeling that living in a non-Muslim land was "dangerous, uncertain and annoying."[9] This accords well with Muslim theology, which divides the world into two spheres of influence: the Dar al-Islam ("The Abode of Islam") and the Dar al-Harb, or Dar al-Kufr ("The Abode of War," or "Unbelief"). Only under special circumstances is the Muslim allowed to live for any length of time in a non-Muslim land. Muzzamil Siddiqui, writing in 1986, enumerated these circumstances:

> Dar ul-Islam is the natural place of residence for Muslims. However, a Muslim is also permitted to live in Dar ul-Kufr as a temporary resident for commercial purpose, as an emissary on a diplomatic mission, or as a student or trainee for a special discipline, subject or craft that is not available in Dar ul-Islam. ... also as a visitor or tourist. ... But in all these cases, he is a temporary resident and must return to Dar ul-Islam as soon as the task is finished.[10]

A Muslim living permanently in the Dar al-Harb is an anomaly. From earliest times Muslims did not generally reside in any country that had not been subjected to Islamic political control through the jihād or that was not becoming Muslim through the activities of traders and Sufi itinerants (as was the case in Malaysia and sub-Saharan Africa). Persons living in violation of such praxis can look to no Islamic precept for guidance concerning how to live in such circumstances, a fact which places North American Muslims at a decided disadvantage in attempting to implement an Islamic lifestyle.

Why then did Muslims choose to immigrate to North America? What mitigated the longstanding tradition that forbade permanent residence in the Dar al-Kufr? The answer is seen in the state of affairs existing in the Muslim world during the latter part of the nineteenth century. Many countries subsumed under the term Dar al-Islam had experienced the humiliation of European colonialist endeavors. There was still in Islam that which interpreted military victories as indications of God's favor, as indeed the early jihāds, Saladin's conquests, and the Ottoman, Mogul, and Safavid expansionary thrusts had been considered. Muslim defeat at the hands of the Mongols had been explained as also being the hand of God but judgment upon the Dar al-Islam for the worldliness it had displayed during the high Abbasid period. At the end of the ninteenth century Islam was again subjected to defeat, this time at the hands of the Christian West. That Allah should allow dhimmis to attain superiority over Muslims was difficult to understand, and though the masses were perhaps not so concerned with the theological and philosophical implications of this state of affairs, they could not fail to understand that the Muslim world was no longer what it had formerly been. But rather than passively submit to European domination, the response of some was to exhort Muslims to pursue and overtake the West by imitating it. Jamāl al-Dīn al-Afghānī, for instance, proclaimed his hope "that Islam will succeed someday in breaking its bonds and marching resolutely in the path of civilization after the manner of Western society. ... In truth, the Muslim religion has tried to stifle science and stop its progress."[11] Such a declaration is indicative of the extent to which the concepts "Dar al-Islam" and "Dar al-Kufr" had become ambiguous, for here was a Muslim scholar recommending to Islamic peoples the adoption of "the manner of Western society." Muhammad 'Abduh (1849–1905), Muhammad Rashīd Ridā (1865–1935), and Sayyid Ahmad Khan (1817–1898) proclaimed similar ideas in various parts of the Muslim world, seeking to create an attitude of openness to Western influences. The "sense of superiority" vis-à-vis the West, which Nyang and Ahmad speak of as characterizing medieval Muslim thought, was thus erased by the progress of Europe and America following the Enlightenment. The Dar al-Harb was no longer a "dangerous, uncertain and annoying" place but was instead becoming a model for Muslim advance.

Having thus removed ideological and theological impediments to residence in a non-Muslim country, the nineteenth century Muslim was free to examine the material advantages of emigrating to North America. Economically the immigrant had prospects of attaining if not riches then at least a comfortable living. The political situation in the United States was stable in the aftermath of the Civil War, and the constitutional guarantees of individual rights—including religious freedom—appealed to citizens of countries in which political oppression was rampant. The availability of personal rights and freedoms in non-Muslim countries further served to break down the distinction between the Abode of Islam and the Abode of Unbelief:

> The changes in the political, cultural, social and economic systems
> and their departures from Islam in the so-called Islamic world have

changed the traditional categorization of countries as Dar ul-Kufr ...
and Dar ul-Islam. What was considered as Dar ul-Kufr traditionally
gave the Muslims more rights than do the regimes which control the
Muslim countries, or Dar ul-Islam today.[12]

The first, second, and third of Haddad and Lummis's waves of
immigration were motivated by such considerations. Personal
survival took precedence over expansion of the religion. According
to Haddad, even the most ordinary Islamic practices were neglected
upon arrival in the Western Hemisphere. Early immigrants "were
less likely to be actively involved in organized religious activities.
Congregational prayer, if practiced at all, was often held in homes
or small mosques, and proselytization was extremely limited."[13]
Apparently the early Muslim immigrants quickly adopted the spirit
of individualism so characteristic of other Americans, and this
enabled them to blend easily into the general society. The earliest
group for which there is documented evidence of having met for
communal prayer was in Ross, North Dakota, in the year 1900. By
1920 a mosque had been built, but within a few years these
individuals had become so integrated into the community that they
had adopted Christian names and married Christians. In 1948 the
mosque was abandoned completely.[14]

The tendency to assimilate was most pronounced among the Arab
communities. Sameer and Nabeel Abraham have observed that

> Arab-Americans, with only a few exceptions, have gone largely
> unnoticed in American society. Their lack of visibility has been so
> pronounced that one writer has characterized them as part of a
> "hidden minority". The reasons behind their lack of ethnic visibility
> lay partly in their small numbers relative to most ethnic groups in
> America and partly in the fact that they were generally well integrated
> [and] acculturated ... into mainstream society.[15]

Not all immigrants abandoned their religious convictions and
practices so readily; in 1919 an Islamic association was established
in Highland Park, Michigan; a similar organization was founded
in 1922 in Detroit. The influence of the surrounding Christian
environment was strong, however, as evidenced by the appearance
of a Young Men's Muslim Association in 1923 in Brooklyn, New
York.

Perhaps the most famous of the nonassimilated Muslim communities in the United States was formed in Cedar Rapids, Iowa. The name that it originally took for its organization in 1925 was decidedly assimilationist in tone (the Rose of Fraternity Lodge), but the mosque, which was built in 1934, has become known as the Mother Mosque in North America.[16] Canadian Muslims were only four years or so behind their southern brethren; their first mosque was established in 1938 in Edmonton.

Maintenance of Islamicity was not limited to the building of mosques. It was common for various groups present in the multiethnic society of America to found lodges, clubs, and associations to represent their individual interests. Muslims began to follow this practice by establishing organizations that reflected the ethnic backgrounds and religious convictions of the Muslim population. Shawarbi, writing in the early 1960s, counted twenty Islamic societies in New York City, "each of them established with the goal of caring for the social affairs of the individuals who trace their origin to one of the regions of the Islamic world."[17] Among these were the United Nile Valley Association, the Nubian Sudanese Association, the North African American Association, the Pakistan League of America, the Yemen American Society, the International Muslim Society, the Indonesian Association, the Muslim League of America, the Islamic Mission of America, the Malay American Association, the Moroccan United Organizations Federation, the Young People Muslim Society, the New York Mosque Foundation, the Young Men's Muslim Association, and the Muslim Ladies Cultural Society.

Eventually an umbrella organization was established to provide a platform for cooperative efforts on the part of as many of these agencies as possible. This became known as the Federation of Islamic Associations and traces its origin to the Cedar Rapids Community mentioned previously. Abdallah Igram was the driving force behind this agency, which held its first national convention in 1952. According to the preamble of the association's constitution,

> Moslems, wherever they are and in whatever age they live are individually and collectively responsible to learn, exercise and spread the ideals of Islam, such as the dignity and supreme worth of every human being, brotherhood, and love among all mankind, and the absolute equality of every person before God.[18]

Here the idea of "spreading" Islamic ideals is mentioned, but the general tone of this document remains introversionist, for it continues as follows: "The Moslems of the United States and Canada shall organize themselves under the present constitution to promote and teach the spirit, ethics, philosophy, and culture of Islam among themselves and their *children*."[19] The outwardly oriented facets of this document are weakened by their classification as merely *attempts*: "They shall try, through publications and otherwise, to expound the teaching of Islam and clarify its ideals and spirit." The insertion of the clarification that "in this endeavor they shall try to point out the common grounds, beliefs, and common ends which other religions share with Islam" removes any trace of exclusivity. There is no sense of the religious superiority that empowered the original Islamic conquests; no idea that Islam has anything to say to non-Muslims other than to point out commonalities between them and Muslims.

It is, of course, possible to see such an orientation as a form of da'wah. E. Allen Richardson believes that "the erection of mosques in America also is a way of spreading the prophet's message (da'wah)" and that "da'wah may also include the distribution of informative literature and the establishment of Islamic presses."[20] But it is difficult to interpret these phenomena as evidence of an expansionary orientation, for Richardson himself admits that

> the proliferation of Islamic publishers shows the evolving strength of the Muslim community to provide for the continuing education of its members. Contrary to the popular impression of Islam, *such organizations rarely proselytize and usually seek their market among persons already within the faith.*[21]

The activity that Richardson refers to is then a "calling," or exhortation, to nominal Muslims, not to the adherents of other religions or to those lacking a religious faith. Consideration of such activity as da'wah is indeed valid if a broad definition of the term is employed. But there appears to be no solid evidence that the mosques and other Islamic institutions established in North America have accomplished the objective of reviving Muslim populations. One of the more visible institutions, the Islamic Center of Washington, D.C., was originally planned as a center for use by visiting diplomatic personnel who did not have the required facilities for Muslim ceremonies in their respective embassies. Of the eight stated objectives of the organization, six may be classified as "defensive" while only two have "offensive" aspects. These two are (1) "to make Islam better known in America by way of delivering lectures and issuance of publications regularly" and (2) "to generally acquaint the American public with the realities about the Muslim world and its importance, and to seek to promote closer relations in all aspects between the world of Islam and the New World."[22] The use of the word "generally" in the second point is suggestive of the overall tone of both objectives: they are indeed ambiguous, and it is difficult to imagine how any measurable results might be obtained. Charles Braden says of the activities of the center that they

> remind one very much of the indirect approach made by Christian missionaries in other lands through some of their great institutions, where the intention is less the immediate conversion of individuals from the other faiths than the leavening of the total life of the surrounding culture with the basic ideals of a Christian culture, thus creating a more favorable atmosphere in which direct missionary work can be done.[23]

Braden's "favorable atmosphere" is the same as Levtzion's ambience, but with an important difference. Levtzion's concept presupposed Muslim control of political, economic, and social structures, first at the uppermost levels of society and eventually at all levels. Within such an environment da'wah activity could be performed with the express consent of the executive, legislative, and judicial branches of government, for each of these had a positive interest in the spread of Islamicity. The conversion of an increasing number of non-Muslims to Islam would (in theory) reduce the potential for tension to arise in societies where differing worldviews competed with each other. Braden assumed that such an ambience can be created with its concomitant results in a society not under Muslim control. Here he has misjudged the effect of the pluralism mandated by the Constitution of the United States. In a Muslim country the government has a vested interest in the expansion of one particular religion, namely, the Muslim faith. In the United

States, however, the government maintains a strict independence from religious matters. Constitutionally it can neither establish nor further any religious sect, and therefore the existence or nonexistence of any specific religion is irrelevant to its basic functions. It is true that protection is afforded all Muslims to both practice and propagate their faith, but initiative is left entirely to them. No bureaucratic aid of any kind, with the exception of protection and in some cases tax exemption, is forthcoming. The eclecticism fostered by this aspect of the American system creates a different kind of ambience. Rather than facilitating the growth of one religion in particular, it dissolves particularistic and exclusivistic attitudes and renders it difficult for *any* religious tradition to claim absolute validity. In such an atmosphere only certain characteristics will cause a religion to expand. These include the appeal of size (i.e., "if everyone else belongs, I should also join"), the appeal of similarity (when the tradition is in accordance with contemporary cultural trends), and the appeal of differentiation (when a culture is generally perceived to be in decline and a religious tradition offers a viable alternative). At the present time, Islam in North America exhibits none of these characteristics to a degree sufficient to attract a significant percentage of the population.

Moving from the national level to the local levels of American society, we find the same problems and additional ones as well. In keeping with the defensive-pacifist orientation, several local communities have established private Muslim schools at all levels of the educational scale. This reflects what the Islamic Circle of North America's *Manual of Daʿwah* calls the North American Muslim's "isolationist, introvert attitude, [which is] mainly due to the fear that if they interact with the non-Muslims of an un-Islamic society, they will lose their identity."[24]

In both Canada and the United States the main crisis of the defensive Muslims appears to be one of leadership. Although other items have given rise to controversy, many of these could be resolved by the presence of stable leaders capable of wisely and authoritatively guiding the community. The difficulties connected with fulfilling this need are manifold. First, as late as 1980 there existed no institution of higher learning in North America which could provide a Muslim with the training requisite to assuming the desired leadership roles. This meant that candidates for leadership had to be sent abroad to study at institutions such as al-Azhar in Egypt. Volunteers were few, and the financial aspects involved made it difficult for even those few to be supported. Further, the training received in Cairo, Mecca, Karachi, and other such cities, was seldom directly applicable to the situation of Muslims residing in the Dar al-Harb. Questions concerning how such Muslims should cope with the problems of living in a non-Muslim culture were either poorly answered or unanswered. The fact that traditional Islam forbids this type of permanent living situation meant that no solutions would be forthcoming from the Qur'ān or the traditions.

Muslim countries such as Egypt, Pakistan, and Saudi Arabia offered to provide educational and living expenses for American Muslims to study abroad, but again, volunteers were few. Another alternative was adopted, which involved sending trained *imāms* from Muslim countries to America. Shawarbi recounts several instances from the 1950s: the large Yugoslavian Muslim community of Chicago received a graduate of al-Azhar, as did the Lebanese and Albanian communities in Detroit. The Muslim World League, founded in 1962 as a service and support organization, had as one of its specific objectives the provision of trained imāms to Muslim communities in the Western World. In the early 1980s some twenty-six communities in the United States alone were receiving the services of leaders provided by this organization; nearly all had been trained in Egypt, Lebanon, or Saudi Arabia.

It is likely that authorities in the Muslim world believed that their countrymen would exhibit a "purer" Islam than an American could ever be expected to attain because of the inevitability of assimilation prior to the studies overseas. The importation of foreign-born and trained imāms has not been without its difficulties, however. Haddad and Lummis note that many of these leaders

> are appalled at what they see as the "Americanization" of Islam. Some of them are now pressing for a more conservative interpretation of Islam, urging members to reject those elements of American culture (such as female attendance of prayer services, the consumption of alcohol, or the holding of social events that include dancing in the mosque basement) that do not accord with the Shari'a ... or with traditional Islamic observance.[25]

Harold Barclay gives a specific example from Lac La Biche, a town 140 miles northeast of Edmonton in which 10 percent of the population is Muslim. In 1962 an imām was appointed who was of Lebanese background and whose training had taken place in Damascus, but "primarily because of his difficulty with the English language, the imām has devoted himself entirely to the local Arab community and has made no attempt to explain the religion to Lac La Biche non-Muslims, nor has he been asked to do so."[26] Besides these features, which serve only to increase the defensive posture of the Islamic community, Barclay comments that the imām has been considered much too strict in his demands of others. Such conservative attitudes alienate young people in particular, exacerbating the already considerable tension existing between Muslim parents and children.

The defensive-passive Muslim is constantly concerned with problems of assimilation. The generational problem previously mentioned is essentially caused by the perceived distancing of children from their religious heritage, and the lack of leadership is in part due to trends associated with assimilationist tendencies. Disunity, in the main attributable to nationalistic and ethnic differences, can also be traced to the degrees of assimilation allowed or disallowed by various sects. Some Muslims take great pride in becoming "Americanized." Barclay attributes much of the decline experienced in the religious sphere to the gradual disappearance of Arabic:

> The Arabic language is closely identified with Islam so that as the Arab moves to greater assimilation in the English-speaking Canadian milieu he sloughs off the Arabic language and in so doing may also be sloughing off the religion as well.[27]

Others do not abandon their religion so much as reinterpret it. In Canada "the prosperous businessmen emphasize the common features of [Islam and Christianity] and minimize the differences," and "for some, Islam appears to have become a kind of unitarian Christianity."[28]

The pressures to conform to the secular society are particularly intense for high school and college-age young people. Although social ostracism is usually attributable more to ethnic than to religious differences, the fact that Islam is usually so closely connected with particular ethnic backgrounds makes the effort to submerge one's ethnicity equivalent to a reduction of religious commitment.

Defensive Muslims are thus plagued by a chronic double-mindedness, exemplifying "an ambivalence between the desire to perpetuate the old and a desire to accommodate to the new."[29] Some are attempting to resolve this ambivalence while others appear to have surrendered to their environment and have focused upon other matters.

But such activity serves only to conceal underlying problems. Gulzar Haider has given a poignant (though tragic) description of this group:

> As you get to know them, you cannot help the feeling that this is a curious assortment of . . . neurotics whose past is a painful memory, however romantically expressed, whose present is comfortable and confused, and whose future is a boundless haze.[30]

Offensive-Activist Muslims

There are Muslims in contemporary North America who have not been content to adopt the defensive-pacifist orientation. They are relatively few in number and they are unclear as to their goals, but they are taking steps to remedy these deficiencies and are gaining in momentum so that one may expect to find them increasingly visible in the years to come.

The adherents of the activist group are of two kinds. They are primarily a radical minority who have resisted the melting pot syndrome and consequently have become only minimally assimilated. Within this group is a large number of students from Muslim countries who enter North America with an awareness that their residence will be only temporary. This consciousness allows them greater freedom to deal with the facets of American culture which they perceive to be un-Islamic, since they do not have to be concerned with their own acceptance into American society.

The second element is composed of new immigrants who are being injected into North American communities at the rate of twenty-five thousand to thirty-five thousand per year. Some of these individuals were committed to activist and reformist ideologies present in their homelands, and such convictions have been instrumental in creating resistance to assimilationist tendencies in the adopted country. Other immigrants would have been considered passive or nominal Muslims in their home countries, but an interesting psychological phenomenon occurs upon their entrance into a non-Muslim country:

> A number of immigrants had never gone to a mosque before being in the U.S. and had believed that adherence to particular Islamic teachings is not a crucial issue. Many have found their consciousness about religious identity enhanced in the American context as people question them about the basic tenets of their religion.[31]

The aspect of American culture that most serves to awaken this consciousness is the perceived lack of ethical values. Observance of blatant immorality imbues new immigrants—all of whom are suffering some degree of identity crisis as a result of their displacement— with a sense of mission, which in turn provides them with purpose and meaning for their lives. Haddad and Lummis describe this phenomenon as an awakening to the supracultural potential of the Islamic faith:

> Many of the more recent immigrants are appalled at what they see as the moral chaos of American society with its high crime rate, drug problems and ready availability of pornography. They see such things as products of a Christian culture that has lost touch with its basic values. These Muslims find little here worth emulating, and consequently turn energetically to the alternative of an Islamic system of values as infinitely superior. Thus they see it as their mission to call America back to faith in God and to work for the establishment of an equitable and just Islamic order in the world, which is above tribal, racial, and linguistic affiliation.[32]

Not only immigrants but also students from Muslim countries recognize the contrast between their own and American society.

> For these students attendance at the mosque is part of an ideological commitment to Islam as a way of life which manifests itself in a concern for the da'wa, or missionary outreach. They see it as their task to attend first to the conversion of backsliding Muslims and then to that of non-Muslims.[33]

Muslims of the immigrant/student category, then, become activists as the result of a specific *reaction* to a cultural or environ-
mental situation. Such reactions are not grounded in a clearly
defined Islamic ethos and thus lack coherency. These Muslims see
a situation and react to it without first giving thought as to the
direction or form the reaction should take. This often results in
confusion between partisan, ethnic, and nationalistic considerations
and what could be considered truly Islamic matters. The fact that
Americans do not reflect the worldview or behavior patterns of
Pakistanis or Egyptians is a matter qualitatively different from the
fact that Americans do not reflect the worldview or behavior patterns
of Muslims. Some of the indigenous activists, however, have begun
to give thought to this and their thinking may in the future serve
to give credence to the reactions of the immigrant/student groups.
Isma'il al-Faruqi was one of the leading pioneers in this area before
his assassination in 1986. He favored the fostering of an "Islamic
vision," which he believed would resolve much of the ambivalence
so characteristic of the defensive-passive Muslim. Such a vision
would assuage any guilt the Muslim might feel with respect to his
emigration, for he would be able to see in the political and/or
economic circumstances that caused him to emigrate the hand of
God leading him to become a *dā'ī* (missionary) in his adopted
country. The vision would also prevent the immigrant from forming
an exaggerated and unrealistic appreciation of his new environment. Through use of the standard provided by Quranic Islam he
would be able to understand that his adopted country is not in
reality characterized by the absolute goodness and superiority he
might be tempted to assign it by virtue of its contrast with his former
surroundings. The immigrant would be provided with the necessary
criteria for correctly understanding and evaluating American society.
It would furnish him with a pattern for transforming this culture
into one more in conformity with the will of God.

Most importantly, the Islamic vision would give the immigrant a
sense of mission, a feeling of being personally called by Allah to
perform a useful and essential function:

> The ... vision lays before the eyes of the immigrant a new challenge
> and a new promise, by imposing upon him the duty to call all non-
> Muslims to Islam, and reminding him that in word as well as in deed
> he is obliged to be the witness of God on earth.[34]

Al-Faruqi thus resolves the problem of the Muslim permanently residing in a non-Muslim society by assigning justification for this residence. All Muslims who have left their homelands to settle in the Dar al-Kufr, regardless of the external factors that led to their migration, are to see themselves as missionaries rather than immigrants in the usual sense of the term.

For the activist, assimilation must remain minimal. The assimilated Muslim is incapable of bearing a credible witness to the society around him. He is unable to offer alternatives to prevailing social conditions because identification with and acceptance of those conditions are implied in his lifestyle orientation. The Muslim must in some sense separate himself from American society and thus allow his lifestyle to present a stark contrast to the lifestyles surrounding him.

But if assimilation is to be avoided, so also is isolation. For the offensive-activist a position advocating separatism in a physical sense from the surrounding society is unacceptable, for this would conflict with his role as a dāʿī. Yunus recognizes this in his statement that

> it is not recommended that Muslims should organize a segregated community. Living in a non-Muslim society, Muslims have to exhibit the principle of cooperation and humanistic altruism to the world that is fast becoming conflict-oriented. By definition the Islamic community has to reach out and be open-ended.[35]

Maher Hathout seeks a middle path between the extremes of assimilation and isolation in what he calls "participation." Neither absorption nor segregation is acceptable for the Muslim in the Dar al-Kufr; rather, a prudent activism is required. Muslims are to become involved at all levels of society and seek to make their voices heard.

In keeping with this idea many activist Muslims refuse to advocate the establishment of private Islamic schools. Their children are enrolled in state-supported institutions of learning and some have begun to agitate for change within these schools in an attempt to bring them into accord with Shariʿa law. The Islamic Society of North America, for instance, disseminates a letter written by Dr. Talat Sultan which advises parents of non-Muslim children as to the needs of Muslim students in public schools. Parents of Muslim children are to distribute these letters in classrooms in the hope that at least some of a long list of demands will eventually be met. Such demands include a strict dress code, separation of the sexes in classrooms and in physical education activities, nonparticipation in plays and proms as well as activities related to Christmas, Easter, Halloween, and St. Valentine's Day, exemption from classes on Fridays between 1 and 2 P.M. and every afternoon of the week for at least fifteen minutes, and alternatives to all food items containing meat of the pig in any form.

Political activism on the part of Muslim organizations has taken the form of lobbying against American support of the nation of Israel. "An Open Letter to the President," circulated at a recent Muslim convention, indicts the Zionist movement for every instance of political chicanery in the United States since the presidency of Eisenhower, the latest being the Iran–contra scandal during the Reagan administration.

Letters such as those mentioned may suggest an overly simplified view of American educational and political systems. At the same time, they represent an increasingly vocal minority which is aware of its lack of sophistication and is seeking to overcome this handicap. The following chapters are devoted to a detailed examination of the offensive-activist groups, including an analysis of the philosophy that motivates them, their vision for the future, the organizations they have established to accomplish their objectives, and the results achieved thus far.

II

TOWARD AN ISLAMIC PIETISM

3

External-Institutional Versus Internal-Personal: Fundamental Strategies of Religious Proselytization

Conquest of the world—be it in a political, economic, or religious sense—requires a carefully designed strategy. Haphazard or spontaneous activity, regardless of its prodigiousness, cannot hope to transform a multiplicity of cultural and linguistic groupings of people, for even if a procedure is discovered to be effective for a single culture, aspects of such a procedure would certainly be inapplicable to other, even neighbouring, societies.

With regard to religion, strategies of "conquest" may be divided into two categories. These are determined by the societal level at which initial entry of a missionary agent is made into a target culture. Generally speaking, the propagation of religious tenets may take place at either the upper, authoritative level of a society, that is, at the level occupied by executive, legislative, judicial, economic, and other bureaucratic structures; or it may begin at the lower, subject level, that is, among the masses. The former approach may be termed "external-institutional" because of its preoccupation with the organizational structures of a society, and the latter "internal-personal" because of its emphasis upon the inner spiritual life of individual persons.

In the history of Christianity these concepts have been associated with varieties of church polity and liturgy and provide a paradigm according to which specific denominations or sects may be classified. The political structure of external-institutional groups generally is hierarchical in nature and includes levels of mediatory agencies which aid the masses in obtaining the grace of God. Liturgical practices are formal and highly structured, their performance strictly controlled by officials within the governmental structure. Roman Catholicism, Anglicanism (Episcopalianism), Lutheranism, and several of the Reformed churches are generally included in this category.

Of particular significance is the eschatology of the external-institutional denominations. All subscribe to the doctrine of amillennialism in some form and its concomitant view of the Kingdom of God. According to amillennial eschatology the establishment of God's sovereign reign over the earth is the specific responsibility of His Church. Jesus inaugurated this reign but knowledge concerning it was to be spread and submission to it accomplished by human agents. Such an eschatology produces a worldview in which the religious and political spheres of life are inextricably bound together. Thus expansion of the political hegemony of a Christian country is tantamount to the expansion of the Kingdom of God. Such a view has been present in the Church since the time of Constantine and is most clearly seen in the early conquest of Europe, the establishment of the Holy Roman Empire, the Crusades, the exploits of the Conquistadores, and post-Reformation colonialist activity.

Immediately prior to the Reformation the Roman Catholic church was involved in defining more precisely its missiological philosophy and objectives. The Demarcation Bull issued in 1493 by Alexander VI divided the world into two spheres of influence. Portugal received patronage privileges in Africa and the East Indies while Spain was given much of the New World, and

> in return for these extensive privileges, the kings of Portugal and Spain were to be responsible for the spread of the faith and the conversion of the heathen in their overseas dominions. Ecclesiastical appointments were to be made by the civil authorities. All expenses were to be borne by the state.[1]

The Reformation gave an added impetus to Catholic missionizing with the appearance of Protestant competitors. External-institutional Protestantism dispensed with certain aspects of the Roman ecclesiastical hierarchy but retained an amillennial eschatology. Several generations passed during which individual Protestant denominations became consolidated and stabilized. It was necessary for them to confront the difficulties presented by the absence of an overarching religious authority. Lack of a papal office or its equivalent and loss of a unified church structure with inquistorial powers had led to doctrinal and political conflicts and subsequent divisions. Although Protestant theology ultimately weakened the bond between church and state, in the immediate centuries following the Reformation the two were still closely tied in Britain, Scandinavia, Holland, and Germany, and the newly burgeoning colonial efforts were accompained by religious activity as well.

Modern Western scholarship has tended to criticize the colonial endeavors and the Third World has been particularly harsh in its condemnation of them. It would be a mistake, however, to attribute to all of the participants the motives which are today considered to be unanimously characteristic of them: a rapacious desire for natural resources, lust for power, and the like. Many of the colonialists were convinced that their nations had been divinely commissioned to transmit the Christian principles under-lying Western civilization and in so doing produce a like civilization in non-Christian lands.

Beginning in the late nineteenth century Christian external-institutional missiology gradually surrendered to the ideoloies of ecumenicity (in the theological realm) and of nationalism (in the secular realm) and the mission of expanding the Church to the ends of the earth by means of sociopolitical conquest was either aban-doned or spiritualized. Although the West still today has the military strength to subjugate other nations to its political hegemony, the pluralism inherent in Enlightenment rationalism has effectively relegated religious beliefs to the private sphere. The mission of Christianity has thus been reinterpreted to mean something quali-tatively different from the establishment of a physical kingdom.

From the examination of Muslim da'wah activity contained in Part I it may be maintained that Islam has traditionally exhibited an external-institutional missiology in its expansionary efforts. Although not specifically formalized in the tenets of Islam, a definite hierarchy is discerned in the structure of the caliphal office. Islamic liturgical practices and beliefs, while not imbued with sacramental power as such, nevertheless are considered effica-cious.[2] More important is the fact that the Islamic view of its earthly mission closely accords with that of Christian amillennialism, that is, that a tangible, material kingdom is to be established.

In Part I the strategic application of this view of the Kingdom was explicated: political conquest gave to a country the status of Dar al-Islam. This was followed by the creation of an Islamic ambience, the purpose of which was to allow Islam to gradually pervade the culture at all levels and thus make conversion more socially acceptable than it would have been had Islam remained a completely alien faith. In short, Muslims entered a society at its uppermost levels and extended their influence downward to the masses.

Whaling considers this strategy as having been determined during Muhammad's lifetime: "At Muhammad's death, Islam was poised to engage in mission outside Arabia, but the model of mission had already been fixed in Arabia, and that model was an integral and triumphalist one."[3] By "triumphalist" he means that Muslims always operated from a position of superiority; the executive, legislative, judicial, and economic institutions were controlled by adherents of the Islamic faith. The Islamized institutions helped both to create the desired ambience and to protect those persons who worked to further it. Thus conversion to Islam became a culturally positive phenomenon. Since the policymaking institutions within the culture had been Islamized, conversion to the Muslim faith came to represent not deviation from but rather conformity to societal norms. When a foreign religion does not control these institutions, conversion is often tantamount to treason and hence much more difficult to elicit.

An external-institutional missiology is regarded as the best vehicle for the propagation of Islamic tenets and is considered by Bausani to be the only strategy for Muslims concerned with fulfilling the Quranic injunctions to perform da'wah.

> The truth of Islam is not, or not chiefly, a theoretical truth, but also and prevalently law and customs felt as given by God, and obviously cannot be spread through personal conversion but only through physical conquest of the region to be converted.[4]

This statement was made during the course of a lecture presented in 1972 at the Centre of International and Area Studies,

University of London. It therefore represents the view of a contemporary thinker who is convinced that the traditional approach is the only viable missiological option available to modern-day Muslims. Turning to the context of the present study (the North American continent) the question naturally arises as to how such a missionary strategy could be implemented in the United States and/or Canada. The possibility of military conquest by a Muslim nation of either of these two countries is extremely remote. Nor is it likely that a minority representing less than 2 percent of a total population will succeed in creating a truly Islamic ambience within that population. This is particularly true when the commitment of the minority has been mitigated to a large extent by assimilationist tendencies.

The Muslim who wishes to perform da'wah activity in North America is thus confronted with a complex situation. He is, on the one hand, commanded by his Scriptures to "call unto the way of thy Lord with wisdom and fair exhortation" (Sura 16:125). No geographical or chronological limitations were set upon this requirement and therefore it must be considered valid for Muslims residing in the United States and Canada during the last quarter of the twentieth century. On the other hand, the conditions which Islamic history has traditionally considered to be prerequisite for such activity are neither extant nor forthcoming. No executive, legislative, judicial, or economic control is exercised by Muslims in America and no ambience has been created. The jihād as traditionally interpreted cannot be conducted since it is subject to a police force which by constitutional law is forbidden to favor one religion over another. The activist Muslim in such a predicament has two options. If he is compelled by his conscience and his view of Islamic history to retain the traditional missiological approach, then he must (at least for the foreseeable future) abandon his mission, for it is clearly impracticable in the Western societies under consideration. Otherwise, he must abandon the external-institutional approach.

If he chooses the former alternative, he may justify his decision in a number of ways. He may appeal to the absence of the conditions his tradition requires for da'wah activity and proclaim his willingness to participate if and when those conditions are actualized. Or he may reinterpret the Quranic injunctions in accordance with an ecumenical paradigm. Isma'il al-Faruqi was one of several who

called for such a reinterpretation. His activist sentiments notwith-
standing, his views were tempered by his conviction that

> the non-Muslim is not a "Gentile", a "goy", an "estranged" or
> "lesser" human being in any way, but a being who is as much the
> object of divine concern as the Muslim, as much *mukallaf* or subject
> of moral responsibility as the Muslim. . . . Islam therefore agrees that
> all religions are religions of God, issuing from and based upon *din
> al-fitrah*, and representing varying degrees of acculturation or attune-
> ment with history. . . . Christianity or Judaism or Hinduism or
> Buddhism is hence, to the Muslim, de jure—legitimate religion—des-
> pite its divergence from traditional Islam. Indeed, the Muslim
> welcomes the non-Muslim as his brother in the faith, in *din al-fitrah*,
> which is the more basic and the more important.[5]

This is not to say that Muslims have no mission to North Americans,
for most of the latter are considered to have become secularized to
the point that their adherence to dīn al-fitrah can no longer be
assumed. Hence the necessity of the "Islamic vision" which al-Faruqi
advocated as being the source and motivation for the modern
Muslim's missionary activity. But this vision in no sense is predicated
upon an external-institutional missiology with its concomitant ideals
of political conquest.

The second option that presents itself to the contemporary
Muslim is to continue the mission of da'wah but to alter or abandon
the traditional missiological approach associated with this mission.
The dā'ī thus accepts the historical circumstances in which he finds
himself and proceeds accordingly. Two forms of this option are
apparent in North America today. The first retains the fundamentals
of the external-institutional approach in that it calls for "conquest"
and the creation of an Islamic ambience. The concept of conquest,
however, has been altered from one employing a military model to
one that focuses upon educational objectives.[6] Recognizing that
domination of American governmental structures is impossible at
this point in history, those who advocate this approach propose to
offer an Islamic worldview at the ideological and epistemological
level. This process, called "the Islamization of Knowledge," involves
the creation of an Islamic ambience through American educational
systems and communications media. Proponents of this strategy

have established the International Institute of Islamic Thought, headquartered in a northern Virginia suburb of Washington, D.C. The organization has produced a "workplan" which calls for a "recasting" of all modern university disciplines "under the framework of Islam." Textbooks are to be prepared which reflect "Islamized knowledge" and these are to be of such quality that they will be accepted for use first by Muslim institutions of higher education and eventually by non-Muslim universities and colleges. Conferences and seminars are to be arranged to explain the texts and to provide training in their use for faculty members. A summation of the workplan is as follows:

> Muslim academicians ought to master all the modern disciplines, understand them completely, and achieve an absolute command of all that they have to offer. That is the first prerequisite. Then, they ought to integrate the new knowledge into the corpus of the Islamic legacy by eliminating, amending, reinterpreting and adapting its components as the world-view of Islam and its values dictate. The exact relevance of Islam to the philosophy (the method and objectives) of the discipline should be determined. A new way in which the reformed discipline can serve the ideals of Islam should be blazed. Finally, by their example as pioneers, they ought to teach the new generation of Muslims and non-Muslims how to follow in their footsteps, push the frontiers of human knowledge even farther, discover new layers of the patterns of Allah ta'ālā in creation, and establish new paths for making His will and commandments realized in history.[7]

Though nowhere specifically stated in the literature of the institute, it is implied that the conditions traditionally created through acquisition of control of governmental agencies have to a large extent been duplicated through the implementation of constitutional law in modern democratic states. Muslim control of a country in the seventh century guaranteed proponents of Islam social mobility and access to all levels of society, freedom to proclaim the tenets of their religion and to construct the institutions necessary for the maintenance and expansion of their faith, and protection from antagonists. All of these conditions are (at least in theory) to be found in the United States and Canada today, and therefore

Muslim political control is no longer the necessary prerequisite to the creation of an Islamic ambience that it was in the early centuries of Islamic expansion.

Complete abandonment of traditional Islamic missiology is much more complex than the option described here. What is proposed is the rejection of the external-institutional philosophy in all forms and the substitution of an "internal-personal" orientation. Further explication of the implementation of this approach by Muslims requires first an analysis of the concept in general.

In the brief description given of the development of Christian missiology it was noted that subsequent to the Reformation a majority of Protestants chose to retain the external-institutional orientation with its concomitant amillennial eschatology and view of the Kingdom of God. But some groups were uncomfortable with the continued involvement of Christians in the political aspects of society, since preoccupation with these affairs was leading to strained international relations and even internecine warfare. Following the Thirty Years' War, which ended with the Peace of Westphalia in 1648, the German Lutheran Philipp Jakob Spener began to propose that the focus of the Christian life be changed from external considerations (including political affairs) to internal matters at the level of the individual. In keeping with these convictions Spener gathered small groups of interested persons in his home for discussion of Sunday sermons, prayer, and study of the Bible. These groups became known collectively as the *collegia pietatis*, from which the movement received its designation as Pietism.

Spener's philosophy was one of continuing reform; for him the teachings of Luther, Calvin, and Zwingli were fundamental but incomplete. Their reforms had been too limited at their inception and had not been developed along proper lines by succeeding generations. The break with Rome was a positive achievement but as long as this severance was confined to the strictly external matters of doctrine and politics, complete reformation of the Church was hindered. The Christian *experience*—not polity or dogma—was the focal point of Spener's teachings:

> [He] was intent upon a moral and spiritual reformation. He was grieved by controversy over doctrine, sometimes bitter as it was and

often arid and having little direct bearing upon everyday living. ...
Spener discounted doctrinal sermons, preached the necessity of the
new birth, a personal, warm Christian experience and the cultivation
of Christian virtues.[8]

Thus a major characteristic of what was to become the underpinning
philosophy of internal-personal missiology was an emphasis upon
experience, upon deeds, upon lifestyle and morality as opposed to
credal orthodoxy and liturgical form.

A second significant element was a novel view of politics in general
and of the state in particular. It has already been observed that
Spener's movement arose in part as a reaction against the political
machinations of the external-institutional Protestants. The wedding
of Christianity to specific political philosophies was for Spener
absurd, for according to his reading of the New Testament, preference
was given to no particular form of government and Christians were
expressly forbidden to do so. As Stein observes:

> In compliance with Romans 13:1ff [Spener] accepted all government
> as ordained by God whether it was Christian, heathen, or Turkish. ...
> God's government abides even when the ruler is evil; just as a jewel
> remains a jewel whether it is in the hands of an honest man or a
> thief. Therefore, subjects are to obey even unjust and oppressive
> governments.[9]

The Pietist is urged to operate at a level qualitatively different
from that advocated by the external-institutional Christian. Rather
than concerning himself with political and economic affairs and the
organizations of social control, he is to bypass these as being
unimportant. For the Pietist, history is operating simultaneously in
two dimensions. There is the physical, earthly dimension, in which
kingdoms and empires rise and fall and in which political structures
are created and dissolved. All such events are controlled by God in
the sense that they occur according to the dictates of His permissive
will, but in another sense they represent a purely human history.
God is *directly* involved with mankind on another plane, which in
contrast to the former is metaphysical and spiritual. Within this
dimension lie the truly important aspects of life: spiritual regene-

ration, moral transformation of the individual, sanctification, and the spreading of the Gospel.

In Pietism the concept of God's kingdom is stripped of its material characteristics. Rather than seeking to produce an outward manifestation of this kingdom through advocacy of specific political, economic, and social institutions, emphasis is placed on the internal and individualistic aspects of the concept. Jesus had spoken of an internal Kingdom (Luke 17:21) and had specifically rejected the idea that this realm had a present physical manifestation (John 18:36). The focus of Spener's movement became therefore the Christian life's internal dimensions.

This division of history into separate spheres was not developed further in Spener's writings. He was, as noted previously, uninterested in theological discussions. However, his application of the Pauline teaching concerning governmental authority as contained in Romans 13:1–7 was significant, for it allowed (albeit in primitive form) a qualitative separation between Church and State. In Spener's thinking the two were no longer inextricably bound as they had been since the time of Constantine. This allowed the formation of a missiology that advocated gaining entrance to a target culture at a level other than that of politics and government and which was unconcerned with obtaining for proselytizing agents an earthly security guaranteed and supported by governmental authority. It is true that the Danish-Halle Mission (a direct outgrowth of Spener's educational center located in Halle) began its work in areas of Danish influence, but this cannot be seen as directly connected with political expansion in the same way that Roman Catholic missions had been joined to the exploits of the Conquistadores and as Anglican missions would be joined to colonialist efforts in North America and in other areas of the globe.

The Pietist emphasis upon the internal dimension of existence does not imply that the external conditions of life on earth are ignored. Latourette notes that Pietism and the movements it spawned—Moravianism, the Great Awakening, and the Wesleyan tradition—"gave rise to many efforts for the elimination of social ills and for the collective betterment of mankind." Political, social, and economic structures were not unimportant. But whereas external-institutional missiology had as its primary concern acquisition of control over these structures in order to facilitate individual conversion, pietistic missiology aimed first at individual conversion at the level of the masses. These converts were to be trained in the moral precepts of the Christian faith and were expected to exhibit a new lifestyle orientation as a result. It was assumed that the gradually increasing number of converted and reformed individuals would have a leavening effect upon society in general. Christianization would thus occur from the level of the masses upward to the controlling cultural structures, rather than from these structures downward.

A shift in eschatology on the part of the Pietists served to further their missionary efforts. The optimistic and triumphalist amillennialism of the external-institutional theologians was replaced in pietistic thinking by a more sober analysis of the course of world history. Through Martin Luther had come the equation of the Roman Catholic papacy with the Antichrist and the belief that the Last Days of the Church were being experienced by Christians living during the Reformation period. The Pietists lent a Christological focus to these teachings, and "the expectation that the return of Christ, which cannot be much longer delayed, will be preceded by a great outpouring of the Spirit of God on Jews and heathen led by a natural gradation of thought to a sense of responsibility for ... missions."[10] This belief served on the one hand to strengthen the preoccupation of Pietists with the elicitation of individual conversions, for upon the return of Christ all further opportunity for salvation would be negated. On the other hand, expenditure of time and effort upon political, economic, and social reform came to be regarded as inappropriate, since the coming of Christ would resolve the problems within these spheres.

The distinctive features of Pietistic missiology may be summarized thus:

1. An emphasis upon individual conversion, personal experience, and the "inner life" as opposed to a preoccupation with religious institutions and liturgical formulas.

2. An activistic, works-oriented approach to sanctification and spiritual growth rather than an orientation emphasizing conformity to an orthodox doctrinal standard.

3. Advocacy of a qualitative separation between the spiritual and the mundane vis-à-vis political, economic, and social considerations, the effect of this being the ability to enter a target society at a level

other than that occupied by the controlling agencies of that society.

4. An eschatological motivation which prompted concern for individual rather than national salvation.

Islam has in the course of its history given birth to a phenomenon similar in many respects to Christian Pietism. So many are the parallels between them that the Islamic movement—known as Sufism—is even described by some authors using pietistic terminology.[11] A detailed history of this phenomenon lies outside the scope of this book, but certain aspects of its ethos which find parallels in Christianity are described.

It has already been noted that, just as Spener and his followers severely criticized Christian political activity, the early Sufis evinced a strong distaste for the preoccupation of the Muslim community with doctrinal controversies, a materialistic lifestyle, and affairs of state. Fazlur Rahman noted that

> ascetic pietism received a further ... impulse from two sides: the environment of luxury and worldly enjoyment that came generally to prevail in the Muslim community with the establishment and consolidation of the vast new empire, and especially as a sharp reaction to the secular and none-too-pious life and attitude of the new ruling dynasty of the Ummayads at their court, the majority of whom behaved in strange contrast to the simple piety of the four early caliphs.[12]

Further, the legalistic tenor that Islam was assuming was unsuited to the temperament of many Muslims—particularly the Persians— and "it was as a reaction against this legal formulation of Islam that ... the early pietistic asceticism changed definitely into what is technically known as Sufism with its proper ethos."[13]

From external considerations the Sufis turned inward, setting the focus of the religious life upon mystical experience. In this they surpassed the Christian Pietists, who did not place as much emphasis upon meditation and isolation as upon moral renewal and purity of life. This is not to say that moral issues did not concern the Sufi. Al-Hasan al-Basrī, for instance, challenged the aspiring ascetic to "beware of this world with all wariness; for it is like to a snake, smooth to the touch, but its venom is deadly ... beware of this world, for its hopes are lies, its expectations false."[14] It was through moral purification that the Sufi sought to attain salvation. This purification, however, consisted primarily of noninvolvement in mundane affairs and this aspect tended to mitigate the movement's message of reform by cutting off opportunities for the common man to observe the Sufi lifestyle.

These separatistic tendencies did have one lasting result in that they served to determine the view of Sufism vis-à-vis civil and legal affairs. The Ummayads were considered to be the epitome of worldliness, and the controversies raised by the Kharijite and Mu'tazilite questions produced a positive distaste for all things political, which continued for centuries. Rahman stated that the isolationism which was characteristic of this early period of Sufist development taught that "men should desist not only from politics but even from administration and public affairs." In this way Sufis (like the Christian Pietists nine hundred years later) separated religion from political structures. An external-institutional missiology that relied upon the military jihād as a means of gaining a bridgehead in a target culture thus found no place in early Sufi thinking. "Warfare" and the jihād were advocated, but these were given an interpretation fundamentally different from that which was traditionally assumed. Rūmī, for instance, spoke of "spiritual combat":

> The prophets and saints do not avoid spiritual combat. The first spiritual combat they undertake in their quest is the killing of the ego and the abandonment of personal wishes and sensual desires. This is the Greater Holy War.[15]

The concept of jihād was thus spiritualized and used primarily as a description of the struggle to purify one's inner self. Political considerations were entirely absent. Sufis were consequently able to move outside the Dar al-Islam and to spread the tenets of their religion in the Dar al-Kufr. Protection and security offered by a Muslim governing agency were immaterial considerations since Allah was seen as all-powerful and well able to protect His own.

It was observed that an alteration in eschatology gave an extra impetus to the evangelical efforts of Christian Pietists; a similar event occurred within Islamic Sufism. From Sunni and Shi'ite theologies the Sufis adopted the doctrine of the Mahdī ("the Guided

One"), a Messiah-like figure who would appear during the End Times, overthrow the Antichrist (*dajjāl*), and assure the spread of Islam over the entire earth. The idea that such events were imminent or that the Mahdī had actually appeared to begin his spiritual conquest of the world imbued Sufis with a sense of mission and purpose that was at various points in Islamic history translated into an intense activism and, in the nineteenth century, warfare. This phenomenon differed somewhat from its parallel in Christianity in that it was periodic as opposed to constant. Martin describes these outbreaks of Mahdist fervor as part of "a millennial scheme that customarily emerged just before the turn of every Islamic century (e.g., in 1785–6 and 1881–2, or 1200 and 1300 of the Hijra)."[16] This motivation was thus not as consistently influential within Sufism as it was within its Christian counterpart, but its occurrences in Islamic history were far more dramatic.

Just as Pietist Christians were able to bypass the external-institutional missiology of their time through the adoption of an internal-personal approach, Islamic history has developed a vehicle in Sufism capable of accomplishing a similar function. Islamic Sufism focuses upon internal experience rather than external observances, advocates an activist approach to sanctification and spiritual growth, provides an eschatological motivation, and, most important, allows for a disjunction to be made between the religious and political dimensions of life. Therefore the traditional missioloical approach requiring political conquest followed by the creation of an Islamic ambience is not held to be a precondition for effective propagation of Islamic tenets.

This is significant, for it offers a solution to the problem outlined at the beginning of this section: how the North American Muslim who is convinced of his responsibility to perform da'wah activity may effectively engage in such activity when the traditional missiological approach is impossible to implement. Sufism provides an alternative in the form of an internal-personal missiology that aims at the conversion of individual persons within society followed by training in Islamic precepts, which will in turn enable each convert to induce further conversions.

The issue of whether Quranic justification is available for such an approach is a debatable one, but at this juncture in Islamic history such a question is perhaps little more than academic. Justification for any practice is necessary only when an authority exists which desires and is able to prevent that practice. In the case of Christian Pietists, for instance, their disavowal of papal authority removed for them the threat of Catholic inquisitorial policies. Although there was initial resistance to some of Spener's practices even in Protestant Germany, this was limited and without major significance for the movement as a whole.

For those Muslims in contemporary America who wish to adopt an internal-personal missiology out of purely pragmatic considerations, there is no authoritative body within the Islamic world that can hinder this action. The caliphal office was dissolved in 1924 in the aftermath of Ataturk's revolution, and no organization has since been able to attain the stature necessary to replace or duplicate the functions of that office. This fact, in conjunction with the constitutional freedoms guaranteed every American citizen, affords the North American Muslim the liberty to conduct himself as he chooses.

It was observed in a previous discussion that Sufism has not (at least in a direct sense) been a significant force in the establishment of a Muslim witness in America. I have found no allusions to any Sufi Order in my discussions with Muslims or in the literature of the various organizations actively involved in da'wah activity. Many of these organizations have nevertheless adopted an internal-personal missiology, raising the question of whether some *indirect* Sufi influence has been exerted or whether this approach has been acquired from some other source (or sources). That Sufism has indirectly played a role in shaping contemporary North American Muslim activity is the thesis of the following section.

4

Hasan al-Bannā' and Abul A'lā Mawdūdī: Pioneers of Modern Islamic Pietism

The offensive-activist Muslims resident in North America have not developed their missiological orientation in a vacuum. The majority of them adopted an internal-personal methodology traceable to two movements in the Muslim world which, despite the fact that they originated and evolved in different countries, display notable similarities in matters of ideology and praxis. The first of these movements was institutionalized in the organization known as al-Ikhwān al-Muslimūn (the Muslim Brothers) and was founded by the Egyptian Hasan al-Bannā' (1906–1949). The second movement took form in the Jama'at-i Islāmī, the brainchild of Abul A'lā Mawdūdī (1903–1979), who resided during the first half of his life in India and during the second half in Pakistan.

Hasan al-Bannā' and the Muslim Brotherhood

Born in 1906, the eldest son of an imām, al-Bannā' was from his earliest days subjected to multiple influences. The encroachment of Western civilization upon his native Egypt, begun by Napoleon and then continued during the reign of Mehmet Ali (r. 1805–1849), had produced conflicting ideologies among the scholars and politicians who shaped matters of public policy. The writings of Muhammad 'Abduh, Rashīd Rīdā, and Jamāl al-Dīn al-Afghānī served to increase the ferment. The expanding activity of Christian missionaries in the Middle East was an additional factor, one that was particularly influential in the formation of al-Bannā''s personal objectives for the organization he was to found.

His education at the University of Cairo gave him the intellectual underpinnings needed to produce a credible movement, but it was never on the plane of the intellectual that he operated. Of much greater importance were the Sufi influences to which he was exposed throughout most of his life. Wendell regards this exposure as intensive, stating that he was "deeply under the influence of Sufism and its distinctive disciplines and observances."[1] Of particular importance was a Sufi merchant, Muhammad Abū Shousha, whom al-Bannā' befriended while a student. This shaykh related stories of "pious and virtuous Muslims" and so inspired the younger man that together they founded the Hasafi Welfare Society. The objectives of this agency were two:

> In the first place it invited the people to build up a high moral character and to prevent from unislamic activities. In the second place it wanted to curb the activities of the Christian missionaries who were actually preaching Christianity in the garb of educationists and social workers.[2]

Al-Bannā''s involvement with this Sufi society continued for three years, while he completed his education at a teacher training college. Despite the intensity of this participation he was somewhat skeptical concerning contemporary esoteric philosophy, holding the view that although mysticism had undoubtedly played an important role in propagating Islam during the Middle Ages, it was now badly in need of reform. Therefore he did not choose to work through the Sufi institutions extant in his time.

The responsibilities connected with the foundation and development of the Hasafi society were doubtless instrumental in the establishment of the activist temperament that became his personal trademark. Al-Bannā' consistently exhibited impatience with those who were content to relegate discussions concerning reform to the classroom. In the institutionalization of his activities he intentionally bypassed the traditional institution of the mosque, which he considered excessively quiescent: "Moral degradation, anarchy and the western culture had overreached the city of Cairo. Hasan al-Bannā' realized this fact and felt that sermons of the mosque would not suffice to curb the ever-growing evil."[3]

He began his movement in a fashion reminiscent of Spener's

collegia pietatis:

> He formed an organization of ... students ... and sent them to the
> coffee-houses and public-places for the preaching of Islam. [They]
> asked the visitors to shun drinking of coffee, story-telling and such
> other idle activities and invited them to come to the fold of Islam.[4]

Political, economic, and social institutions were not the locus of his
activity. These were not disregarded but they did not constitute his
primary focus. In true Sufi fashion he recognized that "the essential
step in the renaissance, and more imporant than 'practical reform',
is a vast 'spiritual awakening' among *individuals*. ... A people cannot
be saved until *individuals* are."[5]

Individuals were both his objective and his method; he aimed to
reach men in order to awaken them and he used men to accomplish
this goal. Upon being asked why he did not write books, al-Bannā'
replied, "I write men." The early excursions to coffeehouses and
other public gathering places produced a following that gradually
spread to towns and villages. As far as possible, he bound these
individuals to him through his personal devotion to them and to
their mutual causes. Mitchell attributes to his "personal and orato-
rical eloquence" and "ability to convey a sense of sincerity, humility and selflessness" the fact that he was acclaimed "the Muslim
leader, the spiritual brother, the Arab struggler, the social reformer,
the powerful believer," and that during his lifetime these personal
qualities "inspired a virtually unlimited personal veneration." Nor
were these feelings aroused solely among simple peasants. Voll
observes that the Muslim Brotherhood (the institution founded in
1928 to lend organization to al-Bannā''s movement) "appealed to
more than the religiously faithful rural people and the urban lower
classes. In terms of its activist members and leaders, it was
a very strong movement of students, civil servants, teachers, office
workers, and professionals."[6]

The appeal of the group's message lay in its holistic and activist
qualities. Under the former rubric was a view of Islam as compre-
hending every facet of human life. In a tract entitled "Our Mission"
al-Bannā' stated that "we believe that Islam is an all-embracing
concept which regulates every aspect of life, adjudicating on every
one of its concerns and prescribing for it a solid and rigorous order."

"Every aspect of life" included society, religion, politics, physical training, economics, education, and culture, the goal being to Islamize each of these and thus to establish an "Islamic Order" (al-nizām al-islāmī). Of significance here is the fact that this order "referred to a set of legal (not political) principles which were re-garded as fundamental to Muslim society *whatever the particular form of political order* [emphasis added]."

The concept of an Islamic Order is nothing more than that which Levtzion calls an Islamic ambience. Islam is to pervade all aspects of a given society and act as a leavening agent. The differ-ence, however, between Levtzion's concept and that of al-Bannā' is not one of substance (for they are substantially equivalent) but rather one of context. Levtzion's ambience was the result of an external-institutional missiological strategy which posited the necessity of a military conquest and capture of influential political, economic, and social institutions. This ambience spread from the upper levels of society downward, the eventual result being the conversion of individuals to the Islamic faith. What al-Bannā' did was to *reverse* this order by beginning at the level of the masses and working upward toward the institutions of social and cultural control. The logical order of the Muslim Brotherhood's four main objectives clearly indicates this reversal in strategy from the traditional jihād:

1. Make every individual a true Muslim.
2. Develop the Muslim family on Islamic lines.
3. Establish a Muslim umma (community).
4. Establish an Islamic state in Egypt.

This order of priorities allowed for participation by the masses in the reformatory activity. Al-Bannā' offered the people an obtainable goal, one that would involve personal sacrifice but not of the kind associated with the military jihād. It would involve the sacrifice of time and money, and possibly one's social status and/or occupation. But such items were expendable given the worthiness of the cause. In order to bolster the commitment of the Brethren and to provide compensation for any loss of status they might experience as a result of their association with the Brotherhood, al-Bannā' implemented a strategy that had but recently been applied in Hitler's New Germany:

an appeal to ethnic superiority. In "Our Mission" he stated that

> we are not denying that the various nations have their own distinct
> qualities and particular moral characters, for we know that every
> people has its own quality and share of excellence and moral fiber,
> and we know too that in this respect the various people differ from
> one another and view with one another in excellence. *We believe that
> in these respects Arabdom possesses the fullest and most abundant
> share.*[7]

Despite less than desirable material circumstances, the devout
Muslim is in no way inferior in terms of status, for in the metaphysical sphere he enjoys superiority over all others. Further,
this status makes incumbent upon all Muslims the fulfillment of a
divine mission. Here al-Bannā' revives an ancient concept intrinsic
to Islamic theology, but one that had been obscured by centuries
of varying political applications. This is the idea that *every* Muslim
is in a sense a *khalīfa*, or vicegerent, placed upon earth for the
exercise of a stewardship entrusted to him by God. Al-Bannā'
declared that "the Noble Qur'ān appoints the Muslims as guardians
over humanity in its minority, and grants them the right of suzerainty
and dominion over the world in order to carry out this sublime
commission." Muslims are not to be content with obtaining for
themselves a comfortable existence and a measure of earthly security
but are rather to be prepared to forgo these luxuries for the sake
of the mission to which they are called: "The Muslim makes his lot
in this world subordinate to his mission, so that he may gain the
next world as a reward for his self-sacrifice."

The individual Muslim is thus assured that his efforts will not go
unrewarded. If tangible consequences are not seen in this life, they
surely will be evident in the next. On the strength of these assurances,
Muslims are to expend themselves in attempting to establish the
Islamic Order.

Al-Bannā' was a master of exhortation and encouragement and
in his speeches always identified himself with the common man. The
following excerpt is representative:

> At that time there will be ready, Oh ye Muslim Brothers, 300
> battalions, each one equipped spiritually with faith and belief, intel-
> lectually with science and learning, and physically with training and

athletics, at that time you can demand of me to plunge with you through the turbulent oceans and to rend the skies with you and to conquer with you every obstinate tyrant. God willing, I will do it.[8]

The appeal of such challenges was especially strong for the young, caught in the aftermath of one war and on the verge of another. The holistic aspects of al-Bannā''s message were easier for them to adapt to since, materially speaking, they had less to lose than their parents. Whatever their motivations, al-Bannā' was pleased with their exertions, for in his tract "To What Do We Call Mankind?" he remarks:

How much do I wish that these brethren who are making inquiries would inform themselves about the youth of the Muslim Brotherhood! Their eyes are wide awake, while other men sleep; their minds are working while the carefree relax. One of them will be bent over his desk from afternoon until midnight, working, striving, pondering, toiling assiduously, keeping at it unceasingly all month long. When the month is over, he hands over his income to his organization, his donation is dedicated to his mission, and his money is put to the service of his goal.[9]

For al-Bannā' this was the epitome of the devout Muslim life. But despite this activist fervor, sacrificial spirit, and talk of praxis, one cannot help but note the absence in his writings of a precisely defined model for the Brotherhood's goals. Nowhere does he state what it means in a concrete sense to be "a true Muslim," to "develop a Muslim family on Islamic lines," to "establish an umma," or to "establish an Islamic State in Egypt." Frustration with such ambiguous objectives is perhaps the reason for the organization's turn to political intrigue following the death of the founder; assassination, at least, was objectively verifiable as to its success or failure. But due to a lack of measurable objectives the internal-personal missiology which al-Bannā' espoused cannot be said to have either succeeded or failed. The holistic concepts espoused by al-Bannā' and his followers contributed to the weakening of Egyptian conservatism and were useful in bringing to a focus questions which Muslims had been voicing with regard to modernization and Westernization. But the lack of a concrete model for the future jeopardized the Movement's credibility.

Abul A'lā Mawdūdī and the Jama'at-i Islāmī

Mawdūdī was born in 1903 in India and, like al-Bannā', was subjected to Sufi teachings at a very early age. His name witnesses to this influence, for Abul A'lā was the first member of the Chishti order to settle permanently in India. On his father's side he was descended from his namesake, and it was to his father that he owed his education in the fundamental precepts of the Islamic faith. He began his career as a journalist, becoming editor of the *Taj* weekly in Jabalpur at the age of seventeen. A three-year stint as editor of the leading newspaper, *Al-Jamiyah*, brought him into contact with several of India's most important figures and exposed him to the contemporary issues with which these men were dealing.

Also like al-Bannā', he was an activist. Charles J. Adams intimates that this characteristic may have been in part a reaction to the sternness of his parental training:

> In spite of the strictness of his upbringing and the father's determina-
> tion to insulate the youngest son of the family against the influences
> of Western culture and education, as a young man Mawdudi had the
> reputation of independent mindedness and of being something of a
> rebel against traditional ways.[10]

He seemed to always represent a contrast to the status quo, a voice of dissent in the midst of unanimity. In the political realm he opposed the partition of India on the grounds that such a division was a concession to Western (and hence infidel) concepts of nationalism, and upon his migration to the new state of Pakistan he opposed the original plans for its political structures in favor of a system more in accord with his own convictions.

He was apparently also opposed to external-institutional mis-siology. Like the Pietists, "[he] came to believe that the best way to transform a society is by the creation of a small, informed, dedicated and disciplined group who might work to capture social and political leadership."[11] He thus began on a small scale but made no secret of the magnitude of his eventual goals: he wished to transform the world. In his *Tadhkira Du'āh al-Islām* ("A Workplan for the Missionaries of Islam") he formulates this objective in political terms:

Our da'wah is to all peoples of the earth, that they may bring about a general revolution in the roots of the present governments, which are ruled tyrannically by despots and profligates, who fill the earth with depravity; that they might tear these leading ideological and practical positions from their hands so that they may be assumed by men who believe in Allah and the Last Day, who follow the religion of truth and who do not desire either grandeur or depravity on the earth.[12]

But to reach *all* peoples he had to first reach *a* people, and therefore he acknowledged that "our da'wah is to ... Muslims especially, that they worship Allah and [submit to] His divine ordinance, and commit no *shirk* in any respect, acknowledging no other god or lord." The adherents of the Islamic faith must first purify themselves if they are to present a credible witness to the remainder of the earth's population. Such a witness is not an option for Muslims; Mawdūdī appealed to Sura 2:143 to claim that "The Qur'ān clearly states that witnessing to the Truth in a manner that would leave mankind with no justifiable ground to deny it is the only purpose behind constituting you as a distinct Ummah ... named Muslims."[13]

He was scathing in his condemnation of the Muslim world for having failed to live up to its calling. "If the Ummah neglects its duty," he said, "or if it gives false witness, it will deserve to be punished more severely than the people." The past and present state of the Jews was evidence of the truth of this contention. A similar judgment might not be far distant for the Muslim world, he warned, for "in almost every respect Muslims ... are giving their witness against Islam and not in its favor as they should ... the persons shaped and moulded by Islam are in no way better than, or different from, those prepared by kufr."

The individual Muslim became the focal point of Mawdūdī's reformatory activity. This was the key to all other facets of his program, for transformation of the political, economic, and social institutions could be achieved only by transformed individuals. In Adams's words, "concentration fell upon the rectification of individual Muslim character and life but not yet upon organized social efforts to transform society." Not until 1941 and the establishment of the Jama'at-i Islāmī did Mawdūdī turn directly to political and social concerns.

Whereas al-Bannā''s personality was lighthearted and magnanimous, Mawdūdī exhibited a more melancholic temperament. Al-Bannā' spoke of "sacrifice"; Mawdūdī predicted "trials." He wrote in a darker, more somber vein than al-Bannā', who was ever the encourager. Al-Bannā' was a friend: Mawdūdī a master. The reformer allowed no illusions to be entertained with regard to the depth of commitment required for the training of an effective dāʿī. He spoke of a "First Phase" in this development, in which a person enters into the dīn of Allah totally and without reservation. This stage is replete with trials, and it will therefore have a filtering effect. Phase One will provide for

> the education of individuals in all that they lack of [proper] behavior for this path, [such as] goodness, devotion, strength, and a pure, strong moral character. Those who are unsuccessful in the ordeals of this first phase withdraw from us of their own accord without us doing anything [to them] by way of testing them or [even] thinking of dismissing them. As for those who meet with success from Allah and come through these trials, they are the successful. They become unshakable, for in them—at the very least—is devotion, freedom, endurance, determination and right conduct, as well as affection for the Truth rather than Falsehood.[14]

Mawdūdī deviates here from the softer philosophy of al-Bannā'. He was convinced that his Islamic workers would meet with persecution in the course of their activities, having himself served time in prison. Opposition is inevitable when the dāʿī reaches Phase Two of his development, in which "those who know in truth the path of God go out and draw to His light those around them who are bound to them by bonds of kinship and friendship or who are neighbors or buyers or sellers." Some will indeed come to the Truth, but not without "drawing the eyes of critics and the lights of investigation to him from every direction."

Individuals who have committed themselves to the task of self-purification are not to remain in isolation, either from society or from each other. They should become aware of the existence of like-minded persons in order to be encouraged and stimulated to more actively pursue Islamic goals. Mawdūdī recommended the utilization of training camps to accomplish this aspect of his plan:

The practical part of the training programme undertakes to provide the workers an opportunity to live together, in a clean, chaste,
Islamic way for a few days to learn punctuality, discipline, good
companionship, fraternity and love, to try to imbibe good qualities
of others and overcome their shortcomings with the help of others.
They must avail of this opportunity to concentrate their mind,
attention and activities exclusively for the pleasure of Allah, getting
rid of all their worldly engagements for a few days at least.[15]

The severity of such a lifestyle of abnegation was mitigated to an
extent by the promises made with respect to the Hereafter. Mawdūdī
exhorted his followers to

give preference to Hereafter (akhira) over this world, in each and
every matter. In every affair in this life, your aim should be to attain
success and blessing in the life hereafter ... we are in this world only
temporarily, to be examined as to who of us are going to prove their
competency of winning the eternal life of Paradise.[16]

Such a focus prevents an improper view of kingdom-building
from developing. By concentrating upon the Akhira rather than the
Dunya ("this world," "material things"), one will avoid the errors
of the Muslim leaders who succeeded the Rashidūn. Mawdūdī constantly reminded his listeners that although Islamic daʿwah definitely
contains political, economic, and social implications, these are not
to assume a position of overriding importance. "We are here," he
said, "being tested not for our achievements in industry, commerce,
agriculture or statecraft, nor for the fine buildings and roads we
construct, nor even for the extent of our success in establishing
culture." In true Pietist fashion he turned the focus of the individual
Muslim *inward*, claiming that life's real tests are by nature qualitative
rather than quantitative. "The true success on which we should
concentrate depends on unflinching loyalty to Allah and complete
submission to His commands, irrespective of the field of our activities
and the responsibilities assigned to us."

These internal qualities were not devoid of external outworkings,
however. The Sufi orientation of Mawdūdī's early life caused him to
emphasize the internal over the external but did not produce an
other-worldly asceticism. More clearly than al-Bannāʾ, Mawdūdī
was able to work out some of the practical implications of the

revolution he envisioned. Whereas the Muslim Brotherhood had emphasized an Islamic Order, Mawdūdī spoke of an Islamic Movement (al-Haraka al-Islāmiyya), and this concept lent a more activist tone to his teachings. An "order" implies a fixed and stable environment which, once brought into existence, exhibits attributes of permanency. A "movement," on the other hand, implies fluidity and mobility. It is continually changing, in constant need of examination and redirection. But significantly, the Islamic Movement conceived by Mawdūdī duplicated the function of al-Bannā"'s Islamic Order in that it provided the masses with interim goals and activities in the absence of an established Muslim community, state, or caliphate. It was not necessary to await the renewal or establishment of these institutions in order to create an Islamic ambience; such an ambience could be created by the people themselves. This would eventually result in a revolution at the upper, controlling levels of society:

> The objective of the Islamic movement in this world is a revolution in leadership. A leadership that has rebelled against God and His guidance and is responsible for the suffering of mankind has to be replaced by a leadership that is God-conscious, righteous and committed to following Divine Guidance.[17]

But no military junta was envisioned. Mawdūdī implemented instead a purely pietistic methodology that made use of an extensive literature campaign:

> [He] began [in Pakistan] to make an appeal to the masses as well as the educated classes, sending preachers and spreading literature in the villages of the West Pakistan countryside. The campaign was very effective; the group consisted of earnest and dedicated men, was well organized, and possessed an articulate ideology expressed in an abundant literature.[18]

Adams reports that "all of Pakistan was swept with enthusiasm for an Islamic order of things." As was the case with al-Bannā"'s movement, opposition grew alongside the enthusiasm and Mawdūdī was jailed in 1948. But by the time he was released in 1950 he was more popular than ever.

He was not, however, content with having set in motion an Islamic movement at the purely local level. Although he realized that the creation of an actual state displaying the characteristics of Islamicity which he desired was not practical after so short a time, the idea of such a state grew to be more and more an intrinsic part of his teachings. He began to confront a philosophical problem as to the sequence of events necessary for the realization of his ultimate goals. He began like al-Bannā' with an internal-personal approach, believing that the transformation of a significant number of individuals would effect changes in the controlling structures of society. But were these expectations concerning individual transformations realistic? If the structures and institutions of a society are actually corrupt to the degree which he and others believed they were, would not the fact that such structures and institutions constantly impinge upon the lives of society's members render it virtually impossible for those members to be truly transformed? Is an Islamic society created by Muslim individuals or does the Islamic society create Muslims? For Mawdūdī these issues were brought to a head when he and his companions failed to dampen the nationalistic fervor that resulted in the creation of Pakistan. To Mawdūdī this was indicative that foreign influence was more deeply rooted than he had reckoned.

He gradually came to believe that for most individuals a personal transformation must be preceded by the establishment of rightly guided social and political structures. He became convinced that

> the natural consequence of what we have said concerning the qualities of perfect worship, sincerity in the religion (dīn) of God and keeping oneself pure from the faults of hypocrisy and [one's] deeds free from the understanding of the wise, is that this [environment for worship] cannot arise unless a general revolution occurs in the system of modern life, which revolves around an axis of unbelief, heresy, iniquity and disobedience. Those who direct and organize the matters [of life] and who pilot the helm are men who have turned from God and His prophet and who scorn His principles and who display arrogance on His earth.[19]

Of course such an environment could never arise on its own. A small group must therefore be prepared for leadership responsibilities, assume control of or at least attain influential positions within society, and then work for the creation of an Islamic

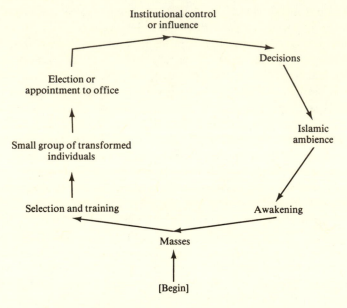

FIGURE 1. Mawdūdī's later missiological strategy.

ambience, which would in turn lead to the awakening of the masses. This small-group aspect was a continuation of his original thinking but this was now refined to produce the concept of a sequence of events which combined *both* internal-personal and external-institutional strategies (see Figure 1). This thinking posited that within the general population would be some individuals radical enough in their convictions to withstand the societal pressures that normally forced one to conform to cultural beliefs and practices. These would be the persons who would undergo the "trials" described earlier and who would come through them victoriously. These few would become members of some organization like the Jama'at-i Islāmī, which had been created long before in India for the institutionalization of Mawdūdī's thinking. In some respects it paralleled the Muslim Brotherhood, functioning as a means of applying Islamic ideals. But it differed from al-Bannā''s organization in that from the first it was politically oriented and early on came to have the status of a political party.

After Mawdūdī's emigration to Pakistan the focus of his Jama'at became even more intensely political than it had been in India; "his programme for the future of Pakistan," says Edward Mortimer, "was the expansion of the Jama'at-i Islami until it had absorbed the state and had, to all intents and purposes, become the state."[20]

Mawdūdī's thought became much more developed than al-Bannā''s, perhaps because he simply had more time than the Egyptian, who was assassinated in 1949 at the age of forty-two. It does not appear, however, that the more politically oriented concepts will be seen as Mawdūdī's chief contribution to the cause of Islam. The concept of the Islamic Movement has had the most significance for the modern world, particularly for Muslims in the West. Like al-Bannā''s Islamic Order, the Movement was appealing for its holistic emphasis, as seen in Mawdūdī's belief that "Islam is a law, or a 'system' of truths and principles forming an integrated and comprehensive whole."[21] The idea that Islam is to affect every aspect of an individual's life transformed the religion from being a mere appendage to particular ethnic backgrounds to being a focal point of daily life requiring personal choice and action. The Sufist emphasis upon the masses (and hence the individual at the level of the masses) contributed to the dissipation of the helpless feeling that the determination of the circumstances of life is completely out of the hands of the common man. Here was something a person could *do*, and according to Mawdūdī's beliefs, these individual choices and activities would eventually have important significance for national, and even international, policymaking.

Despite the fact that Mawdūdī's thinking went beyond that of al-Bannā' in some respects, there is still little concern for the finer points of organization, methodology, philosophy, strategy, material resources, and the like. Adams notes that

> Mawdudi gave but little attention—far too little—to the more practical and mundane aspects of the Islamic state. His discussion is notably lacking in any serious thought devoted to the institutional arrangements in the state that he hoped to see come into existence in Pakistan. At almost every point his views raise more questions than they answer because of the failure to consider the working out of principles in their concrete applications.[22]

Most of the writings of Mawdūdī and al-Bannā' concentrate on developing qualities of the individual: helping the worker to attain closer contact with God and then to strengthen and expand that contact, helping him to focus on the rewards of the Hereafter rather than the here and now, helping him order affairs of the home and family, preparing him for proper relationships with other Muslims in order to produce a unified umma. The assumption is that methods and techniques for communicating the message are not important so long as the life of the communicator is in order. The lifestyle itself should overwhelm others with its religiosity and simplicity; all one need do is display it. In what ways, at what times, and in what locations such exhibitions are to occur remain unspecified. The burden of application is placed squarely upon the shoulders of the individual and the practical outworkings of his faith thereby become the result of his own thinking rather than of mechanical adherence to an imposed system. The value of such a concept is that creative and generative impulses are preserved and spiritual activity maintains a spontaneous character. The disadvantages include the difficulties that arise with respect to the maintenance of unity. But apparently both al-Bannā' and Mawdūdī were so convinced of the advantages of this concept that they were willing to risk the possibility of a splintered movement. Indeed, Mawdūdī advises early on, when speaking of the Jama'at-i Islāmī,

> You may join some other organization, if, for some reason, you are not satisfied with us and find other organizations working for Islamic ideals on Islamic lines ... [and] if you are neither satisfied with us nor with any other organisation, then you should form a party of your own which is devoted to the ideal of establishing Islam fully and witnessing to it faithfully by words and deeds.[23]

Islamic Pietism in North America

The teachings and missionary philosophy of al-Bannā' and Mawdūdī have entered the North American continent by at least three different routes. The first is through the influx of immigrants from Egypt and Pakistan during periods of repression in the recent histories of these two countries. Beshir Rehma states with regard to the 1950s and 1960s that

among these new immigrants were Islamically-trained individuals
from Egypt who were fleeing the oppression of the Nasser regime;
most of these were members of the al-Ikhwān al-Muslimūn ... these
Islamic-conscious individuals, together with immigrants and students
from Pakistan, India, Iran, Turkey and other Middle Eastern
countries, were actively working for Islam in the New World.[24]

The influence of these immigrants has been diffuse, however, since
it is not characteristic of Muslims in America to live in geographical
proximity to each other. But it is significant that more organized
attempts at Islamic activity have a sympathetic group of persons to
draw upon for support and manpower.

The second avenue through which the Muslim Brotherhood and
the Jama'at-i Islāmī entered North America is by way of the Muslim
Student Association, an organization founded in 1963 at the
University of Illinois at Champaign-Urbana. Three of the founding
members of this agency, Dr. Ahmad Sakr, Dr. Ahmad Totonji, and
Jamal Barjinzi, were members of the Muslim Brotherhood. Through
these men the ideology of Hasan al-Bannā' was directly integrated
into the goals and philosophy of the organization. Ihsan Bagby
states concerning the Islamic Society of North America (which was
organized and established by the Muslim Student Association to
oversee operations that were beyond its scope) that "ISNA has
always sought inspiration and guidance from the intellectual leaders
of the modern Islamic movement (Maudūdī, Sayyid Qutb, Hasan
al-Bannā', etc.)."[25] The literature disseminated by the MSA reflects
the ideologies of both al-Bannā' and Mawdūdī:

> Since the 1960s, largely as a result of the Muslim Student Association,
> a growing body of English-language literature has become available
> in the United States, written from a normative perspective by mem-
> bers of the Muslim Brotherhood and Jamaati Islam.[26]

The objectives of this organization are discussed in detail in Part III.

The third significant avenue by which the foregoing ideas entered
into the Western context is through the speech and writings of
Khurram Murad, a disciple of Mawdūdī. Until recently Murad
resided in Great Britain, but his influence has been extensive in
North America as well as in Western Europe. Whereas al-Bannā'

and Mawdūdī were active in specifically Middle Eastern contexts, Murad has taken upon himself the task of interpreting their ideologies (in particular that of Mawdūdī) for application in Western countries, thus providing a philosophical underpinning for the activity of those Muslims residing in the West who desire to carry out the work of daʿwah. The contribution of Murad is discussed at length in Chapter 5.

In addition to the previously mentioned groups, organizations, and individuals, all of which are proponents of Sunni Islam, there is evidence to suggest that Shiʿites have come under the sway of these Middle Eastern influences as well. Yasin al-Jibouri is particularly impressed with Hasan al-Bannāʾ, writing that

> among the Sunnis, al-Ikhwan al-Muslimoon (the Muslim Brotherhood) has been the most active in bringing the Muslim masses back to Islam ... quite a few dialogues were initiated between the ayatullahs and al-Ikhwan of Egypt, Syria, Iraq and other Asian, African and European countries. ... The founder of al-Ikhwan al-Muslimoon, martyr Hasan al-Banna, was one of the founders of Dar al-Taqreeb bayn al-Mathahib al-Islamiyya (Institute for Narrowing the Gap between Muslim Sects) which was established in the 1950s in Cairo. Al-Banna's discourses with Imam al-Qummi of Qum, Iran, are still very well remembered by disciples of both great men.[27]

Finally, the Islamic Circle of North America's *Manual of Daʿwah* contains a bibliography of suggested readings for "Islamic Daʿwah and Movement." Eighty percent of this list consists of books by or about al-Bannāʾ and Mawdūdī. Few (if any) of the activist Muslim organizations in America have been untouched by these two men or the movements which they began.

5

Khurram Murad: Contextualization of the Islamic Movement for the Western Audience

Khurram Jah Murad was born in 1932 in Rai Sen, India. His basic education was completed at the Alexandaria Jahangirya School and he began his college career at Hamidiya College in Bhopal. In 1948 he emigrated to the newly formed state of Pakistan to join the Islamic Movement established by Mawdūdī, to whose works he had been introduced by his mother and sisters.

Upon his arrival in Karachi Murad sought out members of the Jama'at-i Islāmī and within two months he had become an active member of the Jamiat-i Tulaba, the student wing of the organization. Eventually he became president of this group while studying engineering at MD College. In 1957 Murad traveled to the United States to pursue a Master of Science degree in engineering at the University of Minnesota, and upon his return to the Middle East in 1959 became an active member in the Jama'at's East Pakistan Consultative Committee. In 1971 he relinquished his post as president of the Dhaka Jama'at in order to devote himself full-time to da'wah work.

In 1978 Khurshid Ahmad, first director of the Islamic Foundation based in Leicester, England, returned to Pakistan and Murad was asked to succeed him. He remained in this position until 1986 when, due to health problems, he was forced to return to Pakistan to pursue less strenuous activities.

As a disciple and confidante of Mawdūdī, Murad absorbed much of the thinker's vision for a worldwide Islamic movement. His years in the West enabled him to understand the special problems connected with the establishment of such a movement in a non-Muslim context. His thoughts upon these issues gave rise to two treatises published by the Islamic Foundation and marketed in the United States and Canada by the Islamic Society of North America. These works are entitled *Islamic Movement in the West: Reflections on Some Issues* (1981) and *Da'wah Among Non-Muslims in the West: Some Conceptual and Methodological Aspects* (1986). The following summation and analysis of Murad's thinking is based largely upon these two works, though introductory remarks found in his English translations of Mawdūdī's major works also illuminate his alterations and adaptations of the ideas contained therein.

Murad is unequivocal with regard to the ultimate goals of the cause he seeks to further. For him the Islamic Movement is "an organized struggle to change the existing society into an Islamic Society based on the Qur'ān and the Sunna and make Islam, which is a code for entire life, supreme and dominant, especially in the socio-political spheres."[1] On the face of it, this appears to be an external-institutional approach, since social and political trans- formation is plainly envisioned. However, for Murad the idea of "politics" is extremely broad, and the overtly institutional cast of his definition is mitigated by such clarifications as the following: "Any act performed in power perspectives—to influence others—is considered a political act ... thus da'wah, tablīgh, jihād and all interpersonal relations are, to some extent, political; so are all relations within social institutions and structures."[2] Politics, then, is not restricted to the authoritative levels of a society but can exist on the level of the masses as well. Murad's *ultimate* objective may be said to be institutional in configuration, but he realizes the impossibility of attaining this goal in the near future and his methodology for the present is thus distinctly internal-personal. He can state that "the movement in the West should reaffirm and re-emphasize the concept of total change and supremacy of Islam in the Western society as its ultimate objective and allocate to it the highest priority" and yet four sentences later affirm that "the ultimate objective of the Islamic movement *shall not be realised unless the struggle is made by the Locals*. For it is only they who have the power to change he society into an Islamic society."

The Islamic Movement is conceived of as a mass movement because participation in it by all Muslims is obligatory according to the Qur'ān. Murad cites Sura 3:187 and 110, 5:159–160, and 22:77–78 as support for this contention and the idea becomes almost a litany for him:

> Muslims ... have no other justification to exist as a community but that they should bear witness before mankind to the Truth and guidance which God has given them ... those who possess the Book must make it clear before mankind. Otherwise, they deserve to be cursed by God and all those who are deprived of the guidance unless they repent and present its message clearly ... it has been made clear in the Qur'an that this Ummah does not exist for its own self-interest or its own self-salvation, but that it has been brought into existence for the good of all mankind ... it is important to remember that this duty has been laid down upon the whole Ummah and is obligatory on every one of its members.[3]

In this respect Murad's thinking parallels that of al-Faruqi, who maintained that the only justification for a Muslim to remain permanently in the West is as a dāʿī. In this vein Murad states:

> What I am saying is much wider, much more comprehensive and much more profound than merely appending a mixture of daʿwah among Americans to our activities. It is fixing the whole direction of lives, activities, programs, institutions and structures towards the goal of making American society Islamic and Muslim.[4]

This is tantamount to creating al-Bannā''s Islamic Order. It gives Muslims in the midst of a powerful, non-Muslim society an attainable goal by replacing the idea of political and social revolution at the controlling levels of culture (i.e., a military jihād) with the concept of a "political" and social revolution at the level of the masses. How is this goal attained? Each and every member of society is to be confronted with the message of Islam. Such an approach does not violate the "no-compulsion" clause of the Qur'ān because the goal is actually the creation of an ambience, not conversion: "We would not be working to make Muslims of them ... but we shall try to make them understand and accept the values of Islam, if not its forms."

Islamic Movement in the West is an attempt to transfer the concept of daʿwah from the sphere of the theoretical into the realm of the practical. Though only an initial survey, the work seeks to go beyond "objectives and goals" and to outline both a "strategy" and "plans." The first element of this strategy is entitled "Literature" and involves the preparation of materials that can be used for proclaiming the message of Islam. Murad cautions that

> this should be placed first not because it is the most important ... but, because of its role in the present-day world, it will be a necessary prerequisite to some other elements of strategy ... a book can never be a substitute for a man, yet books are crucial to Islam.[5]

This literature should include material prepared specifically for non-Muslims, but it should not be defensive in tone. It is to be designed mainly for two groups, first for the "elite," that is, journalists, politicians, academicians, and writers, and second for children.[6]

The second element of Murad's strategy involves concentration upon da'wah among non-Muslims. Here he wishes to encourage adoption of a new approach, which is detailed in his more recent work *Da'wah Among Non-Muslims in the West*. This approach includes the following precepts:

(1) People are to be invited to "their own religion"—the "oldest" religion—and not to a "new religion." Says Murad: "Indeed ... we may be bold enough to say that we do not invite anyone to change his 'religion', to transfer his allegiance to a rival religion." Here he is plainly advocating the view that Islam is dīn al-fitr—"the natural religion"—which God has repeatedly revealed since Adam. In this sense Islam is not a new religion but rather represents a *restoration* of the one true religion. Judaism and Christianity in their original forms were precisely the same as the Muslim faith is today; alterations and accretions—both intentional and unintentional—made it necessary for God's revelation to be renewed through Muhammad. Thus North Americans, being in the main Christians and Jews, are to be invited to what is actually that which their forefathers believed and propagated. Murad believes that this idea serves to weaken the boundaries between the religions and facilitates a type of ecumenical reform movement.

(2) The starting point and core of da'wah consists of total surrender to God, realizing one's accountability before God for his

deeds, obedience to the Messengers of God, and the construction
of a new world order in which justice will prevail.

The emphasis on justice seen in Murad's interpretation of the
Islamic Movement is original to him. In the works of al-Bannā'
and Mawdūdī it does not appear with regularity and does not
assume the importance that it does in Murad's writings. He
comments, for instance, concerning Sura 57:25 that

> there can be no more categorical a statement regarding the central
> place that the Qur'ān gives to establishing justice among people; in
> social structures, and between nations and to the mission of striving
> for this objective, even using force to dislodge powers that have
> become gods.[7]

The reference to force is characteristic only of Murad's thinking
concerning the later stages of da'wah activity, that is, those which
involve societal transformations. Ultimately the Muslim community
is to aim for "Islamization" of political structures, and this will result
in the establishment of justice. According to Murad, true justice
cannot exist apart from Islam:

> A prophet's mission is not confined to inviting men to worship God
> or condemning, in verbal outbursts, social injustices. It is, additionally,
> to establish justice, by bringing "Iron" or power under God. Power
> is the glue that binds human beings together, it creates and sustains
> social institutions . . . power relations are so closely interwoven into life
> that no life can be just without making them Islamic.[8]

However, the idea of force does not acquire a significant role in
his writings; indeed, he consistently exhorts his readers to exhibit
patience and humility in their dealings with others: "the objective
of Da'wah is not to win an argument, to score a victory, to silence
an opponent; it is to win and activate a heart, a mind, indeed a life for
the cause of Allah."

(3) The Muslim is to begin his witness not with a repudiation of
what is wrong with others but rather with an invitation to reflect
upon commonalities. This is nothing more than a literal application
of the Quranic injunction found in Sura 64:

> Say: People of the Book! Come now to the creed which is common
> between us and you, that we shall serve and worship none but Allah,

and we shall not associate anything with Him [as god], and some of us shall not make others Lords apart from Allah.

Murad makes it plain that he does not advocate an Islamic ecumenicism of the type mentioned previously in connection with Isma'il al-Faruqi, Fazlur Rahman, and others. Christians and Jews must accept the Prophethood of Muhammad in order to be properly "righteous". What is advocated is a change in approach which would initially emphasize the concepts and values rather than the forms of Islam. These should be human values that are universally agreed upon by all, Muslim and non-Muslim alike. Only after these commonalities are established should the invitation be extended to submit to the teachings regarding Tawhīd and the prophethood of Muhammad.

(4) No one is to be compelled to accept the "historical Islam" of the last fourteen centuries. Murad distinguishes between the Islam of the Qur'ān and Sunna of the Prophet and the Islam of historical development. In this way he avoids the need to apologize for or defend the policies adopted by Islamic leadership throughout the centuries following the time of the original Medinese community and the caliphates of the Rashidūn. He declares to his fellow Muslims:

We need not own and justify everything done or said by Muslims in the past, or in our own times. ... We may not be able to change the forms of un-Islamic behavior on the part of Muslims at large or of those within non-Muslim societies, but we can certainly refrain from acting on the precept of "my nation, right or wrong" ... we should not hesitate to repudiate anything in our past or contemporary conduct which is not in keeping with our norms in the Qur'ān and the Sunna.[9]

This philosophy of history allows North American Muslims to apply Quranic teachings directly to their situation without reference to the forms developed within specifically Eastern contexts during the course of Islamic history.

(5) It is essential that Muslims realize that if modern man is going astray, the Islamic community must bear at least partial responsibility for this deviance. Here Murad takes a sympathetic view toward what would otherwise be termed the "unbelief" (*kufr*)

of the West. "*Kafirs* of today," he says, "are not really *kafirs* who have heard the truth and who have rejected it after having known it." It is therefore wrong to begin da'wah activity with a view of the world as divided into two opposing camps: Kafirs and Muslims. Murad points out that the label "kafir" was applied by God's Messengers only to those whose kufr "was demonstrated to be entrenched and deliberate." The kufr that exists today is attributable largely to the failure of Muslims in bygone centuries to fulfill their responsibilities as dā'īs. What this failure implies for the community as a whole is never defined; Murad refuses to issue the dark warnings so characteristic of Mawdūdī.

(6) A qualitative distinction must be made between kufr and the natural characteristics of race and culture. In Murad's thinking, a person may not be considered an unbeliever merely "because he is Western, or white, or Hindu"; he is a kafir only if he is in direct rebellion against his Creator and His Messengers. Murad suggests that the West be critiqued "with the compassion of a surgeon's scalpel, not with the brutality of a butcher's knife." In conjunction with this idea he advocates the use of a "multiple-organization structure" that would organize da'wah activity on the basis of ethnic, linguistic, or geographical background. Saudi Arabian dā'īs would thus work among Saudi Arabians, Lebanese among Lebanese, Egyptians among Egyptians, and so on.

Here Murad reveals his insight into the North American situation with respect to its peculiar multiethnic configuration. He has understood that missiological approaches designed for implementation in countries such as Egypt, Saudi Arabia, and Pakistan are impracticable in a country such as the United States with its lack of cultural and ethnic homogeneity. For Murad the advantages of multiple organizations are incontrovertible:

> The communication within and outside will be effective; there will be greater identification on the part of general people; the leadership and the followers will be homogeneous and able to identify with each other; there will be no language barrier to participation and involvement in activities and decision-making, and the response to "home" situations will not cause any strains.[10]

This idea allows Murad to acccept and even approve the multiplicity of Muslim organizations already existing in North America, the majority of which were formed on the basis of linguistic, national, or ethnic background. Whereas others (Shawarbi, for example) have criticized this phenomenon as a violation of the concept of the umma, Murad incorporates these groups into his strategy.

(7) The message of Islam, though essentially the same in all ages, "must be conveyed through a medium that is understood by the addressees." Murad points out that all of the previous Messengers (i.e., the prophets) spoke in the vernacular of the people of their time. He implies that the presentation of Quranic teachings and Islamic traditions in their medieval forms will be essentially meaningless to the modern listener. These teachings must be re-packaged in order to be relevant to contemporary issues—nuclear disarmament, unemployment, care for the elderly, and the like.

Returning to the discussion of Murad's strategy and plans, the third element (following "Literature" and "Da'wah Among Non-Muslims") involves the support and reinforcement of "home movements." Murad encourages Muslims in North America to remember the countries from which they, or their ancestors, came, and to stimulate the Islamic Movement in those countries by engaging in fund-raising activities and "demonstrations expressing support at times of crisis." Muslims should also seek to influence those persons or institutions in America which affect political processes in Muslim lands.

The fourth and fifth aspects of his strategy involve young people. Murad places high value on imbuing youth with a respect and appreciation for Islamic principles in the hope that these will carry over into the adult years. The children of immigrants and foreign Muslim students are two groups he is particularly concerned about. With regard to the latter he is critical of existing student organizations, which he regards as exhibiting a tendency toward monasticism:

> There just do not seem to be enough efforts to prepare workers for real situation sacrifices and hardships—physical and financial, in giving time and in relations. Detachment from Dawa among non-Muslims, among other Muslims, from campus life, and especially from more than a million-strong Muslim communities around them calls for some immediate remedy.[11]

"Community Needs" is the sixth aspect of his plan. Muslims

must take steps to develop for themselves a secure base by seeking to resolve the problems connected with their legal status, with immigration regulations, race relations, education, employment, cultural identity, and the like. Community organizations, including religious and educational centers, should be established to deal with these issues. Murad does not favor the separation of Muslim from non-Muslim children. He admits that at times private Muslim schools may be useful, but on the whole, "separate schools are not the answer." He encourages instead the establishment of evening and weekend schools in conjunction with the writing and publication of suitable Islamic materials.

His final suggestions include coordination of the thinking, planning, and actions of the various Muslim organizations established in the West. The homogeneous-unit concept is not to be pursued to the extent that wedges are driven between the various expressions of the Islamic Movement. He also suggests that these efforts at cooperation include the establishment of criteria for evaluation of the implementation of the various resources available to Muslims (i.e., time, talent, and money).

Murad harbors no illusions as to the state of missionary thinking in the West. He believes that "it is not difficult to find that the vision of a total change and the supremacy of Islam has been more or less abandoned in the local context, if not theoretically, at least for all practical purposes." Assimilation has occurred on too large a scale, and Islamic activity has been limited to the support of "home movements." Such support, however, "is in fact being utilized to fill the void in the movement created by the abandonment of the 'ultimate objective' in the local context and the need to find some form of continued attachment with it." It is a cover, in other words, to hide the aimlessness of Islam in the West.

Murad believes that many of the problems associated with the Muslim communities in North America are directly attributable to Muslims' failure to pursue missionary objectives:

> Da'wah should be the prime and foremost activity at every level and in every sphere. Only when this objective is relegated to a minor or insignificant position or is neglected, does that movement come to be plagued by diseases like stagnation, selfishness, petty squabblings and dissention [sic].[12]

A renewed concentration on da'wah activity will provide a focus for the community which will so absorb its energies and resources that there will be neither time nor opportunity for differences to arise. Activism, then, is beneficial not only because it represents obedience to God's plan for His umma, but also because it can become a psychological rallying point. Devotion to a "cause" is more effective in creating unity than are direct attempts to foster unity. Giving this "cause" Quranic support and justification lends it an even greater significance and provides additional motivation for its accomplishment.

Part III discusses the multiplicity of forms these emphases have taken in Western society.

III

THE INSTITUTIONALIZATION OF
DA'WAH IN WESTERN SOCIETIES

6

"Paramosque" Structures and Their Development

Jakob Spener did not consider himself a reformer in the tradition of Luther and Calvin. He did not intend to establish a sect in competition with other Protestant churches, and he never formally severed his ties with the Lutheran church in Germany. But his *collegia piatatus* gathered in homes during the week, enjoying an atmosphere of warmth and community that was far more conducive to an emphasis upon Christian experience in daily life than was the foreboding air of the European cathedrals. These meetings, however, were viewed with suspicion by both civil and ecclesiastical authorities, who were aware of the dissent of the Moravians, Mennonites, and other Anabaptist groups elsewhere on the continent. Already troubled by the continuing Catholic presence, Germany did not need additional conflicts at home, and so, while no actual persecution of the kind associated with the Inquisition was instituted, pressure was brought to bear upon the Pietists to keep them from straying too far from the orthodox fold. One of the measures taken was the closing of several universities to persons espousing Pietist convictions. In response, the Pietists opened their own university at Halle in 1694, and out of this institution grew the first Protestant missionary agency, the Danish-Halle Mission. One of the first graduates of Halle University, Ludwig von Zinzendorf (1700–1760), introduced pietistic concepts to a group of Anabaptist refugees he had permitted to build a town on his property. From this group he recruited the first members of what became the Moravian Missionary Society.

Alternatives to traditional church structures had appeared in the past, but these structures had always retained close connections with the established church and were seldom (if ever) considered "lay" agencies. Halle University, the Danish-Halle Mission, and especially the Moravian Missionary Society had no such connections with official Protestant or Catholic denominations. They represent instead the beginning of what is today known as the "parachurch" phenomenon. A parachurch agency is a Christian ministry whose organization is not under the control or authority of a local (Christian) congregation; there is much debate as to the legitimacy of such groups. The criticism directed at them stems from their lack of accountability to traditional ecclesiastical organizations, their nonsupport of the local church, the duplication and lack of coordination of the efforts of each, their focus upon a central figure (usually the organization's founder), and their failure to meet the needs of other than a specific group of people.

For their part, parachurch organizations accuse the traditional church structures of excessive internecine competition, duplication of effort, a distorted focus upon architectural structures, espousal of the clergy–laity division, conservatism, and lack of relevance to contemporary culture. These reasons are generally advanced as justification for the establishment and continued existence of parachurch groups.

It was noted in Part II that both Hasan al-Bannā' and Abul A'lā Mawdūdī deliberately bypassed the mosque and founded agencies of their own. Extensions of their groups are seen in such American organizations as the Muslim Student Association and the Islamic Society of North America. Offensive-activist Muslims have thus constructed "paramosque" institutions, that is, organizations which have been formed as alternatives to those which Muslims established in previous centuries. How has this come about?

In North America the same criticisms leveled at Christian church structures are in many cases applicable to the typical Islamic mosque. "Excessive competition" is a growing problem. This is due not to a development of Islamic "denominations" but rather to differences that exist between Muslims of various ethnic and/or national backgrounds. Competition may even exist within a single mosque, or between different mosques located in the same vicinity. In such circumstances a certain amount of "duplication of effort" is inevitable. As for an "inordinate focus upon architectural structures," the preoccupation seen in the last three decades with the establishment of architectural extravaganzas such as the Islamic

Cultural Center in Washington, D.C. (which includes a mosque) is evidence that such a focus exists on the part of some Muslims. Haddad and Lummis attribute much of this emphasis upon architecture to a resurgence among Muslims of personal identity concepts, which had been repressed for years in order to avoid clashes with American culture. Muslims are today less afraid to affirm their Islamicity, and as a consequence their mosques have become expressions of their pride in being adherents of the Muslim faith.

The clergy–laity division is not intrinsic to Islam, but in America it has proven to be unavoidable. Imāms have been forced to assume a role often indistinguishable from that of a pastor or rabbi:

> Demands for instruction in Islam, for "pastoring" to a congregation many of whose members may be having difficulties adjusting to a new culture, for visiting the sick and bereaved and providing family counseling, all press the imām to enlarge the scope of his functions.[1]

The reason for this transformation is the same as the reason for the alterations made in the function of the mosque itself. In Islamic countries a multiplicity of institutions and officials share the duties of education, administration, and "pastoring." Legislative and judicial needs are met by the Shari'a law courts and officials such as the *qāḍīs*. Educational needs are met by the madrasas, the *'alims*, and the *shaykhs*. Moral ethics are enforced by a combination of governmental decrees and the social pressure created by the Islamic ambience. Consequently the mosque functions (in most cases) as a strictly spiritual institution. It is a house of prayer and the site of the weekly *khutba*. The imām is a prayer leader and on occasion a preacher; even the duties connected with weddings and funerals are conducted by others.

Since non-Muslim countries lack the foregoing institutions and personnel, the mosque must assume functions for which it was not originally designed and the imām must fulfill roles for which he receives no training. The American masjid is a multiplex, combining prayer room, educational center, political forum, social hall, informal law court, and counseling clinic, all under one roof. The imām assumes the role of educator, administrator, accountant, fund-raiser, political agitator, informal lawyer, and counselor. No man can effectively perform so many functions, assuming, of course, that there is even one imām for every mosque.

The transformation of the mosque into an "Islamic Center" has allowed it to meet certain needs but has at the same time weakened its specifically religious character. Some Muslim institutions in America are indistinguishable from a local "country club" or "lodge," and the ethnicity typical of most serves to strengthen this image. In some instances dance halls and bingo parlors have been added, the former in an attempt to retain the interest of young people and the latter to provide funds for general maintenance or for special projects. This adaptationist orientation has resulted in the mosque being relegated to a position of qualitative inferiority; the masjid in America is the institution of the defensive-pacifists.

The imām who serves his mosque on a full-time basis is a "professional." Through the particular circumstances of American life and culture he has become a member of the clerical class and as such institutionalizes an Islamic form of the clergy–laity dichotomy. This is unavoidable because of the equation of his role with that of the Christian and Jewish professionals. But the concept of 100 percent mobilization of the Muslim community is compromised by the imām's professionalism, and the ecumenicism in which he participates mitigates any exclusivistic claims his message might contain. This is characteristic of the defensive-pacifist orientation, and for this reason most imāms would be categorized accordingly.

Finally, "conservatism" and "lack of relevance to contemporary culture" are criticisms aimed at the mosque by such offensive-activists as Khurram Murad, who states that "we have mosque after mosque build on landscapes which had no mosques before, and yet they make no impression on their vicinities."

The examples used to illustrate these criticisms have been drawn from Western contexts, but this does not mean that similar objections have not arisen elsewhere. Hasan al-Bannā' felt that "sermons of the mosque would not suffice to curb the ever-growing evil" of Cairo, and as a consequence he began to send out teams of students to preach fundamentalist Islam in coffeehouses; these young people thus formed an embryonic paramosque organization that later resulted in the Ikhwān al-Muslimūn. Mawdūdī felt himself forced against his will to establish a separate institution:

We have been compelled to form this organization as a last resort. For years I have been calling Muslims to turn away from the wrong paths and to concentrate their efforts on the mission entrusted to them by God. If all Muslims had accepted this call, all of them would have constituted one single organization, an organization which would have enjoyed the status of al-Jama'ah.[2]

There is here a sense of despair that the traditional institutions could not be adapted to a new vision of activism. But there is also an earthy pragmatism; a task must be carried out, and if existing organizations cannot be utilized, then new agencies must be formed.

The dissolution of the caliphate is also used as justification for the founding of paramosque organizations. If this institution had remained intact it could perhaps have assumed a position analogous to that of the Roman Catholic bureaucracy, and individual activist organizations could have been subjected to its authority just as the monastic orders submitted to the authority of the papacy. Since such a possibility no longer exists, Muslims are left to their own devices.

With regard to the paramosque agency as a phenomenon per se, one cannot make a radical division between offensive-activist and defensive-pacifist Muslims, for both have established organizations that operate parallel to the traditional mosque structure. Nor should it be assumed that Muslims who are deeply committed to and heavily involved in paramosque institutions have forsaken the mosque, for this is not the case. The majority either continue regular attendance at a local mosque or form their organizations so that they assume the functions of a mosque at appropriate times, Fridays and Muslim holidays. There is, however, a qualitative difference between the goals and philosophies of defensive-pacifist organizations and those of the offensive-activists. Such organizations as the Federation of Islamic Associations, founded by the Cedar Rapids Muslim community in 1952, evince a distinctly introverted orientation:

This Federation goes out of its way . . . [to work] for the advancement of the religious, cultural and social aspects of all Muslims on the American continent, just as it is working toward Muslims becoming strong through their Islamic heritage, the interpretation of its teaching and the setting forth of its lofty principles, which it shares together with other religions whose adherents are among the non-Muslims of America. In our opinion this Federation will be a powerful agent in spreading Islamic culture to the widest possible boundaries among American Muslims.[3]

Note the final phrase: "among American *Muslims*." Not Americans in general, but rather those who are already adherents of the Islamic faith. Such an emphasis can be seen as preparatory, a contribution to the creation of an Islamic ambience. But the idea that Islam's "lofty principles" are found in non-Muslim faiths precludes the establishment of an exclusivist witness.

A similar institution is the Council of Muslim Communities of Canada, established in 1972. By 1977 it included among its members some forty Islamic associations and mosques from every province. The objectives of this agency are as follow:

1. To present the Islamic way of life as defined by the Qur'ān and Sunna.
2. To strengthen bonds of brotherhood among Muslim communities and individual Muslims.
3. To promote mutual appreciation and friendly relations between Muslims and non-Muslims.
4. To stimulate Islamic thinking and action in the North American setting.
5. To coordinate activities of member communities and communicate with the entire Muslim world.

Of these goals only the third can be considered to be outwardly directed, and its tone is neither exclusivist nor evangelical.

In addition to these national organizations, regional and local Islamic centers have been established in many parts of the United States and Canada. These agencies are also generally defensive in orientation; the Islamic Society of New England, for instance, lists fourteen objectives, none of which can be interpreted as involving non-Muslims with the possible exception of the fifth, which proclaims the intention of the group to "combat misrepresentations of Islam in the media." "Da'wah" is mentioned in the list of the center's activities but is defined as "interfaith meetings held with local, regional, and national religious organizations."

Three of the four main objectives of the Islamic Center in Washington, D.C., are introversionist in orientation. These include the erecting of a house for the service of Allah, use of the center for authentic religious guidance for Muslims, and promotion of "a better understanding of Islam and greater appreciation of its genuine teachings." The fourth objective is outwardly oriented but is not evangelical: "to seek to improve the relationship between the world of Islam and the New World." Muhammad Abdul-Rauf sums up the role of Islamic centers in general: they are, he says, the "forts of Islam in America." This is a significant evaluation, for a fort is a supremely defensive institution.

Most activist paramosque agencies have experienced considerable difficulties with respect to philosophy, strategy, and methodology. The history of North American Islam is dotted with early attempts to propagate the "gospel of Islam,"[4] but most were unsuccessful and were abandoned within a few years of their inception. With regard to more recent endeavors, *Arabia: The Islamic World Review* writes:

> Many of these organizations were created by people who were influenced by Maulana Mawdūdī, Syed Qutb, Syed Nursi and others. But because of the fact that these organizations failed to grasp the nature of western society and its dynamics they have yet to leave any significant imprint on their new countries. Most of these da'wa organizations have now become ethnic groups with an emphasis on preserving their specific cultural identity.[5]

Some organizations, then, which began as activist groups have succumbed to cultural pressures and have been transformed into defensive-pacifist institutions. Other organizations appear to be thriving. In this section statistical information concerning the latter category's establishment, background, and general policies is discussed; following sections will examine in more detail their strategies, methodologies, and literary endeavors.

A Local Organization: The Islamic Information Center of America

Musa Qutub was born in Jerusalem and educated at a Quaker missionary school and a Methodist college, thus becoming well acquainted with the teachings of Christianity. He greatly respects sincere followers of Jesus, but believes that such persons are a minority and that the greater part of the population of America is secularized and "astray." Despite his Christian education, he is convinced that the Islamic faith represents a superior form of religion; this conviction led him to establish the Islamic Information Center of America in 1983. Cooperating with him in this effort were Dr. Ahmad Sakr, former director of the Muslim World League Office to the United Nations and North America and cofounder of the Muslim Student Association in Indianapolis and the American Islamic College in Chicago; and John Merenkov, a medical doctor and convert to the Muslim faith. Qutub is himself a professor of geography at Northeastern Illinois University.

The center, which is presently located in Prospect Heights, Illinois, serves as a meeting place for prayer and an assembly hall for lectures and video presentations. Plans exist for a mosque and fundraising efforts are under way to procure the money needed for construction of this facility. The three main objectives of the organization are indisputably evangelical:

1. To deliver the Message of Islam in its totality and purity to the American people.
2. To inform non-Muslims about Islam.
3. To aid Americans who embrace Islam in delivering the Message to others.

These goals are fulfilled by the following means:

1. Contacting individuals and families to inform them about the Message of Islam.
2. Giving lectures about Islam to schools, colleges, and universities.
3. Conducting seminars and workshops to display Islam as a complete way of life.
4. Writing, publishing, and distributing pamphlets, booklets, and flyers about Islam.
5. Distributing copies of the Qurʿān with an approved translation.
6. Using popular communications media to deliver the Message of Islam.
7. Inviting People of the Book to meet with each other for better understanding of themselves and each other.

Qutub's primary purpose is to "spread the word," and although there is a distinct emphasis upon contacting individuals, lectures, seminars, workshops, writing, television, and radio, he is personally convinced that the spread of the Muslim faith in previous centuries occurred mainly through the witness of Muslim lifestyles and that it should still do so today.

The center is apolitical, and despite the fact that the Ahmad Sakr mentioned as a cofounder is the same Ahmad Sakr through whom a connection was traced between the Muslim Student Association and the Ikhwān al-Muslimūn, Qutub is adamant in his contention that there is no place in his organization for "Shi'ites or members of the Muslim Brotherhood" who attempt to serve their own ends. In keeping with this commitment the center receives no governmental or political help from either America or overseas. It is a nonprofit, lay-oriented organization; neither the director nor the members of the Executive Committee receive a salary. A secretary is the only paid employee. All contributions are placed in the mosque fund or are utilized for materials and to provide scholarships for students at the American Islamic College in Chicago. Each month a list of donors is published in the center's newsletter and readers are reminded on occasion to "contribute without hesitation especially during the holy months of Ramadan," for Allah will reward them up to seven hundred times their offering.

Qutub seeks to provide Americans who are dissatisfied with traditional religious expressions information concerning Islam as a viable alternative. He does not pronounce judgment upon Christians who have deliberately chosen Christianity, and it is not his purpose to argue or debate concerning religious beliefs. He stresses as the chief motivations for his work a profound love for Americans, a desire to draw closer to God, and gratitude for what Islam has done for him.

Two National Organizations:
The Muslim Student Association and
The Islamic Society of North America

On January 1, 1963, some 75 Muslim students representing ten campus organizations congregated at the Urbana campus of the

University of Illinois. A series of meetings was held in which several topics of particular interest to adherents of the Islamic faith were discussed, and out of this gathering was formed the Muslim Student Association. The first official convention of the organization was held in the summer of the same year, and at this conference a constitution was adopted. The document embodied the original goals of the agency, and these included the improvement of students' knowledge of Islam, the perpetuation of the Islamic spirit, the guidance of life in a non-Muslim culture, the explanation of Islam to North Americans, and the restoration of Islam in the students' home countries. The growth that followed was phenomenal, and as of 1983 the organization boasted 310 student chapters with more than 45,000 members.

The founders imparted definite activist elements into the organization at its inception, and their goals mirrored the concerns of expatriate Muslims who had not forgotten the conditions in their homelands. Two of the founders, Dr. Ahmad Totonji and Jamal Barjinzi, were Kurds from Iraq; the third was Dr. Ahmad Sakr. The fact that the organization experienced many tensions during the first years of its existence is due in part to the political convictions of its founders:

> In its early days the MSA competed with the Organization of Arab Students (OAS) for the allegiance of Arab students on various American campuses. The OAS was supported by the Nasserite government in Egypt, which advocated nationalist and Socialist goals. The MSA, with its direct ties to the anti-Nasserite Muslim Brotherhood and the Jamaati Islam, rejected these ideologies as alien to the essence of Islam.[6]

The MSA soon began to produce several influential pieces of literature. The monthly *Al-Ittihad*, its chief organ of outreach, has continued to the present day.

In the early 1970s the MSA underwent an identity crisis and was forced to reevaluate both its objectives and its programs. In 1975 the aims and purposes of the agency were modified, and although these goals have been subject to differing interpretations on the part of commentators, the official rendering of them is as follows:

1. Disseminate Islamic knowledge among Muslims for the purpose of strengthening their commitment to Islam as a complete code of conduct.

2. To present Islam to Muslims and non-Muslims and to promote friendly relations and understanding between them.

3. To develop MSA directions, goals, and structure.

4. To cultivate brotherly relations and foster unity among Muslims in North America.

5. To develop greater understanding and unity among the various language and cultural groups.

6. To conduct social, cultural, religious, and educational activities on campuses in the best tradition of Islam.

On the surface these objectives do not differ from those of the defensive-pacifist groups. Only the second goal has reference to non-Muslims, and the desire to "promote friendly relations" between them and Muslims is not a specifically evangelical goal; it has instead ecumenical overtones. But note the following interpretations of Western writers. Yvonne Haddad states that

> the priorities as reformulated by the planning and organizing committee of 1975 were changed to include: "producing and disseminating Islamic knowledge, establishing Islamic institutions, providing daily requirements, initiating da'wah ... recruiting and training personnel, promoting and nourishing the unity of Muslims.[7]

John Renard is even more specific, contending that one of the MSA's objectives is "the facilitating of Islam's faith-sharing effort among non-Muslims."[8] Perhaps these two authors are referring to other or earlier statements of the organization's goals; the MSA brochure quoted previously has no date of publication, but internal evidence indicates that it was written after 1983. It is also possible that both Haddad and Renard interpreted the stated objectives in light of the actual praxis of the organization, for the MSA has been and remains decidedly missionary in its orientation. Although the "Aims and Purposes" listed previously do not clearly indicate an emphasis upon da'wah activity, the final paragraph of the brochure in which they are contained most decidedly does:

> The most important task which only the MSA can do efficiently is da'wah among non-Muslims. Of all the places in North America, the

campus is the only area where the most curious, the most inquisitive and the most open-minded audience for Islam ... may be found. ... This, according to the recommendation of the Majlis ash-Shura of the ISNA 1983, must be the first priority of the MSA in the future, insha' Allah.[9]

In 1982 a branch organization, the Muslim Communities Association, was formed to cater specifically to the needs of students who had chosen to reside permanently in North America. Also, from the very beginning the MSA was joined by nonstudent Muslims; by 1983 the number of local community groups affiliated with the organization was nearly the same as that of the campus chapters. In keeping with the needs and interests of these groups, organizations such as the Association of Muslim Social Scientists (AMSS), the Association of Muslim Scientists and Engineers (AMSE), and the Islamic Medical Association (IMA) were formed. Such a diversity became increasingly unmanageable and the very name of the association became a misnomer. Consequently the Islamic Society of North America was founded in the summer of 1983 to act as an umbrella organization overseeing the activities of the various agencies mentioned. This was a significant step, for now the MSA could "justifiably confine itself to the campuses and concentrate on students who are going to be the future leaders in their countries."

The MSA works through local, regional, and zonal agencies. Local chapters constitute the association's "backbone"; these are responsible for organizing Jum'a and 'Id prayers, seminars, conferences, Quranic study circles, and social activities. Grouping of these chapters according to geographical location makes up regional divisions, each of which is directed by a president, who is elected by the chapter presidents. The chief tasks of regional management include development of interchapter cooperation and coordination of multiple activities. At the zonal level the United States and Canada have been divided into five sections: The East Coast U.S. (four regions), the Central Zone (five regions), the West Coast (four regions), Eastern Canada (three regions), and Western Canada (two regions). Each zone has a representative assisted by a zonal council, composed of the regional representatives. The council is responsible for the development of general policy and has organized large-scale activities such as summer and winter youth camps.

At the uppermost levels of the MSA is an executive committee, elected every two years by mail ballot. This committee consists of a president (from the United States), a vice president (from Canada), the preceding president, and one zonal representative from each of the five zones. The group meets at least three times each year and more often if necessary.

The association is divided not only geographically but functionally as well. The Islamic Book Service (the North American Islamic Trust) is a division which is responsible for the dissemination of Muslim literature in the United States and Canada. The catalogs of this agency boast hundreds of titles in both English and Arabic, and an increasing audiovisual emphasis is indicated as well. The Islamic Teaching Center is another division which has in recent years attained high visibility among offensive-activist Muslims in North America. This center is responsible for the training of young people in the principles of the Islamic faith and for preparing "Islamic workers," individuals who will be effective in communicating the message of Islam to non-Muslims. The Teaching Center lists among its primary activities the arranging of lectures and study groups concerning da'wah, the preparation of correspondence courses, and the organization of training camps for aspiring dā'īs. During 1986, for instance, the center claims to have presented more than 80 lectures and to have held 12 study groups. More than 200 students participated in correspondence courses and in addition to the literature included in these the center distributed 5,800 copies of the Qur'ān, 175,000 brochures, 26,000 booklets, and 5,000 books. Ten workshops were held in addition to two training programs in various Islamic disciplines for older Muslims and one training program for new Muslims. In 1987 several summer programs were offered, including courses in the Arabic language and separate training camps for older and younger Muslims in the principles of da'wah. The Teaching Center also contains a Department of Correctional Facilities, which in 1981 contacted 4,000 inmates in 310 prisons, enrolling more than 500 in an Islamic Correspondence Course. And in 1987 the organization sent out a request to every Islamic Center in the United States and Canada to sponsor the placement of at least four books in every school, university, and public library. The recommended literature includes Yusuf ʿAlī's translation of the Qurʾān, Malik's *Al-Muwatta*, ʿAbd al-Atī's *Islam in Focus*, and *Toward Understanding Islam* by Abul Aʾlā Mawdūdī.

In recent years the association has concentrated upon building a facility in Plainfield, Indiana, costing $21 million; 124 acres of land have been acquired and construction has already been completed of a mosque capable of seating 500 individuals and with expansion capabilities for up to 1,500. Included in this complex is a library containing 80,000 volumes along with microfilm and audiovisual facilities. The location is ideal for the association's training programs since it also includes classrooms, a day-care center, a cafeteria, dormitories, and recreational facilities.

As was indicated previously, the MSA and its constituent agencies, the Islamic Teaching Center and the Islamic Book Service, have been subsumed under the Islamic Society of North America. This agency also assumes responsibility for the Muslim Communities Association of the United States and Canada, the Association of Muslim Social Scientists, the Association of Muslim Scientists and Engineers, the Islamic Medical Association, the Islamic Services of Canada, and the Foundation for International Development. Membership is open to "any Muslim, aged sixteen years or more, living in North America, who endeavors to practice Islam as a total way of life." An emphasis on holism previously noted as characteristic of al-Bannāʾ and Mawdūdī is evident in this description, as it is in the definition of Islamicity contained in ISNA's membership brochure. Under the heading "Islam and Muslims" is contained the following paragraph:

> Islam is the universal religion for all mankind. Muslims who have willingly and freely accepted Islam have committed themselves to a comprehensive re-ordering of their responsibilities and relationships according to the Qurʾān and Sunna. They have accepted as uncompromising principles of their organizational work the facts that Islam is a total way of life (2:208), that Muslims are one brotherhood (49:10), that they are righteous in action (3:104), that shura is a cornerstone of Islamic conduct (42:38) and that Muslims are mutually interdependent.[10]

A statement of "Aims and Purposes" continues the holistic emphasis and in many ways echoes the objectives of the MSA: "The aims and purposes of ISNA shall be to advance the cause of Islam and serve Muslims in North America so as to enable them to adopt Islam as a complete way of life." The organizational structure consists of a General Assembly, which is composed of all the members of the society. Its duties are to elect a president and two vice presidents, to elect a Majlis ash-Shura, to adopt resolutions, and to amend the constitution as necessary. The Majlis ash-Shura is composed of general members and ex officio members which total in number between twenty-four and one hundred. Qualifications for this office include being "an adult, practicing Muslim known for his Islamic manners and morals in his community and organizational dealings"; being committed to regular participation in educational and training programs as well as regular financial contribution to ISNA of not less than 1 percent of gross income; having been involved in Islamic work in the United States or Canada a minimum of three years; having been a member of ISNA a minimum of three years; and not being "an active position seeker." The Majlis adopts policies and formulates plans for ISNA as a whole, confirms appointments of members of the Executive Council, raises and allocates funds for projects, and approves the affiliation of organizations with ISNA.

The Executive Council is composed of the president and vice presidents and any other members appointed by the president. Its duties include the implementation of decisions made by the Majlis ash-Shura, preparation of budget proposals, supervision of the General Secretariat and functional committees, and formulation and initiation of specific projects. The General Secretariat is composed of a secretary general, a number of directors determined by the Executive Council, and the Secretariats of affiliated organizations. This committee handles the administrative, financial, legal, educational, and training activities of ISNA and its affiliated organizations; it is also responsible for conducting the day-to-day operations of the society as a whole.

One would expect that an organization with such decidedly bureaucratic functions would more easily fit into the defensive-pacifist category than into the offensive-activist. Thus far this has not turned out to be the case. At the convention held by the society in September 1987 one lecture topic was "Our Mission," which included discussion of the question of whether ISNA would be "consumed by a dominant culture" or "make an impact on the future shape of events in this continent." Muzzamil Siddiqui and Siraj Wahaj discussed "The Qur'ān and the People of the Book," grappling with the question of "what we who live as a minority in a society administered by such people can draw from the Quranic passages to guide us in our present circumstances." In the keynote address, "Qur'ān: Guidance to Live By," Khurram Murad exhorted Islamic workers to expand their vision for making America a Muslim continent.

Shiʿite Organizations: The Islamic Societies of Georgia and Virginia

As indicated earlier, the Shiʿite population in North America is quite small. It is interesting to note, however, that Nyang and Ahmad list among the leading contributors to Muslim intellectual life in America the name of Yasin T. al-Jibouri.[11] This individual was born in Baghdād in 1946 and was for a time a schoolteacher in both Iraq and Saudi Arabia; in the early 1970s he moved to Atlanta, Georgia, to pursue graduate studies. His literary accomplishments and erudition resulted in his being appointed imām of the Islamic Center of Atlanta, but he was summarily dismissed from this position when it was discovered that he was "of the Jafari School of Law." This experience (from all accounts an unpleasant one) led him to found in the fall of 1973 the Islamic Society of Georgia, Inc., "primarily to propagate Islam without emphasizing sectarian differences or preferences." Almost immediately publication was begun of the newsletter *Islamic Affairs*, which al-Jibouri considers to be "the mouthpiece of Shiʿite Islam and the most powerful advocate of Shiʿism in the country."

The organization grew rapidly through proselytization, and the objects of this daʿwah activity included Sunni Muslims as well as unbelievers:

> Due to the zeal of the Society's founders and the literature they circulated, several Sunnis did, indeed, find in Shiʿism the answers they had sought since embracing Islam. They became Shiʿites, and before too long began disseminating the faith to others. Entire

families, mostly black, became Shi'ite, and their number slowly but steadily grew.[12]

Literature for distribution to both black and white Americans was sent from Iran (by the World Organization for Islamic Services), from East Africa (by the Bilal Muslim Missions of Tanzania and Kenya), from India, and from Pakistan. Al-Jibouri claims that by 1977, some 55,770 copies of books and booklets had been mailed, free of charge, mostly to African-Americans who could not afford to buy such literature.

A great number of theological questions which were raised by the converts could not be answered by any of the American Shi'ites with whom al-Jibouri was in contact. In subsequent correspondence, Ayatullah al-Uzma Abul-Qasim al-Khoi of Iraq was asked to send a trained Shi'ite *alim* to the United States. Shaykh Muhammad Sarwar of Quetta (a small town on the Afghanistan–Pakistan border) was chosen and arrived in 1976. Fluent in six languages (including English), Sarwar had little difficulty in adapting to his new environment.

After a time the emphasis of the society shifted from outreach to defense: "Rebutting attacks, implicit and explicit, on our Islamic faith in general and Shi'ism in particular [came to] receive the top priority in our consideration."[13]

Al-Jibouri appears to have been subjected to a case of "burnout" in the late 1970s and decided at that time to relocate.

> The burden of running such an organization fell mostly on my shoulders, although I was neither the president nor the vice president, but simply the general secretary. I decided that I had to move from the city and make a fresh start elsewhere. . . . There are other reasons for making such a decision which I prefer to keep to myself.[14]

On May 20, 1982, he founded the International Islamic Society of Virginia, Inc., located in the Northern Virginia suburb of Falls Church. The purposes of the new organization are as follow:

1. To promote the Islamic teachings of brotherhood and foster religious awareness and spirituality.
2. To serve Muslims by providing social services and education.

3. To establish unity within the Muslim community and link Muslims with their brethren inside and outside the United States.

4. To promote Islam, providing reading material for interested non-Muslims.

5. To raise funds for needy Muslims.

6. To serve as liaison between Muslim and non-Muslim communities.

7. To defend Islam when attacked unjustly by the news media.

The last objective is a carryover from the Atlanta-based operation, and al-Jibouri states that "exposing the ugly role played by the newsmedia in distorting Islam, and of books misrepresenting our faith is on the top of the list of our priorities in the Da'wah work." With this in mind, *Islamic Affairs*, which had been discontinued in 1979, resumed publication in 1984.

A Canadian Organization: The Islamic Circle of North America

The Islamic Circle was originally established in the United States in 1971, but its headquarters has since been relocated to Montreal and its book service to Scarborough, Ontario. The circle was founded "to call Muslims and non-Muslim alike to the path of Allah. It strives for Iqāmah al-Dīn ('the establishment of religion') in this part of the world." The stated objectives of the group are decidedly evangelical in tone:

1. To acquaint Muslims with the call of ICNA, and to disseminate the message of Islam among non-Muslims in North America.

2. To organize those who agree with the call of ICNA, according to the methodology contained in the constitution of ICNA.

3. To provide intellectual, moral, and physical training from an Islamic perspective to those who are associated with ICNA.

4. To cooperate and coordinate plans with other Islamic organizations to achieve the aim and objectives of ICNA.

5. To make every effort to contact, cooperate with, and coordinate the Islamic movements outside North America.

The organizational structure is well developed. A nāzim is elected from among the members of the circle by secret ballot each year.

Qualifications for this office include being among the best in *taqwa* ("piety"), never desirous or ambitious to seek this responsibility, knowledgeable, able to make wise decisions according to the Qur'ān and Sunna, having rendered great sacrifices for the sake of Iqāmah al-Dīn, and possessing good administrative capabilities. A Majlis ash-Shura, composed of five men, advises the nāzim, who is also assisted by a mu'tamid (secretary general). Finally, there are the central departments, which include Training and Da'wah, Information and Publication, the Bait al-Māl (Treasury), Planning, External and Internal Relations, Organizational Affairs, Book Services, and the Ladies Wing.

In order to effectively carry out the purposes of the organization, North America is divided into four organizational zones, each headed by a nāzim who supervises the work of local units. These units are established where there are three or more members and each is headed by a local nāzim elected by those members. Associate membership in a unit is open to any Muslim individual who agrees with the aim and objectives of ICNA, and honorary memberships are available to non-Muslims interested in the work of the organization. Full membership is awarded only to the Muslim "who sincerely tries to lead an Islamic life and at least observes the obligatories [sic] of the Shariyah ... and obstains from major vices and pledges to abide the constitution of ICNA."

In accordance with its emphasis upon outreach to non-Muslims the organization has commissioned and published a book entitled *Manual of Da'wah for Islamic Workers*. This work contains the following sections: "The Concept of Da'wah," "Techniques of Da'wah," "Da'wah at Different Places," "Means of Da'wah," and "A History of the People of the Book."

A Nonorthodox Organization: The Ahmadiyya

The Ahmadiyya Movement calls itself "The True Islam" but is considered by the majority of other Muslims to be a heretical sect. Ghulam Ahmad, the founder and namesake of the group, was born in 1839 to a well-to-do family living in Qadian, India. As a minor government official in Sialkot, Ahmad engaged in several discussions with Church of Scotland missionaries, and these talks played an important role in the formation of his doctrinal convictions. Returning to Qadian he began to experience visions and dreams through which he received revelations leading him to believe that he had been appointed the *mujaddid* ("renewer") of Islam's fourteenth century. By 1889 he had in effect established himself as a new khalīfa and in 1891 he expanded his role to that of the Christian Messiah and the Hindu Krishna. The extremity of these and other claims led both Sunni and Shiʿite Muslims to repudiate his teachings and organization.

Ahmad and his followers continued undaunted and the sect became noted for its unrelenting castigation of both Christianity and Hinduism. It became estranged from nearly every group within Indian society, but for some the controversy surrounding the founder added to the attractiveness of the group.

One of the sect's most interesting doctrinal teachings concerns jihād. According to Ahmad the concept of a military "holy war" was entirely in error and Islam was to be preached instead "with reasoning and heavenly signs." This was an acknowledgment of the impracticality of an external-institutional missiology for modern times and the need for an internal-personal alternative. For this the sect turned unashamedly to its Christian opponents and borrowed freely from the strategies of the denominations with which it was familiar. This methodology was imported to North America when the group entered the United States in 1920. In that year a mission was founded in Chicago, and in 1923, 1925, and 1928 additional missionaries were sent from the Indian headquarters of the Qadianis. The movement in the United States was led by Mufti Muhammad Sadiq, who also began publication of *The Moslem Sunrise*, which remains today the leading periodical of the Qadianis.

By 1933 the Movement had expanded to include six major cities: Chicago, Pittsburgh, Cincinnati, Indianapolis, Detroit, and Kansas City. In the following decade centers were established in New York, St. Louis, Dayton, Washington, D.C., Philadelphia, Teaneck (New Jersey), Waukegan (Illinois), and Baltimore. As of 1981 there were twenty-six chapters (jamaats) active in United States and four in Canada, each one directly responsible to the director general of the Ahmadiyya Muslims Foreign Mission Office in Pakistan. This organization is an outgrowth of two societies that were formed during the early outreach endeavors. The Sadr-Anjuman-i-Ahmadiyya was created to direct the executive and educational aspects of the movement, and the Anjuman-i-Tariqi-i-Islam was to handle its propaganda efforts. Missionaries were sent from the Pakistani center and this practice has been maintained to the present day. In this respect the Ahmadis differ from such organizations as the Islamic Information Center, the Muslim Student Association, and the Islamic Circle of North America, which are not controlled by institutions in foreign nations.

The missionaries who were sent to North America earlier in the century had received their education in Ahmadiyyan principles from the Missionary Training College originally located in Qadian and now located in Rabwah. This institution presently consists of a high school affiliated with Punjab University and a theological college. The training program consists of a seven-year course of studies, divided into six different categories. These include linguistics (it is required that each missionary learn Arabic, English, and one other language), world religions, contextualization of the Ahmadiyyan message, apologetics, utilization of the mass media, and the doctrines of the Ahmadiyya. The college receives converts from other countries besides Pakistan, though it appears that at the present time the majority is still recruited from the home country. The principal feeder group is the Khuddam-ul-Ahmadiyya (Servants of Ahmadiyya), organized as a young men's association to encourage teenage males to become actively involved in the missionary outreach of the movement.

The term of service for an Ahmadiyyan missionary may be as long as ten years. During this period he is financially supported by the sect, which requires every adherent to designate a minimum of one-sixteenth of his monthly income for the missionary program; many give more than 10 percent. This practice in combination with the general frugality of the missionaries has resulted in the availability of a large missionary force.

The Ahmadiyya Movement in North America has become sufficiently well established to make possible increasing self-sufficiency. This is evidenced by the fact that although strong connections are maintained with Pakistan, the American Ahmadis have in recent years shown a tendency to adopt specifically American approaches to religious proselytization such as "blitz" campaigns and city-wide evangelization programs.

North American Islam, then, has given rise to a multiplicity of paramosque organizations which are proliferating and adapting themselves to the particular circumstances of American culture. What strategies and methodologies are they employing in their missionary endeavors? Chapter 7 explores this subject.

7

Paramosque Strategies and Methodologies

Muslim missionary endeavors during the first half of the twentieth century exhibited an almost purely educational emphasis. Mohammed Alexander Russell Webb, the first American convert to Islam and founder of the American Islamic Propaganda Society in the early 1890s, had as his chief aim "to teach the intelligent masses who and what Muhammad was and what he really taught, and to overturn the fabric of falsehood and error that prejudiced and ignorant writers have been constructing and supporting for centuries against Islam." Webb evinced a profound optimism that the Islamic faith would spread rapidly throughout Western civilization and wrote in 1893 that "its adoption as the universal religion seems only a question of a comparatively short time." His da'wah efforts were limited to the publication of a journal (*The Moslem World*), the construction of a lecture hall and library, and the establishment of a book publishing house. Very little direct contact with non-Muslims was ever established, and all three of Webb's operations were halted within a few months of their inception.

The Ahmadiyya imitated in its da'wah endeavors the Christian Missionary movement. Charles Braden observes that there were some five hundred converts by the year 1959. Of these, 30 percent were Orientals, 5–10 percent of "Muslim" extraction, and the remainder mostly blacks. No more than 5–10 percent were white. According to Khalil Nasir, one of Braden's students at Northwestern University who later became the head of the Ahmadiyya in the United States, the chief appeal of the movement lay in its presentation of Islam as nondiscriminatory with regard to race, as a simple and rational religion, and as a viable alternative to blacks dissatisfied with their treatment at the hands of Christian churches.

There are at present other approaches besides that of education. Each of the organizations discussed in Part II exhibits its own distinct philosophy of outreach. In addition, several Muslim writers have taken up the subject of daʿwah apart from any specific organizational application. The following remarks are compiled from a combination of these two sources.

No one strategy or methodology is held to be inherently "Islamic." Amin Islahi, a disciple of Mawdūdī and deputy chief of the Jamaʿat-i Islāmī from 1941 to 1958, holds that "the prophets never insisted on any one exclusive method in their missionary work."[1] Common sense dictates that the dāʿī "should abstain from methods detrimental to the dignity of the message of the Truth or his own dignity and prestige" and on this there is general agreement. Contrary to the philosophy of the Ahmadiyya, however, many Sunni and Shiʾite groups hold that imitation of Christian practices is unacceptable for Muslim workers. Islahi condemns borrowing because of a situation in India with which he was familiar in which a Muslim leader allegedly adopted a Christian practice in urging "Muslim whores" in Delhi to preach Islam to their non-Muslim customers.[2] The Muslim World League, however, is not so negatively disposed toward the methods of other religious groups; at a 1974 convention held in Mecca the organization stressed vigilance of foreign missionary activities but noted that "much could be learnt [sic] from these such as the establishing of Islamic broadcasting stations, the production and distribution of literature on Islam in various languages, etc."

If the issues of strategy and methodology are then relatively unrestricted, what forms have been adopted by modern Muslim activists? It was noted in a previous chapter that certain Muslims (e.g., Ismaʿil al-Faruqi) preferred to adopt a form of what may be called "lifestyle evangelism." This implies that the Muslim lifestyle is in and of itself so highly attractive that non-Muslims will convert to Islam upon observing pious Muslims living in local communities. According to the proponents of this concept this is the only acceptable form of conversion. Islahi, for instance, states that

God has not given [the Islamic Worker] power to convert anybody to his way of thinking ... he should not care whether people listen to him or not ... he does not worry himself with the questions whether other people will accept or reject his message and whether God will allow it to be established or not.[3]

For other Muslims this approach is far too passive, for in a pluralistic society what guarantee is there that non-Muslims will even notice Muslim lifestyles, let alone be attracted to them? For this reason such writers as Fathi Yakan are scathing in their denunciation of the "lifestyle" concept. Yakan refers to it as Jamāl al-Dīn al-Afghānī's "have-your-say-and-leave" approach in that it "guarantees nothing, it is slow, and it has little effect." Criticism of the lifestyle approach is also implied in Akbar Muhammad's claim that having conversion as a conscious objective is what has made Christians so much more effective in their missionary activity. Since conversion is such an intrinsic part of their own experience, they seek to elicit similar phenomena from those to whom they convey their message. The proof of this lies in the fact that American converts to Islam, who of necessity must experience some form of conversion, are infinitely more effective in their proselytization efforts than are those who boast Muslim parentage or ancestry. The American converts actively seek to produce an experience in others which duplicates their own, and this lends an effectiveness to their efforts which is not observable in the case of "lifestyle" advocates.

Given the disagreement that exists with regard to these approaches, proponents of each are sufficiently numerous that both may be treated as characteristic of American Islam.

Indirect Da'wah: "Lifestyle Evangelism"

Muhammad Imran summarized the view of the proponents of indirect da'wah in his exhortation to "let us ... take Islam to the West not by pulpit preaching and mailing Islamic literature but by doing what Muslims ought to do, living, drinking, eating, sleeping and behaving as Muslims are enjoined to do."[4] Embodied in this statement is both a criticism of Christian methodologies and a contention that the witness of the Muslim life is the ordained Islamic method of da'wah.

It is certainly a more comfortable means of propagating the faith from a psychological standpoint, since it is not necessary for the witness to actually confront a targeted individual with exclusivistic claims and thus risk the trauma of scorn and rejection. Going about one's daily activities in the hope that these will arouse curiosity eventually leading to inquiry can never be counted as a total loss even if no conversions are effected, for one always has the satisfaction of completing these activities as ends in themselves. This is not the case with one who concentrates upon a verbal witness, for if his message is rejected, his effort in its entirety has been in vain.

While many of the proponents of direct daʿwah are critical of what they consider to be the inadequacies of the lifestyle approach, Islahi reveals a concern that the method of verbal witness is by itself insufficient. He criticizes those who "utilize the agency of the word of mouth as the only means of propagation of the faith," for in his opinion "they never make any attempt to practically demonstrate the true Islamic life." Here stress is placed on the word "only," for Islahi is speaking as a champion of direct witness. But he calls for a balanced viewpoint, a combination of lifestyle and verbal witness that together make for credible proselytization.

This idea of balance is a common theme among the more thoughtful Muslim writers and reflects the emphasis on holism that was noted in the discussions of Hasan al-Bannāʾ and Abul Aʾlā Mawdūdī. Both Islahi and Khurshid claim that one of the reasons for the inadequacy of earlier daʿwah attempts in America was a lack of holistic orientation. Khurshid castigates dāʿīs for having gotten caught up in "abstract and theoretical discussions" rather than "presenting Islam as a complete way of life for all." Such a presentation, says Fathi Yakan, requires tremendous sacrifice on the part of the dāʿī, who must submerge his own identity for the sake of others' interests:

> The humble dāʿī is the one who lives together with the people, receives the people, speaks with the people, visits the people and loves the people. He is one who serves the people, and does not use them. He is bonded together with the people and does not divide them or treat them harshly. ... The dāʿī is in truth one who lives for others, not for himself, and his habits revolve around society [in general] and around Muslims, not around himself. He is one who works to increase the ease of others while taking no account of his own ease. Rather, the dāʿī is in truth one who rejoices at the happiness of others, is saddened by their misfortunes, is satisfied when they are satisfied and is content when they are content.[5]

This kind of incarnational thinking is typical of the more profound thinkers who advocate indirect da'wah. Akbar Muhammad believes that it was mainly "social intercourse and similarities in interests, especially in local areas, which substantially account for the early spread and reinforcement of Islam."[6] Islam, he says, "would not have spread much beyond the Arabian peninsula had it not stressed social contact." This stress upon contact with the common people in one's local area is in many respects a viable strategy for outreach. Personal contact with a devout adherent of a religious faith is nearly always instrumental in the conversion of individuals to that faith. The ability of a Muslim to identify with day-to-day joys and sorrows (i.e., to enter into life's emotional realm as opposed to interacting on a strictly intellectual plane) exercises a profound appeal. The question arises as to whether such interaction is sufficient to produce submission to Allah on the part of a non-Muslim. Is it not possible, and, in pluralistic America, probable, that one who is religiously devout and socially empathic will be admired and appreciated as simply "a good neighbor" without inquiry as to the causes of the observed devotion and empathy? Are there not "good people" who exhibit concern and philanthropy apart from religious motivations? And, given the stereotypes existing in modern America, would it not be easier to attribute Muslim characteristics to the fact that they are the products of foreign cultures than to the fact that they represent alternative religious beliefs? In the same way that "everyone" knows that Southerners are more slow-paced than Northerners and that Third World people are more "family-oriented" than are inhabitants of the First World, might not Arabs, Lebanese, Egyptians, and other Middle Eastern peoples be naturally (read "culturally") more empathic than Westerners? In order to produce a witness who will pinpoint *Islam* as the root cause of one's lifestyle orientation some verbal interaction must inevitably occur. Traditionally, formal conversion has consisted of a sincere recital of the Shahada: "There is no God but Allah and Muhammad is His Prophet." But would it not be difficult for a non-Muslim who is attracted to the lifestyle of a Muslim family living in the midst of his community and who wishes to adopt that lifestyle for himself to discover the formula for becoming a Muslim without ever having spoken to an adherent of the Islamic faith? It is true that such a person might begin by imitating those aspects of the Islamic lifestyle that he has admired, but is this sufficient to make him a Muslim?

Must not one be aware of the doctrines concerning Tawhīd and the prophethood of Muhammad to make a valid commitment to the religion and does not such awareness presuppose an intellectual contact at some point? If one answers in the affirmative, then a commitment to a purely lifestyle philosophy of ministry is not possible; one must include at least some measure of direct contact between the Muslim and the non-Muslim.

For some advocates of the indirect approach the idea of Islamization or Muslim education has offered a middle path between a lifestyle approach and verbal proselytization. In an earlier section some of the ideas of the International Institute of Islamic Thought were examined. This organization aims at creating an Islamic ambience through writing, publishing, and disseminating textbooks giving the Islamic viewpoint concerning every major academic discipline in the hope that such textbooks will eventually be adopted for general use by American students. This cannot be viewed as a direct approach unless one posits the utilization of these texts by a Muslim teacher in every classroom. But such contact, though admittedly desirable, is not essential, for the knowledge contained within the texts would be sufficient to enable any inquirer to convert to Islam independently of direct contact with a dāʿī. The IIIT gives priority to those who are already Muslims, since many Westerners of Middle Eastern or North African extraction are only ethnically or nominally "Muslim" and their Islamicity consequently has neither foundation nor depth. The institute's organizational brochure reveals the influence of al-Bannā's holistic emphasis, for it recognizes the need of a unified vision on the part of Muslims with regard to "man's relation with nature" and of "the social, political, economic and international order, of man's function and destiny." It is the goal of the institute to create this vision and to work toward its fulfillment, and toward these ends a strategy consisting of four major steps has been proposed by Robert Crane. These steps include conducting a paradigmatic analysis of Western thought, developing a Shariʿa paradigm as an alternative, utilizing this paradigm to create "Islamic disciplines," and developing a "new science of Tawhīd Cybernetics." This last aspect has been made possible by the computer age and involves the creation of "a computerized databank, assembling all human knowledge in a form suitable for the introduction of purpose in artificial intelligence."[7] Upon completion of such a databank, one would be able to submit any conceivable question in the areas of politics, economics, law, morality, and so on, and receive instantaneously an "Islamic" answer or solution. In effect one would have a computerized Majlis ash-Shura or ʿulamāʾ. Crane realizes that this is not an objective that could be accomplished in a short while; his time frame allows for a twenty-year period during which twenty "ummatic scholars" would work full time in assembling the necessary data. "Insha'Allah," he says, "this process would be a powerful tool of daʿwa and of cultural transformation through paradigmatic revolution in the world academic community."

That which separates Crane and the IIIT from the proponents of direct confrontation of non-Muslims is the willingness of the former to forgo individual conversions in the interest of producing a national (and eventually international) ambience. But is it reasonable to believe that an ambience with obviously religious overtones can be created and maintained in a nation that is by constitutional mandate a secular state? Nowhere in its literature does the institute propose or anticipate the political changes that would be necessary at some point to create their ambience in its fullness.

While the IIIT operates at the college and university level, other Muslims are involved in primary and secondary education. It was observed previously that Muslims who take a separatist position by advocating the establishment of Muslim private schools are generally categorized as defensive-pacifists. This is not the case with all, however. Some agree that *by themselves* "weekend schools, Quranic schools, correspondence courses or other supplemental education will *not* accomplish what Muslims seek."[8] But there is also a belief that daʿwah efforts are useless as long as traditional public education facilities are allowed to remain, since the godless teaching which takes place in these institutions undercuts efforts to establish an Islamic ambience. Islamic institutions must therefore be established as alternatives to secular schools, but the motivation for these institutions must not be to separate Muslims from non-Muslims. Instead, the purpose must be to create havens to which even non-Muslims may be invited. Islamic schools thus become tools in the hands of trained and dedicated dāʿīs.

It was the Muslim World League that first suggested such a use of educational institutions at its meeting in Newark in 1977. The conference participants recommended that "programs be developed and implemented for integrated Muslim adult and family education for both men and women, and that such a program be related to Islamic Da'wah." In keeping with this objective the league has supplied funds for several training institutions, including the American Islamic College located in downtown Chicago.

Direct Da'wah: Activistic Preaching

Activistic preaching involves the confrontation of non-Muslim individuals with specific precepts of the Islamic faith in the expectation that this information will evoke a decision on the part of those individuals either to submit (*aslama*) to Allah and the cause of Islam or to consciously and deliberately refuse to accede to Allah's demands (*kafara*). The Muslims who are proponents of this type of da'wah are convinced that the Islamic lifestyle, although essential as supportive of one's witness, is nevertheless insufficient to bring non-Muslims into the fold of Islam. Living a Muslim lifestyle is consequently only a part of the dā'ī's responsibility; he must also confront non-Muslims with the implications of that lifestyle. Islahi narrates the procedure to be followed:

> The fact[s] should also be taught in such a beautiful language and in such elegant form, that those with any capacity for the acceptance of the Truth may accept it, and those turning away from it, may be left with no other excuse save their own perverted tastes and obstinacy.[9]

From Sura 16:125 Allal al-Fasi draws three principles of missionary activity, the second of which is "gentle preaching with reasonable and acceptable ideas which will attract the people." In modern contexts "preaching" connotes the sermonizing of a minister to an assembly of people. But this is an overly restrictive use of the term. It may also refer to the activity of the itinerant, that is, the wandering mendicant who proclaims the tenets of his faith from the street corner and in the marketplace. This is the idea which Islahi attempts to convey in his *Call to Islam and How the Holy Prophets Preached*. His thesis contains seven principles which he believes are universally applicable to Islamic dāʿīs. First, the preacher must begin with the people of his own nation; until they have heard the message it would not be proper for him to go elsewhere to preach to others. Nor should he think in terms of reaching the largest number of people; quality is of greater importance than quantity. The preacher's call to Islam should be clear, self-evident, dignified, and effective. He should present arguments in many ways, and be "replete with emotion and zeal." Preachers and their colleagues should exhibit uniformity and unity of purpose. They should never be obstinate or antagonistic and should always have regard for the feelings of listeners.

Itinerant preachers are still active today. Fathi Yakan tells of the Tablighi Group, a division of the Islamic Group in Lebanon with which he is associated. Members of this organization are required to free themselves for a specific period of time (one hour a week, one day a month, one month a year) in order to "promote daʿwah all over the Muslim world." Some Middle Eastern itinerants reach the United States. Haddad speaks of "scholars from India, Pakistan and Saudi Arabia, who travel throughout the country proclaiming normative Islam." Those who are sent from overseas are apparently limited in number, however.

More common among Muslim groups in North America is a strategy that concentrates upon local areas. In each district daʿwah in many forms is pursued at various societal and educational levels. This is considered superior to true itinerancy, an approach that allows only minimal personal contact for a short period of time.

Within a specifically defined locale, lectures, seminars, and the like are arranged in schools, mosques, libraries, and other facilities to which the general public is invited. The Islamic Circle has a plan according to which

> ICNA workers individually and in groups meet and establish contacts with the people around them, invite them in [*sic*] meetings and seminars where the Quranic and the Hadith studies and lectures on Islamic topics are presented. Pamphlets and books on Islam are also distributed [at these meetings].[10]

The Muslim Student Association also makes use of this method in its campus ministries. The college and university setting is particularly conducive to lectures dealing with a broad spectrum of topics which will attract different kinds of people. Refreshments are made available following such gatherings so that Muslim students and/or Islamic workers can circulate freely among those in attendance, engaging in conversation and answering general questions that may arise concerning Islam.

The Islamic Information Center of America has determined specific boundaries within which it seeks to carry out daʿwah activity. Within a year of the organization's establishment it sent a form letter to every Protestant and Catholic church and every public school within its targeted district, introducing the organization and suggesting the possibility of arranging lectures for the purpose of increasing general awareness concerning the Muslim faith. Although few institutions have extended invitations, several high school students have visited the center's facilities to make inquiries.

The Ahmadiyya is the most practiced of the Muslim sects in the art of arranging seminars and using them as platforms for daʿwah. Tony Chi describes the procedure by which debates are arranged. First a lecture upon a scientific topic is announced. At some point during the course of the lecture Ahmadiyyan teaching is introduced, and at the conclusion of the talk the floor is opened for questions. At this point the speaker finds opportunities to debate key issues. Chi reports that in the late 1960s and early 1970s Billy Graham was repeatedly invited to debate an Ahmadiyyan scholar and that his refusal to do so was construed in Muslim circles as typical of the cowardice of Christians everywhere.[11]

Public assembly halls and auditoriums are preferred over religiously oriented buildings for meetings of this nature. Just as Christians and Jews have experienced difficulties in attracting adherents of other faiths and nonbelievers to churches and synagogues, so have Muslims been unable to entice non-Muslim Americans into mosques. If anything, the Muslims have operated under an even greater handicap, for whereas churches and synagogues have dotted American landscapes for centuries, the mosque remains an exotic novelty. It may be appreciated for its architectural splendor, and a visitor may occasionally enter and inquire out of curiosity concerning the dome and minaret, but general invitations to lectures or debates held within its environs elicit little response from non-Muslims.

The IICA advocates a form of secular dialogue in its initial invitation to other groups. In October 1985 the center formally invited each "esteemed Christian community" within a defined area to participate in dialogue. The letter of invitation stated that "we feel our organization has some goals in common with yours," listing such items as "the goal of leading people into a pattern of godly living through following the commandments of God and the examples of His Holy Prophets," "not compromising with godless secularisms or any other similar –isms," "countering atheism wherever it exists," and "the fact that all our commitments are to God alone." The writer went on to say that "we feel strongly that by pooling our efforts jointly we can effectively deal with the problems [of society] that are confronting us ... together we can accomplish much more than as individuals living apart." It is clear that secular dialogue is not the only goal envisioned by the center, for the letter also states that "we hope to present a clear view of Islam to you and also the Islamic view of Christianity; these dialogues, hopefully, will lead us all to the same Right Path that has been revealed to us through His Chosen Prophets." The ultimate goal is thus conversionist in tone.

The Islamic Circle lists as the second phase of its da'wah process "serious dialogue and acceptance of Islam." It implies that such interaction can take place on the individual as well as the group level. A dā'ī should first "develop friendship and win the trust and confidence of any individual who shows inclination towards Islam" and then "engage in serious dialogue, inviting him and his family for tea or dinner." At this time the concepts of Tawhīd, the prophethood of Muhammad, and the Day of Judgment should be presented, along with an explanation of the erroneous teachings of such religions as Christianity. The dā'ī is advised to be patient, for these contacts can extend over a long period of time. It is stressed that each non-Muslim must make his own decision to accept or reject Islam.

At the far end of the spectrum stands Muhammad Khurshid, who is adamantly against dialogue in any form. "Nothing can be more dangerous for a dā'ī," he says, "than getting entangled into a dialogue, because the very spirit of a dialogue is not to unravel the truth but to create a myriad of confusion and enigma." Khurshid appears to be convinced that nothing short of direct, confrontational preaching is acceptable from a Quranic point of view. Dialogue is "entangling," for in order to participate according to the rules of propriety (i.e., exhibiting a nonjudgmental attitude), the dā'ī must relinquish the freedom to preach which is his by right of Allah's appointment of the Muslim ummah to be "witnesses unto mankind." A Muslim does not bandy words with unbelievers; "his sole aim is to convince any and every person of the Truth."

Lectures, seminars, and dialogues in most contexts involve comparatively large numbers of people. Although the personal character of da'wah is preserved in these contexts to a greater extent than in radio or television broadcasts, they do not allow for the adaptation of the Islamic message to individual circumstances which a one-on-one contact usually permits. This has been recognized by some Muslim leaders, although this conviction is usually accompanied by a reluctance to adopt methods that are perceived as being invasive of the privacy of individuals. "Door-to-door" visitation of the kind associated with Jehovah's Witnesses, Mormons, and similar Christian sects, is seldom encouraged. Imran counsels dā'īs to "go door-to-door in your locality at least once a week," but it is clear from the context that he is speaking of visiting Muslims who have become neglectful of the pillars of their faith. The Islamic Circle encourages workers to go in groups of two or three to "Muslims, new Muslims and non-Muslims," but all such visits should be by appointment only.

Maryam Jameelah (an American convert to Islam who emigrated to Pakistan after becoming a Muslim) does not encourage door-to-door work but proposes instead the establishment of "small study circles" to be held in private homes. This method is significant in that it would allow Muslim women to fulfill their responsibility with regard to da'wah. Missionary activity for a woman "should start with her own children and closest female friends and their small children."[12]

Personal contact is emphasized in another strategy adopted by some paramosque agencies for the purpose of reaching a key element of society: the young people. Youth camps and summer schools have been developed as ways of attracting elementary and high school children. The Muslim Student Association's summer training camps offer a variety of short-term courses (usually one week in length) dealing with a number of Islamic subjects. The complex in rural Plainfield, Indiana, provides excellent facilities. Such camps are not restricted to the MSA; in 1977 it was reported that the Muslim World League had rendered "considerable help to various Islamic centers—for [their] youth camps, summer schools [and] other programs."

In contrast to youth camps, prison ministries have proven to be highly effective in disseminating information concerning Islam to nonbelievers. Ahmad Sakr reported in 1977 that the Muslim World League was involved in "carrying the message of Islam to our Afro-American brothers who are unfortunately in prisons." Prisoners are technically a "displaced people" and are therefore more susceptible to religious transformation than are persons who enjoy a measure of earthly security. The Muslim Student Association has recognized this and has devoted a relatively large amount of its resources to proselytization efforts among prisoners. The Islamic Teaching Center contains a Department of Correctional Facilities which in 1981 alone contacted approximately 4,000 inmates in 310 prisons and enrolled more than 500 inmates in an Islamic Correspondence Course "under which a graduated Islamic instruction is provided by mail, coupled with visits by daʿwa workers."

Television, radio, and similar communications media are gaining proponents among Muslim activists in North America. Islahi has been swept up by the implications of concentrating on mass media:

> Just as a schoolmaster can make himself heard in his classroom, so can we make ourselves heard the world over, if we are so pleased. Today we can, with the modern scientific aids, make the masses and the classes alike erudite in the teachings which would have taken months and years to impress upon them and perhaps with no great success. It is imperative that these media of mass communication be made use of for the preaching of the Truth.[13]

At the Muslim World League's international meeting in 1974 the suggestion was made that the league study foreign missionary techniques in order to eventually be able to establish Islamic broadcasting stations. At the 1977 meeting in Newark, Ahmad Sakr reported that "the Rabita [had] also helped some Islamic television and radio programs on a small scale." In July 1987 there appeared in *Arabia: The Islamic World Review* an editorial written by Fathi

Osman entitled "Towards a Better Presentation of Islam." Among his suggestions was an exhortation to Western Muslims not to limit themselves with regard to communications techniques. "Written composition and oratory" are not the only ways of reaching others, he says. "Basics of journalism, audio-visual aids, public relations, community leadership and social work should [also] be studied by all propagators of Islam, even if they are not specialized in mass communications or media." One of the most sophisticated of the television shows has been the series entitled "Islam at a Glance," sponsored by the Islamic Information Service of Los Angeles. It began in 1985 with the program "The Concept of Shahadah," followed by "Articles of Faith," "Sirah," and "Aspects of Islamic History." Documentary profiles are presented of Muslim communities in different parts of the world, and a direct telephone contact facility allows viewers to call in to request literature as well as to make suggestions and comments.

Muslims in North America have for decades concentrated upon developing various types of literature for the purpose of disseminating information about their religion. All of the paramosque agencies discussed here are involved to some extent in a literature ministry. Most produce a serial such as a newsletter, magazine, or journal, as well as tracts and/or brochures to be used in proselytizing efforts. Many have sponsored educational materials, mostly in the form of small booklets; a few have become involved in the publication and distribution of full-length books.

The Muslim World League has contributed to the establishment of newspapers and Muslim journals in North America and has in addition published "a vast amount of Islamic literature for free distribution," including "a large number" of Qur'āns. The literature ministry of Yasin al-Jibouri's Islamic Societies of Georgia and Virginia is explicated in detail. Apart from the publication of *Islamic Affairs* (which in al-Jibouri's opinion has become "the mouthpiece of Shi'ite Islam and the most powerful advocate of Shi'ism in the country"), the Georgian society undertakes to distribute literature received from foreign organizations such as the World Organization for Islamic Services. It is noted that "one shipment carried the largest number [of books and pamphlets] ever received from one Muslim organization: 7500 items." From East Africa, Shi'ite literature was sent from Bilal Muslim Missions and the Muslims of India and

Pakistan contributed as well. "By July 1977," says al-Jibouri, "as many as 5,770 copies of books and booklets had been mailed out."

The International Institute of Islamic Thought concentrates primarily upon the production of academically oriented books. No indication is given as to which of these have as yet been produced other than al-Faruqi's *The Islamization of Knowledge*, which is actually a workplan rather than a scholarly text. One would expect such an organization to concentrate upon authorship of a scholarly periodical, but although this appears upon the list of the organization's objectives, such a journal has not yet appeared.

The Islamic Information Center of America has published small tracts such as Ahmad Sakr's "The ABC's of Islam" in addition to its monthly newsletter *The Invitation*. It has also been instrumental in disseminating literature produced by the Islamic Propagation Centre of Durban, South Africa.

The Islamic Circle publishes the bimonthly *Tehreek*, and its *Manual of Da'wah* contains instructions regarding the distribution of pamphlets "at public places: waiting rooms of offices and hospitals, shopping centers, airports, and bus stations." The Circle also boasts its own publishing arm, the ICNA Book Service, with offices in Montreal and New York City. The *Manual* contains a list of recommended titles for Islamic workers, all available from the book service; these include works on tafsīr (commentary), hadīth (tradition), sirah (history), fiqh (jurisprudence), Islamic da'wah, Islamic ideology, comparative religion, and books specifically dealing with "The American Scene" and "The Canadian Scene." Although the *Manual* gives preeminence to the spoken word, it concedes that concentration upon written materials is nonetheless essential and suggests that Islamic workers prioritize the writing of articles "in beautiful English" concerning such topics as American civilization ("its fallacies and shortcomings"), American family life, "Americans on the way to destruction," a "profit and loss accounting of modern civilization," a survey and analysis of the American financial system; "modern slavery" (which would discuss the bondage of Americans to modern trends), "modern idolatry" (an explanation of how Judaism and Christianity are distorted forms of the Prophet's teachings), the Way of Salvation in Islam, the necessity of having only one code of life (namely Islam), and a discussion of "the life hereafter."

The Muslim Student Association has concentrated upon literature since its inception. Its magazine *Al-Ittihad* has been one of the leading Islamic serials in America. The MSA also boasts a large publishing agency, formerly the Islamic Book Service and now known as the North American Islamic Trust. The catalogs for 1987 contain over four hundred titles in English and an additional five hundred titles in Arabic. Writings of and about al-Bannāʾ and Mawdūdī from a large proportion of the MSA's offerings: forty-five of the works listed were written by these men or proponents of their teachings. The MSA has also produced a great amount of material for its outreach ministry, including *The Islamic Correspondence Course* and *A Manual for Islamic Weekend and Summer Schools*. Small booklets containing expositions of various aspects of Islamic theology and praxis have been published for use by converts or by those wishing to deepen their knowledge of the religion.

In addition to the foregoing organizations, agencies have been established which have as their sole purpose the publication and distribution of Islamic literature. Examples of such groups are Kazi Publications of Chicago, which supplies books and materials to Muslims in both the United States and Canada, and New Era Publications of Ann Arbor, Michigan, specializing in works of a more academic nature. Through these agencies several hundred works are made available to the Muslim population of America and new titles are being added each year.

100 Percent Mobilization of the Muslim Umma

There is no ambiguity concerning North American Muslims' views with respect to a clergy–laity dichotomy. They are unanimous in their opinion that the traditional Islamic rejection of such a distinction is essential to the Muslim ethos. There is no Muslim clerical class. All Muslims without exception are responsible for carrying out the duties enjoined by their faith and these include the Quranic injunctions to engage in daʿwah activity.

For Muhammad Khurshid these responsibilities have been incumbent upon all Muslims since the time of the Prophet. "With the advent of Rasul Allah," he says, "Muslims were charged with the responsibility of being the model of right conduct for all mankind for all time to come." Islahi adds that the Islamic mission is not an option but rather a duty *demanded* of each Muslim.

The concept of 100 percent mobilization is grounded in the view that the Muslim umma has inherited the apostolic mission of the Prophet Muhammad. This is expressed by the Islamic Circle in their *Manual of Da'wah*:

> Da'wah ... in reality stands for a universal movement that was carried on by all the prophets and messengers of Allah. ... After the Prophet [Muhammad] ... the Ummah... has been entrusted to carry on his mission. Every member of the Ummah has to bear this responsibility.[14]

This is held to be true by the Ahmadiyya as well: a spokesman for the organization writes that "previously Allah used to raise prophets to do the work. Now that the prophethood as come to an end, it is the Holy Prophet's followers that are honored by being given the mission of the prophets."[15] This concept has become a common theme in recent years and the training programs established by the MSA, ICNA, and similar organizations aim at providing the resources necessary for fulfillment of these responsibilities. Most recognize, however, that for a variety of reasons not all can be involved to the same degree. Fathi Yakan acknowledges that "it becomes incumbent upon each of the individuals in an organization to carry out his productive role *within the limits which his possibilities, his powers and his capabilities allow* [emphasis added]." In accordance with this conviction he recognizes three categories of workers: (1) those "who have the best abilities and dispositions in terms of understanding, believing, interacting and following instructions"; (2) those whose abilities "hover between strength and weakness"; and (3) those in whom natural abilities appear to be nonexistent and who appear to be incapable of productivity. All of them need to receive training. Only rarely will a Muslim be able to attain the necessary skills through his own private study; a more formal and organized program is almost always necessary. This need not involve extensive schooling, for quality rather than quantity is the aim. Ahmad Von Denffer illustrated this concept in 1982 at a World Assembly of Muslim Youth (WAMY) conference held in Nairobi, claiming that "it may take months and years to prepare people for their tasks ... as far as their respective skills are concerned," but that it is a misconception to believe that "in order to be a 'real Islamic worker' you need to be a graduate from Medinah University, or an 'alim' or at least work full-time in a mosque or an Islamic Center. Hardly anything is more wrong and more damaging to our daʿwah than such an idea."

Training

An acknowledgment of three separate stages of growth and development can be discerned in the writings of Muslim theorists and in the programs of the paramosque agencies. Stage One involves the conversion of the non-Muslim to the religion of Islam; Stage Two "the reinforcement, strengthening or deepening of Islam in the individual"; and Stage Three the development of an "Islamic Worker," or "dāʿī." Fathi Yakan describes each of these in his work *Kayfa Nadʿu ilaʾl-Islām?* (How Do We Call [People] to Islam?). The first phase involves the "building of principles which produce a sound ideology concerning existence, man and life, from which come faith in God and the remainder of the five pillars." The second phase

> is that in which it is desirable to transmit new elements [of Islamic doctrine] to [the convert], when his faith is in a proper state, his basic principles are firmly established, and his understanding of Islam is complete. It is the phase of practicality; the phase of the concrete, material appearances of faith and of sound Islamic behavior."

The third phase "is that in which it is desirable to turn [the convert's] attention from the establishment of his faith, the perfection of his understanding and the excellence of his [own] work to the phase of entering into the work of the Islamic Movement."

The intellect is the chief focus of paramosque training programs. This is because "intellectual richness enables the worker to be a continuous transmitting power. Those who are conscious of their intellectual feebleness will avoid people and society and avoid assuming any responsibility." This conviction leads to an emphasis upon education and appears in the writings of the Muslim World

League, which in 1974 recommended the establishment of "educational and cultural centers" and "institutes for training of Muslim workers"; the Ahmadiyya, with its missionary training college at Rabwah and its contention that "Islam wants the [*tabligh* worker] to utilize his faculty of reasoning as well as his power of judgment as he directs his appeal to the intellect of man"; the Islamic Circle, which states that all converts "will be involved in intensive Islamic education and training ... to prepare for jihād—the struggle to establish Allah's Dīn Islam on the earth"; the Islamic Information Center, which provides scholarships for its converts to attend the American Islamic College in Chicago; and the Muslim Student Association, whose Islamic Worker Training Programs provide training in such areas as Arabic skills, the beliefs of Islam, the goals of the Islamic Movement, Islamic legal reasoning, fiqh of Salah and marriage, and issues of da'wah.

Fathi Osman notes that "several Islamic universities have now either a special faculty or a department which is concerned with da'wa throughout the entire course of study right from the beginning, while others may have it included in the program of the Faculty of Theology." He recommends that da'wah studies "include the necessary and relevant knowledge of psychology and sociology, especially that which is related to religion" and that other disciplines be at least touched upon, such as social work, mass media communications, public relations, center management, and community leadership. In addition to these, the major world religions should be studied thoroughly from their own sources.

There are also individuals who have taken it upon themselves to contribute to the training process by preparing literature for use by Muslims generally. Ahmad Shafaat has prepared a two-volume work entitled *Missionary Christianity and Islam*. This is "a series of studies of religious issues that arise during Christian missionary preaching among Muslims. It is written primarily to aid Muslims who are the target of missionary preaching or who want to participate in dialogue with the churches or do da'wah among Christians." In preparing this work Shafaat examined manuals used in training Christian missionaries and then proceeded to deal with the suggestions for preaching to Muslims and assertions regarding Islam contained within these point by point. He lists inconsistencies and inaccuracies in the Christian Scriptures, quotes from church fathers who allegedly did not believe in the inspiration of the Bible, and proves that the doctrine of abrogation (a chief target of criticism from Christian missionaries) is found in the Bible as well as in the Qur'ān.

Certain writers, however, are careful not to allow academic orientation to completely dominate the training of Islamic workers. Osman is adamant in his contention that "da'wa studies should have successful practitioners of da'wa among the teachers." A program in da'wah should include supervised fieldwork, and this is not to be restricted to sermons in mosques:

> Visits should be arranged to social workers, schools, hospitals, prisons, the press, TV and radio stations, non-Muslim foundations, and so on. They should be trained to work in all these fields, make surveys, produce questionnaires and measure attitudes. Journeys inside the country and abroad should be organized to widen the perspective of a da'iyya and let him know about the experiences of Muslims and non-Muslims.[16]

Yakan also believes that Islamic workers must be self-critical; they must be "keener than anybody else to know their shortcomings and to discover their sins so as to be always rightly guiding and guided and to set the best example for all people." The Islamic Circle holds "night vigils, study circles and training camps at different intervals on central, zonal and local levels to help its workers in improving Islamic knowledge" and holds organizational meetings where "evaluation of previous work, planning for future work and other organizational matters are discussed."

8

Contemporary Apologetics:
The Literature of Proselytization

Muslims rely almost exclusively upon the printed word for their proselytization. Beginning with the collection of Quranic materials under 'Umar and 'Uthman and the gathering of hadīth by such men as al-Bukharī and Muslim, Muslim authors have produced an imposing array of literary works. This practice continues unabated even today.

The popularity of works by Hasan al-Bannā', Abul A'lā Mawdūdī, Khurram Murad, and others, has been mentioned, but these are generally not used to propagate the message of Islam. The only exceptions are three booklets containing addresses by Mawdūdī which have been published by the Islamic Foundation of Leicester and the Muslim Student Association in America. *Towards Understanding Islam* is a brief exposition of the Five Pillars. Of more depth is *Islam:An Historical Perspective,* which gives a panoramic view of history as interpreted by a Muslim. Islam began with Adam and Eve but became lost "in a maze of paganism and pantheism." Subsequently Allah ordained a series of prophets who attempted to steer people back to the correct path. Muhammad was the last and greatest of these messengers, and the path was most fully explicated in and through his life. This sets the stage for a common Muslim appeal: in choosing to follow Islam, one is not "converting" but rather "reverting" to the worldview and state of being that is innate in every person, To submit (aslama) is thus painless; it is analogous to coming home after a long and perilous journey.

What Islam Stands For is in many respects a continuation of the previously mentioned work. Here the appeal of Islam lies in its universality and its holism. Muhammad's mission "was for the whole world and all times", and his prophetic task included the prescrip-

135

tion of a moral code, the enunciation of principles of culture and civilization, the laying down of a mode of worship, the establishment of a framework of belief, and the determination of rules that would serve as a basis for social and cultural relationships, as well as economic, judicial, and political dealings, matters of war and peace, and international affairs. For the American dissatisfied with the abstractness and other-worldliness of Christianity and the nationalistic and materialistic preoccupations of the Jewish race, Islam stands as the alternative that will meet every need, be it philosophical, theological, social, political, or economic.

The Muslim Student Association's Islamic Teaching Center has prepared two brochures and a correspondence course designed specifically for use in proselytization. *Islam at a Glance* begins by defining and explaining the terms "Islam" and "Muslim." Like Mawdūdī's booklets, it emphasizes that Islam is not new but in actuality is the only true religion. Each of the Five Pillars is explained, and the importance of the Qur'ān and hadīth is affirmed. The idea of Tawhīd is presented as intrinsic to the Muslim faith and the concept is made to include a rejection of the idea that there is a particular "chosen people." This appeal represents a theme common in Muslim literature in which Islam is presented as a panacea for the problem of race relations. The brochure also explicates the Muslim concept of worship and makes the point that Islam contains no ritualism and that it instead emphasizes "intention and action."

Man is considered to be a free agent. He is, however, accountable to God, and his freedom is therefore not without limitations. The brochure goes on to proclaim the Islamic view of human rights and contends that science and technology are not inimical to Islamic teachings but are rather supportive of them. Finally, Islam is presented as "the cure for modern ills" such as family problems and alcoholism. The brochure ends with a list of booklets recommended for further study; these include Mawdūdī's *Towards Understanding Islam* and Syed Qutb's *Islam and Universal Peace*.

In *Ten Unique Features of Islam* one finds a completely different approach. Whereas the preceding brochure was reserved in its presentation of Islam and subtle in its contrasting of the Muslim faith with competitors, this tract is unabashedly direct. "Unlike other religions, Islam is the only religion which was given a name by its prophet and its holy book"; "no other religious denomination carries a meaning or conveys any sense of its outlook on life as does Islam"; "Islam alone of all religions has provided a multipurpose institution in the form of 'mosque' to serve the religious, social, educational and political needs of the community"; as a divine and democratic institution, it has no parallel, either in the past or the present"; "of all religious books, the Qur'an alone has remained unaltered, unedited, unchanged"; "of all the prophets, Prophet Muhammad ... alone has a historical existence"; "no other religion has provided a platform which can be used by the people to overthrow oppressive-imperialist powers"; "Islamic teachings are plain, simple and explicit and do not lend themselves to more than one interpretation of basic issues"; "Islam has never witnessed any large-scale defections from its fold during the last 14 centuries"—these are the claims made for the religion of the Muslims.

The Islamic Correspondence Course contains eleven units of study designed for use with persons above the age of eight years. The sections deal with Basic Principles of Islam, the Life of Muhammad, Salat (including the text of the Fatiha and photographs of the prayer positions), Fasting, Hajj, Zakat, the Prophets of God, the Rightly Guided Caliphs, the Moral Teachings of Islam, the Qur'ān and Hadīth, and Muslim Holidays and Ceremonies. The 247-page textbook/workbook contains an impressive amount of doctrine and history and its use in prison ministries has apparently met with a great deal of success.

Islam at a Glance is also used by the World Assembly of Muslim Youth (a subdivision of the MSA) as the first in a series of brochures designed for use among Muslim young people and interested non-Muslims as well. They are intended to "arm Muslim youth with full confidence in the supremacy of the Islamic system over other systems" and they have apologetical value when presented to non-Muslims. Brochures 2, 3, and 4 have been designed contextually for a Western audience in that they contain numerous quotations from Western writers concerning various aspects of Islam. These are entitled *What They Say About the Qur'ān, What They Say About Islam,* and *What They Say About Muhammad.* Other brochures include *The Moral System of Islam* (emphasizing individual responsibility and accountability), *Life After Death, Prophethood in Islam,* and *Concept of Worship in Islam* (which espouses the holistic view that everything, including purely natural functions, become worship when they are performed in accordance with God's regulations). Brochure number 9 deals with *The Concept of God in Islam* and number 10 speaks of *Human Rights in Islam*, including an exposition of the "universal rights" conferred by God upon all men.

The Institute of Islamic Information and Education in Chicago specializes in brief tracts written to arouse curiosity on the part of non-Muslims. Neither Islam nor Muslims are ever mentioned; all that is mentioned is a "Last Divine Book," available to persons interested in obtaining further information about the topic contained within the tract, and an address for ordering it is given. Each tract ends with an appeal to send for this book because "it was written for you, and you have the right to know." A tract entitled *You Love Freedom, Don't You?* contains a short exposition concerning moral ethics; *So You Don't Believe in God* exhorts the reader to be "God-conscious"; and *AIDS* is again an appeal to the idea of moral absolutes. Breaking the pattern set by these tracts is *A Strange and Unique House*, which narrates the history of the Kaʿba. Much more Islamic in tone, it mentions several points of Muslim doctrine. This is also true of the larger brochure *Introducing Islam to Non-Muslims*, which speaks of Allah and Tawḥīd, Muhammad, the Qurʾān and Sunna, the Messengers of God, Angels and the Day of Judgment, the state and religion, the Five Pillars, the Islamic calendar, celebrations, diets, places of worship, and holidays. These brochures are made available at such meeting places as the Muslim Community Center in Chicago; Muslims are then to distribute them among friends and acquaintances.

A much more sophisticated work has been prepared by Nur al-Islam's Ahmad Shafaat, who has taken the ninety-three verses of the Qurʾān which speak of Jesus and collated them with the verses contained in the New Testament Gospels he considers to be historically accurate, forming what he calls *The Gospel According to Islam*. Shafaat's fundamental premise is that "Muslims believe Muhammad to be a messenger of God to all mankind, while most Christians would perhaps deny it. But this difference is not too much more serious than the one between those Christians who believe that [the] pope infallibly speaks the word of God and those who deny it." The book is written to a Christian audience and "is an attempt to bridge the gap between Christianity and Islam, since the distance between the two faiths is not as great as a lack of dialogue tends to make it." In order to gain a wider readership Nur al-Islam published the work through a nonreligious publishing agency (Vantage Press).

One of the most famous (and most prolific) of modern Muslim apologists is Ahmad Deedat. Born and raised in Gujarat, he emigrated in 1927 to Durban, South Africa, where he took up work in a shop across the street from Adam's Mission, an evangelical American mission station. Continued discussions with Christian missionaries led him to seek answers to the questions which they raised and in 1958 he founded the Islamic Propagation Centre as an organization specifically designed to combat Christian proselytization. After more than forty years of preaching, Deedat continues today to speak out against Christian missions. Early on he made a decision to help Muslims defend themselves against proselytizing efforts:

> It made me ponder as to how many unwary Muslims are being constantly assaulted by Christian evangelists who carry out a door to door campaign, and being invited in by the proverbially hospitable Muslim, I thought of how the merciless missionary munched the Samoosas and punched the wind out of the Muslim with snide remarks against his beliefs. Determined to bring home to the Muslims their right to defend themselves and to arm them with enough knowledge to counter the hot gospeller, the door to door peddler of Christianity and the shameless insulter of Islam and its Holy Apostle; I humbly undertook to deliver lectures to show the Muslim masses that they had nothing to fear from the assaults of Christians.[1]

Deedat does not go door-to-door. His booklets and videotapes have made him a famous figure and he is in constant demand as a speaker and debater. On screen he exudes a charismatic and saintly appearance and his wit and charm temper what might otherwise be considered an acid tongue. Christianity is his chief enemy, and it is against this religion that his attacks are directed. But it is clear from his writings that his main encounters have been with Jehovah's Witnesses (whom he characterizes as "the fittest missionaries among the thousand-and-one-sects-and-denominations of Christendom"),

Seventh Day Adventists, and the Worldwide Church of God, none of which are exemplars of orthodox Christianity.

Deedat gives alternative renditions of the story of the crucifixion and resurrection, the meaning of "the sign of Jonah," the inspiration and inerrancy of the Bible and the name of God. His booklets are filled with accounts of his ability to make Christian professionals highly uncomfortable and to expose their alleged ignorance of the Bible and history. Debates, which are organized by his center between Christians (usually missionaries) and Muslims (usually himself or one of his colleagues such a Yusuf Buckas, a young South African lawyer), draw crowds composed of the adherents of both religions. It is expected that Christians will become convinced of the errors of their faith by the poor showing of their representatives.

Deedat's booklets include *Crucifixion or Cruci-fiction?*, *Is the Bible God's Word?*, *What Was the Sign of Jonah?*, *Resurrection or Resuscitation?*, *Christ in Islam*, and *What the Bible Says About Muhummed* [*sic*]. These are made available free of charge to all inquirers. They are distributed from the central office in Durban but are also available through Muslim groups in several Western countries.

Deedat's style is often vitriolic, much to the delight of the crowds which he never fails to attract, even in England and the United States. He has been described as "a man of the masses" and "a people's scholar" and has in recent years accepted challenges from or has asked to debate some of America's leading evangelists (at a reported remuneration of $10,000 per appearance).

Deedat's writings are full of pleas to "help the poor Christian missionaries escape their ignorance" and his consistent references to evangelicals as "hot-gospellers" and "Bible-thumpers" are designed to induce an emotional rather than intellectual reaction. The following is typical:

> Why don't you (dear reader) memorize just this one verse [Luke 24:39–40] ... with just this one verse you can take the wind out of the missionaries' sail. You can CRACK HIS SKULL, exactly as young David, with his little pebble did to Goliath. The pleasure is yours.[2]

Deedat is critical of missionaries for their "harassment of the heathen," for their "glamourization of despicability and ignominy" (referring to the testimonies of converts with criminal backgrounds), and for the "cheapness" of the salvation they offer. He interprets their tactics as evidence that they are indeed "modern-day crusaders who aim at making [Africa] a Christian continent ... by the turn of the century," and he sees his own ministry as a kind of countercrusade.

Deedat has become particularly critical of some of the more recent missiological strategies employed by North American Christians. In one context he criticizes evangelical relief organizations such as World Vision, accusing them of "stealing Muslim children in the guise of feeding the hungry." Josh McDowell, a popular Christian apologist, is accused of being one of a group of "sick people," for whom "every trick in the bag is permissible to clinch a convert for Christ."

Deedat is by no means the only Muslim who has found occasion to criticize Christianity and Judaism. Another writer who has gained fame among North American Muslims is Maryam Jameelah. She has written prolifically against both the West and Christianity. Representative of her thinking is this excerpt from a study of the *'ahl al-kitāb*:

> When Jesus returns to earth, where will he go—to the church or to the mosque? We are quite confident that he would scorn the church as having nothing whatever to do with him; he would surely smash the images of the Crucifixion as a malicious lie and destroy all the paintings and statues representing him, his mother and the saints as idolatry. I am certain that when Jesus Christ returns to earth he will go straight to the Bait ul-Muqaddas in Jerusalem and lead the Juma salat as our Imam! ... Nowhere would he feel more out of place than in the Vatican! He would be the last man ever to seek an audience with the Pope! And to the sleek, sophisticated, complacent, smug and arrogant church and synagogue-goers in Europe and America, he would tell them as he did the stiffnecked Pharisees two thousand years before: "... Ye serpents, ye generation of vipers, how can ye escape the damnation of Hell?[3]

Those aware of Jameelah's background and psychological difficulties (which she herself describes in the introduction to each of her works) would find it relatively simple to dismiss her polemic as coming from one who, having become an outcast in her native country due to her failure to achieve normal adolescent development, opted for a radical change and now heaps execration upon the society that rejected her. Such a dismissal is complicated, however, by the fact that her criticisms are molded into works that are excellently written and appear to be well documented.

IV

THE DYNAMICS OF CONVERSION TO ISLAM

9

Religious Conversion:
The Traditional Western Paradigm

Religious conversion is by no means a neglected topic among the various fields of the social sciences. The thirteen-page bibliography by Lewis R. Rambo which appeared in the April 1982 edition of *The Religious Studies Review* attests to the popularity of this subject among psychologists, sociologists, and historians as well as theologians. The titles listed reveal the existence of a tremendous variety of approaches to and theories concerning the phenomenon in general.

William James's *The Varieties of Religious Experience* is widely regarded as the cornerstone of research dealing with the phenomenon of conversion but in actuality James owed a great deal to the research of his contemporaries James H. Leuba and Edwin Starbuck. The latter was particularly influential. At the end of the nineteenth century Starbuck administered a questionnaire to 192 "converts" to the Christian religion. These 72 males and 120 females were individuals who had undergone "sudden changes of character from evil to goodness, from sinfulness to righteousness, and from indifference to spiritual insight and activity." His findings first appeared in *The American Journal of Psychology* in 1897 and were later expanded in his *Psychology of Religion*, published in 1900. Starbuck found that conversion experiences were characteristic of certain age groups; for females, the key age was thirteen to fourteen and for males, sixteen. He concluded from these statistics that the years of greatest frequency of conversions correspond with the periods of greatest bodily growth for both males and females and that there is a correspondence between the periods of most frequent conversions and puberty in both sexes.

William James was the first to emphasize the *integrative* function of religious conversion in his definition of the concept. It is a process, he says, "gradual or sudden, by which a self hitherto divided, and consciously wrong inferior and unhappy, becomes unified and consciously right superior and happy, in consequence of its firmer hold upon religious realities." James refers to Starbuck's contention that conversion "is in its essence a normal adolescent phenomenon, incidental to the passage from the child's small universe to the wider intellectual and spiritual life of maturity." The experience shortens "the teenage metamorphosis," for when the subject reaches a certain point in the development process, conversion becomes a viable solution to what is perceived to be a universal afflction of mankind: the difficulty of arranging into a coherent whole the various influences impinging upon the self from the different spheres of one's environment. International, interracial, and interethnic concerns along with political, social, and economic alternatives must be combined with specific cultural factors and individual idiosyncrasies. The number of possible combinations of these factors is bewildering and the individual is essentially alone in the struggle to adopt a worldview and life view. But a religious system can become both a paradigm of classification and a bonding agent according to which these factors can be separated, analyzed, and then joined together into what is for each individual a rational and logical system of belief. Since failure to accomplish this task of integration in some way (not necessarily by means of adopting a religious faith) can result in psychological malformation and mental illness, conversion has, according to James, an essentially positive function.

The foregoing accords well with Starbuck's findings concerning the most common ages for conversion experiences. Since adolescence is the period during which individuals are most intensely involved in forming a worldview and life view, it is logical to assume that if James's theory of conversion as a solution to the problem of intergration is correct, then adolescence would be the period most conducive to this phenomenon and this indeed turns out to be the case. In order for there to be a *religiously* oriented integration, however, two things must be present in the mind of the individual. One must experience a sense of incompleteness or wrongness concerning one's life in general and there must be a positive ideal which one desires to attain. Both of these must be expressed in terms of *religious* tenets (i.e., "sin" and "righteousness," respectively) or the integration process will result in adoption of a nonreligious alternative. "Conversion" may indeed occur but it will not be to a religious faith.

Again referring to Starbuck, James distinguishes between two types of conversion, one conscious and voluntary, which he calls "volitional," and the other involuntary and unconscious, characterized as "self-surrender." The latter form takes place in the subconscious and subliminal part of the mind and is often labeled "spontaneous" conversion. James posits that the sudden convert may be "one of those subjects who are in possession of a large region in which mental work can go on subliminally and from which invasive experiences, abruptly upsetting the equilibrium of the primary consciousness, may come." Spontaneous conversions, then, are not really so spontaneous. Subliminal mental cogitations suddenly break forth at a moment of "crisis" precipitated by either natural or supernatural causes.

Leon Salzman's 1953 essay entitled "The Psychology of Religious and Ideological Conversion" was groundbreaking in that the author assigned value judgments to his categories of conversion. Like James, Salzman distinguished between progressive or maturational conversion, which he described as the end product of a reasoned, thoughtful search, and what he termed regressive or psychopathological conversion, characterized by an emotional experience nearly always seen in conjunction with attempts to solve deep-rooted problems. This latter form is the spontaneous conversion attributed by James to the subliminal workings of the mind. But whereas James interprets the experience positively in that the individual is able to assemble his identity constructs and form a worldview, Salzman sees it as only a "pseudo-solution" most likely to occur in neurotic, prepsychotic, or psychotic persons. Spontaneous conversion does not perform a proper integrative function and is at best only an interim or short-term solution to psychological problems. Salzman observed that many of his psychiatric patients who experienced this form of conversion had suffered from backgrounds filled with "hate, resentment and hostile, destructive tendencies." Rather than being characterized by a "unified and consciously right, superior, and happy" personality, the postconversion lives of Salzman's subjects revealed a sublimated or transferred hatred as seen in (1) the exaggerated, irrational intensity of their belief in the new doctrine;

(2) their concern with form and doctrine rather than the principles of their new belief; (3) their attitude of contempt, hatred, and denial toward previous beliefs; (4) their intolerance toward anything or anyone deviating from their new faith; (5) their crusading zeal for new conversions; and (6) their masochistic/sadistic tendencies as evidenced by their desire for martyrdom, their preoccupation with self-denial, and the like. Starbuck's observations with regard to age groups were again upheld in this study, for Salzman reported that the experiences of his patients had occurred mainly during adolescence, and that this was only to be expected since this is the period of greatest turmoil in life and attitudes of resentment and hostility are common. But conversion does not help one to resolve these attitudes, for "overt cruelties and hatreds now receive acceptance under the cloak of a divine goal." He blames evangelical revival meetings and tent campaigns for stirring up an atmosphere of hate and fear and for unleashing resentment and "unconscious destructive feelings." He concludes that spontaneous conversions are detrimental to the mental health of an individual and that the situations which produce them are best avoided.

In 1965 F. J. Roberts conducted a study of forty-three theology students, twenty-three of whom had experienced "sudden conversions." He found that both extraversion and neuroticism were normally distributed in this group and drew the conclusion that neuroticism was not significantly related to the type of conversion experienced. This would seem to contradict Salzman's findings. He did note, however, that those who embraced the faith in which they were raised were significantly more neurotic than those who came from homes of dissimilar faith. He believed that this may have been attributable to the fact that the latter made a conscious and deliberate choice with regard to their personal convictions and in doing so underwent a successful integrative process. The former group, however, may have felt themselves unduly pressured to conform to their parents' desires and their maturational process was consequently stunted. "Conversion" for these was perhaps only a pseudo-solution since anxiety continued to characterize them. But Roberts did not believe that the incidence of their anxiety was significantly higher or more intense than in the population ar large.

Charles Spellman, Glen Baskett, and Donn Byrne attempted in

1971 to resolve the apparent contradiction between Salzman's and Roberts's findings. With the help of local ministers, three groups of residents in a predominantly Protestant town were classified according to their having experienced sudden conversions, gradual conversions, or no conversion at all (this last group was labeled "nonreligious"). Each individual was then psychologically measured according to the Taylor Manifest Anxiety Scale. The thesis being tested was that if as Salzman claimed conversion was only a pseudo-solution to adolescent integration problems, a reduction in anxiety should *not* be observed on the part of those who had experienced spontaneous conversion. This proved to be the case, for the resulting means of anxiety were as follows: sudden converts, 26.65; gradual converts, 17.81; and nonreligious, 18.40. Salzman's observations were thus confirmed: the anxiety level of spontaneous converts was not reduced and, in certain cases, was perhaps even raised. The concluding hypothesis contained a prediction that when sudden converts realized that their anxiety remained high, they would probably backslide or seek a new solution to difficulties.

In 1965 John Lofland and Rodney Stark introduced a theory in which conversion was attributed to a form of reverse psychology. After studying a millennarian cult on the West Coast of the United States they proposed that in highly individualistic Western societies it is often the case that persons "relinquish a more widely-held perspective for an unknown, obscure and often socially devalued one." Conversion thus becomes a form of protest against familial or social conditions deemed to be less than ideal. According to this study seven factors, or "predisposing conditions," are necessary for conversion, the first being the experience of *tension* between an imagined ideal and one's actual situation. This may involve feelings of frustration, rage, or helplessness. Second, the subject must possess a *religious problem-solving perspective.* All of the participants in the study were uninformed about conventional psychiatric and political perspectives for defining problems; all had come from small towns and religious communities and thought only in terms of religious faith as a solution to life's difficulties. At the same time, each was convinced that conventional religious institutions offered no viable solutions to these difficulties, and that alternatives must therefore be sought. This leads to the third characteristic, that of *seekership.*

Each member of the sect classified himself or herself as a pilgrim, as one breaking new ground and seeking new possibilities in terms of lifestyle and worldview.

Each subject eventually reached a *turning point*; a moment when "old lines of action were complete, had failed or had been disrupted." New involvements became both desirable and possible. At this stage *cult-affective bonds* were formed: relationships were established with individuals who had already made the decision to adhere to the sect's teachings. The influence of such persons was profound and played a key role in attracting others. But *extra–cult-affective bonds* were significant as well, wherein the *disapproval* of a person or persons with whom the subject had a negative relationship (e.g., parents) through a reverse psychological process became a motivation for an even deeper involvement with the nontraditional group. Finally, the new member was drawn into *intensive inter-action* with other group members through being given specific tasks connected with the group's purposes and objectives. This active (as opposed to purely verbal) participation served to solidify the convert's feelings of belonging.

According to this model, conversion does not perform an integrative function but serves rather as an escape mechanism from and a way of "getting even" with that which is perceived to be a hostile environment. In some respects this parallels Erik Erikson's concept of a "moratorium alternative" as interpreted and applied by V. Bailey Gillespie in his 1979 study entitled *Religious Conversion and Personal Identity: How and Why People Change*. According to Erikson, young people struggling with the adolescent integration process sometimes opt for a "retreat" to a situation in which they are able to work out a plan of self-reorganization and integration without disturbance from the more mundane realities of life. Martin Luther's monastic interlude serves as an example of this. Gillespie expands on this idea and proposes that an adolescent conversion experience may function as an entrance to a kind of psychological moratorium and that for some individuals it may actually serve to postpone the genuine integrative crisis to a later time. He cites the following passage from Erikson in support of this contention:

> They are marking time before they come to their crossroad, which they often do in their late 20s, belated just because they gave their

all to the temporary subject of devotion. The crisis in such a young man's life may be reached exactly when he half-realizes that he is fatally over-committed to what he is not.[1]

The teenage conversion experience, then, would be nothing more than a pseudo- or interim solution, albeit a positive and even essential one. It would be classified by James Fowler as merely one of what he termed in a recent study "stages of faith." Fowler distinguishes between "conversion," which he defines as a change in the *content* of faith (a qualitative change), and what he calls "the developmental growth of faith" (a quantitative change). According to this paradigm many of the earlier studies mentioned did not actually deal with conversion at all, since, strictly speaking, no crossing of religious or ideological boundaries was involved. Thus people who are raised within a Christian environment and who make a voluntary decision during adolescence to adopt formally the precepts of Christianity do not "convert" but merely ascend to a higher stage of faith. In Fowler's reckoning this would be a movement from Stage 2 ("Mythic-Literal Faith") to Stage 3, which he terms the stage of "Synthetic-Conventional Faith." At this level the individual synthesizes values and information, thus acquiring a basis for the formation of his identity and outlook on life—another way of describing James's integration process. The significance of Fowler's thesis is that this stage is not the culmination of the religious life but may (and should) be followed by three additional phases. Following the level of synthesis is the fourth stage, that of "Individuative-Reflective Faith"; this spans the period from young adulthood to age thirty-five and is described as a "demythologizing phase" in which the self claims an identity no longer defined by a composite of roles or meanings to others. Stage 5 involves "Conjunctive Faith" and usually begins around midlife. It involves the integration into one's self and outlook on life "much that was suppressed or unrecognized in the interest of Stage Four's self-certainty." In this phase one is aware of paradoxes and apparently contradictory truths and strives to unify opposites in the mind and in experience. One is ready for "that which is different and threatening to self and outlook, including new depths of experience in spirituality and religious revelation." The paradoxes acknowledged in this stage are resolved in the sixth and final phase, that of "Universalizing Faith." On this level occurs "a desciplined, activist *incarnation* of the imperatives of absolute love and justice," in spite of any "threats to self, to primary groups and to institutional arrangements of the present order" which may be involved. Few attain this level; it is reserved for those willing to pay the ultimate price for their religious commitment.

Among the more recent studies of conversion as it was previously defined by Starbuck and James is that of Max Heirich, who in 1977 published an article entitled "Change of Heart: A Test of Some Widely Held Theories About Religious Conversion." His findings appear in many ways to contradict all previous research. Heirich first categorizes studies prior to his own under three different rubrics. Conversion may first of all be "a fantasy solution to stress, in which the threatening situation is dealt with either by making an alliance with supernatural forces or by changing one's frame of reference so that previously distressing material no longer seems important." The conclusions of Salzman, Spellman, and Gillespie would fall into this category. According to the second rubric, conversion is attributable to "previous conditioning that leaves one right for the plucking." Parental orientations may affect the eldest child, sex role education may explain the dominance of female converts over males, and so on. The theories of Starbuck and James would be included here. "Interpersonal influence and encapsulation" form the third category, "whereby inputs from others become so mutually consistent and reinforcing that one begins to see things through others' eyes." Lofland and Stark would recognize in this statement an allusion to their observations of the efficacy of cult-affective bonds. But Heirich is critical of his predecessors' failure to employ control groups against which their findings could be measured. His own studies indicated that when compared with such a control group, persons experiencing religious conversions showed no significant difference in the amount of personal stress, the environment of their upbringing, the significance of peer influence, and the like. Very few of his subjects reported a devout upbringing, a parochial education, or being eldest in a devout household. His conclusion was that the process of conversion occurs through use of available social networks for those who are *already* seekers. In other words, while one can account for the *route* that conversion takes within a population, that which *prompts* the religious quest is still a mystery. No single factor or even group of factors provides a motivation. Heirich came away convinced that a great deal more research was needed to produce new and alternative theories.

As if in answer, the following year brought a new thesis by Flo Conway and Jim Siegelman. Abandoning the strong reliance upon psychological and sociological theories that had characterized previous studies, this team proposed a physiological cause for the phenomenon they chose to call "snapping." This is in actuality a synonym for the concept of spontaneous conversion, which for these authors is an experience of far graver significance than others had previously recognized. They reported that psychological and sociological factors do indeed play a role in the conversion experience but that they actually lead to biochemical alterations in the structure of the brain itself, resulting in altered states of consciousness. Such alterations can be produced "by means of simple techniques of communication: age-old tools of rhetoric and persuasion, refined methods of propaganda and mass-marketing and as yet little-understood elements of group dynamics and non-verbal communication." Using the work of Stanford neurophysiologist Karl Pribram as a foundation, they proposed that the brain functions as a holographic storage and retrieval system and that a "holographic crisis" can be brought on through use (or misuse) of the previously mentioned communications techniques. These can induce "emotionally-charged mental conflicts demanding urgent resolution." Here again James's integration process appears, but Conway and Siegelman imbue it with an essentially hysterical character. The crisis results in the brain finally succumbing to a "physiological dysfunction which renders it receptive to new ideas and physically incapable of judging or evaluating the wisdom or correctness of those ideas." In other words, something "snaps." The aftermath of this experience is all-important, for if the brain's attempt to reorganize itself is thwarted, the change may become permanent. If the person remains in an alien environment, for instance, he will almost certainly be reorganized in conformity with that environment. Reversal of this dysfunction can be accomplished only by a process equally crisis-oriented and abrupt (a controversial form of which is the procedure known as "deprogramming"). Conway and Siegelman are convinced that "snapping" is characteristic of the conversion process found not only in connection with extremist cults but even with the more "orthodox" Christian denominations that specialize

in "revivals," "tent-meeting campaigns," and "born-again experiences."

What may be gleaned from the foregoing studies? A primary
observation is that each was conducted from a Christian perspective
and in a Christian environment. Even the allegedly "neutralist" or
"secularist" approaches are characterized by either Christian
presuppositions or a confinement to distinctively Western (and hence
in some sense Christian) case studies. Very little research appears
to have been conducted concerning conversion to non-Christian
religious traditions apart from a few works such as Nock's
Conversion (1933), Levtzion's *Conversion to Islam* (1979), Bulliet's
Conversion to Islam in the Medieval Period (1979), and Rosen-
bloom's *Conversion to Judaism: From the Biblical Period to the
Present* (1978), all of which approach the subject from a historical
viewpoint. New ground will therefore be broken in approaching the
subject of conversion to Islam phenomenologically.

Second, previous conclusions regarding religious conversion must
be considered tentative due to the contradictory nature of those
findings. Theological, sociological, psychological, and physiological
causes have all been suggested as giving rise to conversion
experiences, and though it is possible that each of these may play
at least a small part in the overall process, it is impossible on the
basis of the research which has hitherto been conducted to specify
with any precision the way in which this process functions in
complete detail.

Despite the difficulties associated with these studies, one can
construct from them a model of conversion that will be useful for
comparative purposes. Setting aside exceptional cases, certain
characteristics do appear with marked regularity.

(1) William James's *integration factor* appears to play a key role
in the conversion process. Conversion to a religious belief involves
commitment to a theology, a worldview, an epistemology, an
ontology, a moral ethic, and the like. One receives personal identity
constructs in addition to a pattern according to which the various
aspects of life may be organized into a rational system. "Religious
converts" are those persons who in their struggle to integrate these
factors choose a religious as opposed to a nonreligious solution to
their difficulties.

(2) Conversion in Western contexts occurs most often during

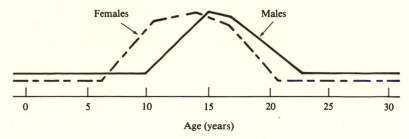

Females   Males

| | | | | | | |
| 0 | 5 | 10 | 15 | 20 | 25 | 30 |

Age (years)

FIGURE 2. Age of conversion for males and females.

adolescence or in a period immediately following adolescence. The average age according to Starbuck was 14.8 for females and 16.4 for males, according to Roberts 15 years, and according to Gillespie 16 years. Gillespie also reported that in a survey conducted in 1958 of thirty-two other studies of religious conversion, sociologist Michael Argyle concluded that the dominant age of religious conversion in America was 15 years. Starbuck's observation that female conversion occurs slightly earlier than that of males has been attributed to differences in physiological maturation; these findings are portrayed graphically in Figure 2. As mentioned in a previous context this age factor may be positively related to the "integration struggle" mentioned earlier. Adolescence is usually the period of time during which individuals are most intensely involved in constructing a worldview and lifeview as well as forming a personal identity. Since adoption of a religious faith contributes to each of these, it is only logical to expect that the highest rate of conversion will take place during the time when the struggle to integrate reaches its peak intensity.

(3) Some form of *personal stress* or *anxiety* was found to be a factor in nearly all of the studies mentioned. Although Roberts and Heirich do not believe this to be a significant factor, the preponderance of the evidence supports the observation that this psychological state (attributable to a variety of causes) plays a part in the conversion process. It is my belief that it is neither the quality nor the quantity of anxiety that is important here (for according to Heirich's research the difference in anxiety levels between the subject [convert] group and control groups was not great) but rather the psychological ability or inability of the subject *to deal with* stress

that is significant. Here again the integration struggle may play an important role. Most individuals are apparently able to deal with this conflict and its concomitant anxiety through commitment to nonreligious worldviews and life views, since the majority of people do not experience religious conversion. Only a minority seek a religious solution and for many of them it is apparently a satisfactory one. It is obvious from Spellman's findings that gradual (as opposed to spontaneous) converts did indeed experience a reduction in personal anxiety and that therefore the conversion experience of these people was a viable solution to the difficulties experienced in connection with the integration process.

(4) *Interpersonal relationships* are significant in the conversion process, and it appears that the effect of these is the same whether they are of a positive or negative nature, given the presence of the other factors mentioned. The conversion of an individual may be due to the influence of other individuals who have themselves been converted and with whom one enjoys a positive relationship or it may be a reaction to or protest against persons for whom one feels hatred or disrespect. The point is that people do not convert in isolation from other individuals; some personal influence, either positive or negative, is always present.

(5) One or more of a number of *conscious motivational factors* are influential at the time of conversion. Starbuck delineated a set of such factors, and no one has improved upon his list since the time of his research. He listed eight items which he observed most often among his subjects, and these were as follow:

> *Fears*—involving a general insecurity concerning life, in particular with regard to death and the afterlife.
> *Other self-regarding motives*—a desire for status, an aspiration to a profession in the ministry, desire to see a loved one in Heaven, and the like.
> *Altruistic motives*—involving a desire to be a part of a religion perceived as being based on an ethic of love, of sacrifice, and of service to mankind.
> *Following out a moral ideal*—which presupposes that religion upholds the highest of such ideals.
> *Remorse for and conviction of sin.*
> *Response to teaching*—which involves an "intellectual" or "rational" decision.
> *Example and imitation*—which involve the influence of family, relatives, and/or peers.

Urging and social pressure—which are akin to the last-mentioned motivation but are of a more direct and intense nature.

All of the case studies conducted by various researchers since Starbuck reveal one or more of the preceding motivations. The majority of Roberts's seminary subjects appear to have been motivated largely by example and imitation along with urging and social pressure. The adherents of the cult that was the subject of Lofland and Stark's research were following out a moral ideal which they had been unable to find in traditional religious institutions; the fact that the cult is described as "millennarian" is indicative that "fears" might have played a role as well. Bragan reported that one of the subjects of his research displayed "a vague, guilty awareness of having used his conversion for personal gain," implying that "self-regarding motives" were involved in his decision-making. Salzman criticized evangelical revival meetings for "stirring up an atmosphere of hate and fear." Heirich noted that an entire segment of conversion research is devoted to experiences attributable to interpersonal influences which create a situation "whereby inputs from others become so mutually consistent and reinforcing that one begins to see things through the others' eyes," obviously a form of example and imitation. Starbuck's list thus appears to be exhaustive, at least from the standpoint of conversion to Christianity.

The "typical" religious convert in the West, then, is a person between the ages of 12 and 18 (average 15 or 16). The individual has grappled with the need to integrate the various internal and external factors impinging upon his or her life into a unified whole and has simultaneously, perhaps as a result of this conflict, experienced some form of personal anxiety or stress. A religious as opposed to nonreligious resolution to both the integration struggle and the anxiety is sought and is found through a relationship with another individual who has opted for or is positively disposed toward a religious solution. The final commitment, which is more likely to be made spontaneously than it is to be made as the result of a prolonged process of reflection and consideration, may be attributable to one or more of the motivational factors observed by Starbuck. To what extent does this profile accord with a description of the typical Western convert to Islam? This is the question that is taken up in the next chapter.

10

Conversion to Islam

The topic of conversion to Islam has been very little explored. T. W. Arnold remarked in *The Preaching of Islam* that "Muslim literature is singularly poor in those records of conversions that occupy such a large place in the literature of the Christian Church," and Richard Bulliet observed in 1979 that "although interest in the subject has grown in recent years ... the great conversion experience that fundamentally changed world history by uniting the peoples of Middle East in a new religion has had few modern chroniclers." Neither of these authors offers a reason for this neglect. The theory may be proposed that since Muslims do not emphasize supernatural phenomena in connection with conversion (as does Christianity in its recording of the Apostle Paul's experience on the road to Damascus, Constantine's hearing of the voice from heaven prior to the Battle of Milvian Bridge, and Augustine's radical departure from his early lifestyle), historians of Islam considered the experience of conversion to be normative and therefore not necessary to report. For Christians supernatural conversion experiences have had apologetical value and it has been helpful to record as many as possible. But the Muslim believes that the propositional tenets of his faith are self-evident if they are properly presented and understood, and the focus of his proselytization is the proclamation of these tenets rather than the experiences of human beings. Another possibility is that the external-institutional missiological approach explicated earlier produced in many localities an intergenerational change which was so gradual that there was simply nothing tangible to report.

As Bulliet mentions, however, there has in recent years been increasing interest in this subject. His own *Conversion to Islam in the Medieval Period* and Nehemia Levtzion's *Conversion to Islam* are two of the most detailed studies that have appeared. The latter is an edited work containing articles of a general nature as well as essays dealing with a wide variety of geographical areas, including Iran, Anatolia (modern Turkey), South Asia, Indonesia, China, and Africa. Levtzion emphasizes the significance of the "ambience" created by a combination of the newly established Islamic institutions and the immigrating Muslim populations and shows how this environment gave rise to conversion. He deals with the importance of traders as agents of Islamization and also devotes a few paragraphs to a discussion of the role of the Sufi movement in spreading Islam outside the territories captured during the original jihāds. He concludes with a brief section concerning the distinction made by A. D. Nock between the concept of "conversion," which Nock limited to prophetic religions that are exclusive and require an unqualified commitment, and "adhesion," which he considered typical of nonprophetic religions and which is based upon a pragmatic attempt to satisfy "natural needs." Levtzion maintains that although Islam is a prophetic religion, its expansion throughout the Middle East and North Africa can be explained only in terms of a process of adhesion, thereby undermining Nock's categories. This is the closest that Levtzion comes to a phenomenological consideration of conversion.

Bulliet's work is not as geographically oriented as Levtzion's but deals rather with general trends in Islamic conversion processes. He discusses the subject of "individual" as opposed to what he calls "communal" conversion; these concepts are substantially the same as Nock's in that individual conversion would be true "conversion," whereas the communal phenomenon would be considered "adhesion." Bulliet also makes some sociological observations. He considers it axiomatic that "the convert's expectations of his new religion will parallel his expectations of his old religion" and that "no one willingly converts from one religion to another if by virtue of conversion he markedly lowers his social status." He also contends that from a political standpoint conversion to Islam leads "almost inevitably to a weakening or dissolution of central government" and that a clash of interests usually arises between elements of the population that convert at different times.

These are excellent studies, but they are of little use in research involving Islam in America. This is mainly due to the fact that these authors approached the topic from a historical standpoint, noting when various populations became "Muslim" and certain aspects of the process by which this occurred. Very few phenomenological observations were made and even these are questionable. Lofland and Stark's study, for instance, does not bear out Bulliet's claim that the convert will expect from his new religion the same things that he did from his old; their research revealed that the convert often seeks something radically different from his former faith. Nor would they agree that no one willingly converts if by so doing he will lower his social status, for their findings showed that converts to cults such as the one they were studying often seek to escape the upper or middle-class values with which they were raised and actually welcome a more primitive living standard. Also, while Levtzion's and Bulliet's studies offer some suggestions as to the motivational factors involved in conversion to Islam (i.e., Levtzion's observation that at the time of the original jihāds upper class populations converted in order to maintain status and wealth while lower classes sought to gain these items), descriptions of these factors are general and are applied to populations as a whole. Individual factors are left untouched. Finally, the studies were confined to geographical areas that have been under the domination of Muslim peoples for centuries. Neither dealt with the subject of conversion to Islam in the West, in either Europe or America. Nor was any of the research by the various social sciences regarding religious conversion in Western contexts used for purposes of comparison by Bulliet, Levtzion, or any of the authors in Levtzion's collected work.

Research Methodology

The objective of the research conducted for this chapter was to determine the nature of conversion to Islam within Western contexts with respect to the sociological characteristics of converts (i.e., age, gender, religious background, etc.) and the motivational factors involved in their decisions to become Muslims. The source material for this study became of necessity a composite of different kinds of information. Originally the analysis was to be based on the results of a questionnaire that was developed for use in ascertaining certain facts regarding the experiences of North American converts to Islam. A general letter was mailed to twenty Muslim organizations which, on the basis of the goals and objectives outlined in their publications, could be considered offensive-activist agencies. The letter described the proposed project and included a sample questionnaire. Inquiry was made as to the feasibility of distributing the questionnaires through the organization and having the agency then either collect and return the completed forms or recommend that the individuals to whom the forms were given return them. All participants were assured of absolute anonymity. The majority of these agencies did not respond or were unwilling to cooperate. Eight organizations, however, were agreeable and questionnaires were mailed in varying quantities.

The results were disappointing. Only twelve of the questionnaires were completed and returned. This was probably due to the suspicion that exists among American Muslims regarding research into their lifestyles and religious experiences. There is a lack of confidence in the ability of non-Muslims to properly understand and portray those who adhere to the Islamic faith. Other researchers have met with similar difficulties. In a recently published study of Islam in the United States, Yvonne Haddad and Adair Lummis stated that

> some mosques were reluctant to cooperate, and others simply refused, out of fear of misuse or distortion of the information. Many immigrants are suspicious of researchers because they come from countries where the only people asking questions are government agents or spies. One of the major difficulties we encountered in collecting our research was that of establishing sufficient trust that our questions could be answered openly and honestly. Assurance of anonymity was helpful, but the bitter experience that some in the Muslim community have had in the American context made many of those interviewed suspicious of our motives and watchful of our methods.[1]

Yasin al-Jibouri of the International Islamic Society of Virginia gave the following response to an inquiry concerning the feasibility of distributing questionnaires through his office:

> You probably will not find too many Muslims who would respond to your inquiries simply because of trust. Muslims during the last few years have become the target of a very cruel, systematic, well-organized, funded and publicized campaign aiming at discrediting

them and their beliefs. For this reason, and for others, Muslims have become more cautious, withdrawn and alerted than ever before. They would not trust their own Muslim brethren unless they know them for a lengthy period of time.

Thus alternative sources of information were needed, so I began an extensive examination of Muslim periodicals, booklets, and books, seeking written accounts of the conversion of Westerners to Islam. This research yielded sixty separate testimonies from a variety of sources, including the newsletter *Invitation* of the Islamic Information Center of America; the periodicals *Islamic Affairs, Muslim News International, The Arab World, The Whole Earth Review, The Islamic Order, Islamic Horizons, The Islamic Review,* and the *Chicago Tribune*; booklets by Maryam Jameelah (Margaret Marcus), Muhammad Webb, and Nishikanta Chattopadhyaya; and books such as al-Jindī's *Āfāq Jadīda lil-Daʿwah al-Islamiyya fī ʿĀlam al-Gharb,* Peter Clark's *Marmaduke Pickthall: British Muslim,* and Muhammad Asad's *The Road to Mecca.*

The use of these sources changed the nature of the study from one dealing exclusively with American converts to one which involved a composite of both Americans and Europeans. Of the subjects, 34 were Americans (47 percent of the total) while 38 were Europeans (53 percent). Of this latter figure 28 were British citizens, 5 were Dutch, 2 German, and 1 each Hungarian, Austrian, and Polish.

A possible objection regarding this methodology concerns one of the chief sources used in gathering these testimonies. *The Islamic Review* is published by the Ahmadiyya sect, considered by most Muslims to be heretical in its doctrines and beliefs. The question may be raised as to whether adherence to the Ahmadiyya may truly be considered adherence to Islam. But the Ahmadiyya Movement was included in the discussion of offensive-activist groups and its conversion dynamics are therefore significant. Also, *The Islamic Review* is a publication not of the Qadiani but rather of the Lahori division of the Ahmadiyya. The latter is considered to be far closer to orthodoxy than the former due to its view of Ghulam Ahmad as a *mujaddid* (a "renewer") of the Muslim faith rather than a prophet. The main teachings of the Lahoris with regard to Muhammad, Tawhīd, the Five Pillars, and other significant aspects of the religion, are indistinguishable from those of traditional Sunni doctrine. Finally, *The Islamic Review* does not indicate whether the individuals whose testimonies it publishes are actually members of the Ahmadiyya. It is certain that at least two of the accounts included in the magazine concern people who had no connection whatsoever with the movement (Muhammad Webb and Margaret Marcus), and it may therefore be assumed that other accounts involve persons generally known to be converts to Islam but not connected with the Ahmadis.

Admittedly, the sampling is not large. Yvonne Haddad claims in her article "Islam in America," written in 1982, that 5,000 individuals of European background have converted to Islam. She gives no documentation for this figure, but if its validity is assumed, the 34 Americans represent less than 1 percent of the total. Recall, however, that Starbuck's study involved only 192 subjects, surely an even smaller percentage of the total number of Christian converts in America at that time.

Results of the Study

Of the 72 testimonies examined, 50 (69 percent) concerned males and 22 (31 percent) females. These statistics indicate that men are attracted to Islam at least as much as and perhaps more than women. The survey conducted by Starbuck and upon which his *Psychology of Religion* was based consisted of 192 cases, 120 of which were females (62.5 percent) and 72 of which were males (37.5 percent). These proportions are nearly the opposite of those observed in the survey of Muslim converts. While this differentiation may be attributable to the random nature of the survey, it may also be due to the nature of the Islamic faith. Although this religion upholds a theoretical equality between male and female, traditionally it has been characterized by male orientation and domination. The veiling and seclusion of Muslim women, the fact that their attendance is not required at mosque functions, and their exclusion from official positions of leadership are evidence of the accuracy of this characterization. There exists no general perception of the mosque as being essentially an organization for women and children. The stereotypical image of the Muslim male emphasizes his virility and masculinity, and this may well be a source of appeal to Western men. One British convert, for instance, noted that he had been raised in Christian surroundings but that he actually worshiped "nobility and courage" and it was due to his observation of these traits in Muslim men that he converted to Islam.

Aside from the positive influence such characteristics may exercise upon males, a correspondingly negative effect may be aroused in females. The media presentation of the Muslim woman as veiled, secluded, uneducated, and little more than a material possession of the male finds little to commend it in the eyes of the contemporary Western woman, and although traditional Eastern standards of dress and social interaction are not as a rule enforced in Western contexts, the stereotypes regarding female subjugation to the male have exercised a wide influence, which has perhaps contributed to the relatively low proportion of female converts. Note that the proportional disparity is greater in Western Europe than it is in America (see Table 1). This may be due to the fact that a large proportion of European males attribute their conversions to wartime experiences that brought them in close contact with Muslim cultures (33 percent of European male converts mentioned this factor in their testimonies). The women, who remained at home during the world wars, did not come under such influences. As for the nearly equal proportions of male and female converts in America, the larger number of females is possibly attributable to one of three factors. First, it may be that just as Christianity has been accused of being a religion of women and children, religion *in general* has come to be perceived as a female-oriented phenomenon, and thus women in America are found to adhere in greater proportions to *all* expressions of faith. Second, it is possible that some women have reacted negatively to the feminist movement (including its effects upon the Christian church) and have deliberately sought a more conservative alternative. Third, it may be that American women are less opposed

TABLE 1.   Conversion to Islam According to Gender

Gender	Americans	Europeans	Total
Males	18	32	50 (68%)
Females	16	6	22 (32%)

to marrying Muslim men (which nearly always involves conversion to Islam even though the official precepts of the religion do not require it of Christians and Jews) than are European women, but no statistical information on this subject is available.[2]

The religious background of the converts was predominantly Christian. Of the 72 converts, 41 (57 percent) mentioned that they had been Christians or raised as Christians; 10 stated specifically that they were Roman Catholic, 8 that they were members of Protestant denominations, and 23 simply called themselves "Christian" without specifying rite or denomination. In addition 5 persons (7 percent of the total) spoke of Jewish backgrounds, 2 (3 percent) claimed to be "agnostic," 1 (an Indian residing in Great Britain) had been a Hindu, and 23 (32 percent) did not mention a religious background at all.

The converts were quite explicit concerning their general dissatisfaction with their previous religious beliefs. Eleven individuals mentioned that at a specific point in their lives they consciously and deliberately rejected the faith in which they had been raised. Six gave an age at which this occurred, the average of these being 16.8 years. Other testimonies were indicative of a relatively young age of rejection, although no specific figures were given. As noted previously, the average age of conversion to Christianity is 15–16 years; thus the testimonies of converts to the Islamic faith reveal that there is a body people who, at almost precisely the same time when other persons are committing themselves to adhere to the faith in which they were raised or which is dominant in their culture, choose deliberately and conciously to *reject* that religion.

For a significant number of converts rejection of the faith of their parents or culture did not imply a rejection of religion in general. This is evidenced by the fact that many proceeded to explore other religious alternatives following their initial rejection of a particular faith. Eight individuals spoke of brief encounters with Buddhism, four with Hinduism, two with Taoism, two with Unitarianism (apparently not considered a division of Christianity), two with Judaism, and one each with Ba'hai, Confucianism, and Sikhism. Five individuals recounted experiences with a multiplicity of religions before deciding upon Islam.

Few were explicit with regard to their reasons for rejecting particular religious faiths. Of the Christians, six expressed dis-

TABLE 2.   Religious Background of Converts to Islam

Background	Number of Converts
Christian	
Roman Catholic	10
Protestant	8
Denomination not specified	23
Total Christian	41
Jewish	5
Hindu	1
Agnostic	2
No indication	23

satisfaction with the "irrationality" of the concept of the Trinity, the doctrine of transubstantiation, and similar teachings. Some were disappointed with Christianity's inability to speak to modern social issues and one rejected the religion's exclusivistic claims. Most, however, reported that they had simply "left the religion."

It is in the statistics concerning the age at which conversion to Islam occurred that the greatest deviation from the previously mentioned studies of religious conversion in the West is found. Forty-one of the converts reported their exact age or gave sufficient biographical information to allow determination of it within three to five years. The average age of all the converts at the time of their conversion experiences was 31.4 years. For the twenty two Americans whose ages could be determined, the average was 29; Europeans were slightly older at 33.7. These figures indicate that a significant amount of time elapsed between an individual's rejection of the religion of his culture or upbringing and his decision to become a Muslim. If the figure of 16.8 years is used as the age of rejection, and that of 31.4 years as the age of conversion, this gives an average of 14.6 years during which the individual either was experimenting with religious beliefs other than Islam or was neglectful of religion altogether.

Erik Erikson's observations regarding a "moratorium period" may be of use here. Recall that Erikson posited that many adolescents struggling with the integration process opt to "retreat" for a period of time in order to work out a plan of self-reorganization or integration without disturbance from mundane realities. His remarks concerning the time span connected with the moratorium concept are particularly applicable, for he states that individuals are "marking time before they come to their crossroad, which they often do in their late 20s." Erikson is referring in this passage to Augustine and Luther, who eventually returned ("converted") to the dominant religion of their environment. But in the case of the converts to Islam a different outcome is seen. The rejection of a religious faith at the precise time when many were converting *to* the religion of their parents marked for them the entrance into a period of spiritual moratorium. Rejecting all commitments to a specific religion allowed them to explore other religious alternatives, something they could not have done had they undergone conversion during adolescence due to the exclusivistic claims of Christianity and Judaism.

How did this rejection of a religious solution affect the integration process? The individuals merely adopted "secular" identities and worldviews in the same way that persons do who accomplish integration without resort to religious conversion. But this was only a temporary or incomplete integration, for the subjects eventually sought a religious alternative with which to replace the nonreligious. Figure 3 shows the spiritual development of the religious convert according to Western research compared with the findings concerning the convert to the Muslim faith. In a Christian context the individual typically experiences conversion at age fifteen or sixteen and this becomes a period of maximal commitment to the religion. Researchers have noted that this is usually followed by a period of lesser commitment, or "backsliding," during which the convert concentrates upon other aspects of life (education, choice of career, marriage, etc.). When some measure of occupational, marital, and financial security has been attained, and in particular when children have reached school age, there is usually a renewed commitment to religious values, church attendance, and the like.

Note the differences between this profile and that of the convert to Islam. This individual inhabits the same spiritual environment and may even make some initial progress toward a conversion experience but then rejects completely the religion of his upbringing or environment. There follows a moratoriumlike period which lasts an average of 14.6 years during which other spiritual options are sometimes explored. Conversion to Islam, a faith entirely divorced from the religion of the environment of upbringing, occurs in the late twenties or early thirties.

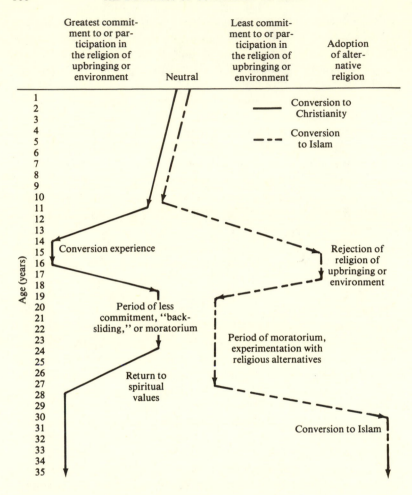

FIGURE 3. A comparison of the development stages of converts according to standard Western research and converts to Islam.

Of what does the conversion experience consist? What must one do to become a Muslim? The testimonies offered very little explanation of what was involved. Most individuals merely stated that they had become Muslims at such and such a time after a particular event. A few referred to a public recitation of the Shahadah ("There is no God but Allah and Muhammad is His messenger") as their *formal* conversion, but a number of converts felt that they had *always* been Muslims without knowing it or that they had gradually realized that they had become Muslims at some indeterminate point in the past. Muhammad Asad records that he came upon a man in Afghanistan who, after conversing with him for a time, declared that he was already a Muslim in his heart and that he should formally repeat the Shahadah. Evelyn Cobold, a British writer, stated that "it is probable that I have been a Muslim since my earliest years."[3] Margaret Marcus (now Maryam Jameelah) remarked that she had "always been a Muslim at heart." Daniel Moore felt that he had accepted Islam "in his bones" long before his formal profession, and Jamil Abd al-Shukoor Plant came to the conclusion after being stationed in Singapore that "in actual fact ... I had been a Muslim at heart for at least two years before my return." These statements indicate that conversion to Islam did not involve an upheaval in the lives of these individuals. On the contrary, it appears that it is possible for one to slip effortlessly into the religion; that one can take on the characteristics of Islamicity without being aware that a significant transformation is taking place.

This observation accords well with the fact that seventy-one of the seventy-two conversions under investigation must be categorized as "process" as opposed to "spontaneous" experiences. They are not the result of an emotional reaction to pressures brought to bear by the atmosphere of a revival or tent-meeting campaign. In most cases there was no crisis, no sense of desperation, no abject feeling of lostness or hopelessness driving individuals to seek religious solutions to their difficulties. There was no occurrence of what Conway and Siegelman call snapping, since there were no "emotionally-charged mental conflicts needing urgent resolution." The converts did not become "dull and glassy-eyed" or "mindless zombies" who isolated themselves from society. On the contrary, most were warm and open individuals who were fully conscious and aware not only of their own local environment but of the international aspects of the faith they had adopted. Their conversion experiences were the end result of a long process of seeking, a deliberate choice made after careful examination and consideration of alternatives. This is a rational as opposed to emotional approach to religion, and as such stands in clear contrast to Starbuck's description of his Christian subjects' "intensity of emotions." He noted that "the whole nature [of the convert] is in a high state of tension, and that the senses are much more acute." The emotion is more often in terms of feeling than sight or hearing, as of being bound to the seat, having a choking sensation in the throat, carrying a load on the shoulders, and the like. Sometimes, however, the emotions gave way to "the presentation of unusual sights" and "voices of condemnation and assurance." Such occurrences are apparently typical of contemporary conversions, for Conway and Siegelman wrote in 1978 that among those who are "born again" in America "a tingling of energy appears to be common, along with alternating feelings of heat and cold. Frequently, the individual will have the impression of a cleansing flow of water, which is usually accompanied by an uncontrollable surge of tears."[4]

Such expressions are not characteristic of Muslim converts. Of the seventy-two testimonies under consideration only three reported what may be called "supernatural experiences." Abd al-Karim Germanus of Hungary wrote that the prophet Muhammad appeared to him in a dream and that he felt a vivid fear upon seeing and hearing this personage. Jim Olson, a British military officer, also wrote of a dream in which he saw smoke rising from the earth to heaven, out of which shone "a marvelous light."[5] The word "Islam" was formed from this light on the smoke and this "filled his sight and senses"; shortly afterward he became a Muslim. And Luzita Fatima Aitken awoke one morning to find at the foot of her bed a "dazzling bright light like a great star," out of which came the "beautiful voice of a young man." This voice quoted two verses from the Christian Gospel of John but Aitken believed that the contents were an indication that Jesus desired her to convert to Islam. The overwhelming majority of the converts, however, speak of a gradual process involving conversation with Muslims, reading of the Qur'ān and/or other Islamic literature, and in some cases journeying to Muslim lands. At some point a conscious, rational decision was made to formally declare the Shahadah and to begin to follow fundamental Islamic practices. Half of the respondents to the questionnaire noted that they had experienced "a feeling of peace and happiness," but half noted no emotional response whatsoever. They had experienced no visions, voices, bright lights, "tingling," or "warmth," and apparently not even "peace and happiness." Conversions to Islam, then, differ significantly from conversions to

Christianity in that they appear to be "conversions of the head" (i.e., the intellect) rather than "conversions of the heart" (i.e., the emotions).

Careful examination of the testimonies reveals that very few of Lofland and Stark's conclusions regarding conversion to minority ("deviant") cults related to Islamic conversion. Their study involved individuals who had "relinquished a more widely-held perspective for an unknown, obscure, and, often, socially devalued one." Such a description would seem to be applicable to Islam, for the majority of the subjects indeed rejected a more widely held perspective (e.g., Christianity) and adopted Islam, which in the West is relatively unknown, obscure, and perceived by some to be socially inferior. However, most of the predisposing factors mentioned by the researchers as leading to conversion are diminished or entirely absent among converts to Islam. The first (tension or stress produced by disjunction between an imagined ideal and actuality) is discernible in only a few of the accounts. The overwhelming majority experienced no crisis, and this may be attributable to the fact that the subjects were, due to their age, beyond the stresses that normally accompany adolescence and the integration struggle. These individuals had resolved this struggle by rejecting the religion of their upbringing or culture and entering a "spiritual moratorium." Interim solutions were adopted which allowed the individual to function during the fourteen years that on the average were devoted to the mundane concerns of life before turning to Islam. The majority appear to have attained successful positions in various professional fields such as teaching, journalism, foreign service, and the military. Any problems that remained were limited to the metaphysical sphere and these were not of crisis proportions.

Lofland and Stark also posited that converts to a minority religion think exclusively in terms of a religious problem-solving perspective as opposed to psychological or political perspectives. This is true of converts to Islam insofar as they continue, even within the moratorium period, to seek a religious solution to questions of ultimate significance. But there is a difference between the subjects of Lofland and Stark's study and those of the present study. The converts to the millennarian cult had failed to integrate their society and culture into their worldviews. They had opted instead for a religious belief in a future paradise and resigned themselves to await the advent of this period, separating themselves in the meantime as much as possible from their political, social, and economic surroundings. It may be that integration of these factors of life was never truly accomplished in these individuals and that their cult experience was itself a type of moratorium. But if this is the case, conversion was for them *to* a moratorium period, while for the converts to Islam it was *from* such a period. The Muslim converts did not leave society, however, in all but one instance they continued with the careers adopted during the time before they converted to Islam.

"Seekership" is equally characteristic of both groups. Many converts to Islam characterized themselves as "seekers," and fourteen mentioned specifically that a number of years passed during which this search took place. Nine gave a specific number, and the average of these (excluding two which were extreme) was 5.7 years. For these subjects a sizable portion of the period between rejection of the old religion and acceptance of the new was spent in active searching. Unfortunately, Lofland and Stark did not record any figures for the average length of their subjects' seekership and therefore no comparison is possible. It may be assumed that the adherents of such a cult were older than the average age of conversion (15–16), and so a period of searching can be posited. This would not be the case for Starbuck's subjects, however; they were simply too young and too immature to have engaged in a profound metaphysical search for a number of years.

The fourth factor, called "the turning point," involved coming to a place in life where old lines of action were complete, had failed, or had been disrupted. For the millennarian subjects this occurred just prior to conversion and formed an integral part of the process. One finds, however, that in a number of cases of conversion to Islam no such point appeared in connection with the conversion experience. The transition was often so effortless that realization of a change came at a much later time. If indeed a "turning point" exists in the process of becoming a Muslim, it is more likely to be located at the time of the individual's rejection of the religion of his parents or culture, and this is usually followed by a decade or more before conversion occurs.

Cult-affective bonds are extremely significant for Muslim converts. Lofland and Stark observed that the conversion of their subjects was ultimately attributable to their having come to accept "the opinions of friends." Of the converts to Islam, forty-three (60 percent) specifically mentioned the influence of a Muslim friend or an acquaintance in their decision to convert. Ann Abu-Ghosh tells of a best friend who converted to the Muslim faith; W. Ingram relates how impressed he was by a Muslim actor he was directing who would pray between takes;[6] folk-singer Cat Stevens tells how his brother gave him a Qur'ān he had purchased while visiting Palestine; Hussain Rofe befriended a Muslim missionary in London; J. F. Ruxton treated a Muslim patient and was impressed by his faith in the midst of suffering; Thomas Clayton met an Algerian Boy Scout while attending an International Boy Scout Jamboree in France. As previously mentioned, several military officers had come in contact with adherents of the Islamic faith during their tours of duty in Muslim countries.

There is evidence that "extra–cult-affective bonds," through which the disapproval of a person or persons with whom one has a negative relationship can become motivation for deeper involvement with the group that is disapproved of, played a role in only two cases. A certain amount of bitterness is detectable in the accounts of both Muhammad Asad and Maryam Jameelah with regard to the secular lifestyles of their Jewish families. Their rejection of Judaism may have been in reaction to their parents' abandonment of the metaphysical element of their ethnic heritage, and their adoption of the religion of the Arabs could be interpreted as a retaliatory act. There is too little information available in the remaining accounts to say whether or not similar situations might have played a role in the experiences of others.

The last of Lofland and Stark's predisposing factors (that of "intensive participation in the activities of the group") was not an important factor in the conversion of these subjects. It is said of Marmaduke Pickthall that he "went native" during his residency in Palestine, but this may refer only to matters of dress, eating habits, choice of residence, and the like. Since Islam forms such an integral part of the people's lifestyle in these regions, there was certainly exposure to Muslim practices on the part of Pickthall and all others who spent time in Muslim countries, but it is doubtful that many actually participated in prayers, the giving of alms, or the fast of Ramadan. Only one of the converts in the sample spoke of participation prior to conversion: R. L. Mellema, former director of the Islamic Hall of the Tropical Museum, Amsterdam, relates how he asked some Muslim friends if he could take part in the Friday prayers. The research by Lofland and Stark concerning conversion to a minority religious belief is thus only partially applicable within a Muslim context and their paradigm needs to be considerably refined before it can be used as an explanation of religious conversion in general.

The same is true with reference to Starbuck's list of motivational factors in the conversion process. As for the first ("fear of death and hell"), only Maryam Jameelah mentions a fear of death, while Abd al-Karim Germanus mentions a feeling of fear accompanying the vision of Muhammad which contributed to his conversion. No other convert mentions death, the Judgment, the Fire (al-Nar), or any other eschatological subject.

Under the rubric of "self-regarding motives" Starbuck listed such sentiments as "I wanted the approval of others"; "Father had died and I thought I would get to meet him"; and "Ambition of a refined sort influenced me." One searches in vain for any such phrase in the accounts of conversion to Islam.

"Altruistic motives" were of greater significance. As examples of these in the context of Christian conversion Starbuck recorded such phrases as "I felt I must do better and do more good in the world." This is similar in tone to the conviction of Mohammed Webb that Islam "develops higher and nobler elements of humanity." Twelve other converts mention that in Islam they saw the only hope for uniting mankind and creating equality among the races. The prevalence of such motives may be due in part to the age of the subjects; having experienced much of life they wished to contribute in some measure to the resolution of humanity's difficulties. Fourteen out of seventy-two represents nearly 20 percent of the sampling (four times the percentage which Starbuck records in his study) and yet this is still a relatively small figure and indicates that other motivations were of greater or equal significance.

One might suspect that a desire to "follow out a moral ideal" would be particularly characteristic of those who adopted the ethical religion of Islam, and generally speaking this is true. Daniel Moore mentioned that he was attracted to the "spiritual existentialism" which involved "how you enter a room, which foot you entered with, that you sip water but gulp milk, etc."; Maryam Jameelah, who had been repulsed by the immorality of her New York surroundings, found a haven in the "strictness" of her new faith. Michael Hames mentioned "morality" as an aspect that should attract everyone, as did R. L. Mellema. In addition to these, five of the twelve respondents to the questionnaire answered the question "What was the characteristic that most attracted you to Islam?" with "moral and ethical standards."

"Remorse for and conviction of sin" were entirely absent in seventy-one of the seventy-two cases. Only Luzita Aitken remarked that her decision to convert was in part due to "many sins and mistakes" which she had committed. Many other converts, however, maintained the exact opposite; they did *not* believe that they were "sinful" in the sense that Christianity claimed that all men were. Indeed, the doctrine of original sin was repulsive to several individuals and they mentioned that one of the precepts of Islam that most attracted them was the innate goodness of man.

Nor was "social pressure and urging" a factor in conversion. Starbuck's subjects converted to the dominant religion in America and it is expected in certain religious subcultures that one will choose to make a "profession of faith" when he or she reaches adolescence. The fact that one's peers are under the same social pressures creates a subtle desire not to be left out or left behind. This dynamic had great significance for Starbuck's converts; indeed, those listing "social pressure and urging" as their chief motivation for conversion formed the largest percentage of his converts (19 percent). This was not the case with Muslim converts in the West. The social pressure and urging which they received was in many cases to *reject* Islam as a religious alternative. Amina Benjelloun admitted that her sister, a psychiatrist, had become "quite worried" about her mental health. Hussain Rofe remarked that "people came to explain that I had taken a step backwards." Two of the respondents to the questionnaire indicated that their marriages to non-Muslims had ended in divorce when they began to adopt Islamic practices. Others stated that while family and friends attempted to understand and accept their decision to convert, it was apparent that they could not wholly comprehend the reasons for such a decision.

There remain the factors of "example and imitation" and "response to teaching," and these are the only two that are significantly characteristic of converts to Islam. With regard to the first, forty-three of the seventy-two converts mentioned specific individuals or groups that had influenced them in their decision. These persons furnished living examples of the Islamic faith that were attractive to those with whom they came in contact.

"Response to teaching" was the chief motivating factor for only 10 percent of Starbuck's subjects. But it was mentioned by the overwhelming majority of Muslim converts as figuring significantly in their experience. Fifty-four of the seventy-two converts (75 percent) mentioned either aspects of the teachings of Islam in general or some specific teaching (or teachings) of the religion as being instrumental in their decision to convert. This appears to inhere in the "process" nature of these experiences. The moratorium period between rejection of the parental and/or cultural religion and acceptance of Islam provided a time for careful reflection upon the precepts of a variety of alternatives. In a number of cases various teachings were examined comparatively and those of Islam were considered to be qualitatively superior.

In a careful analysis of the subjects' testimonies, five separate items related to the teachings of Islam appeared consistently. The first of these was *simplicity*; the precepts of Islam were perceived to be much less complicated than those of Christianity, Judaism, Hinduism, and Buddhism. The pronunciation of the Shahadah was all that was required to become a Muslim; no baptismal ceremonies or catechetical classes were necessary. Afterwards it was recommended that one participate in the five daily prayers, almsgiving, the fast of Ramadan, and the Pilgrimage, but none of these is complicated and none involves engagement in theological or philosophical speculation. Some 20 percent of the converts mentioned "simplicity" as a motivational factor, a majority using this very word. The Prophet, said Daniel Moore, was a "perfectly balanced master of wisdom and simplicity." H. F. Fellowes stated that Islam "is simple and straightforward, free from eleborations which cannot be believed." And former Anglican minister R. J. Flowers attributed his decision to convert to "the simplicity of truth and the sincerity of the Muslim people and Islamic doctrine." These Westerners viewed their own traditions as needlessly complicated and intricate. Some of the more educated converts alluded to the syncretistic tendencies inherent in Roman Catholic Christianity and stated that Christianity had become so corrupted by pagan accretions that it was impossible to give the present form of this faith credence as a revelation of God. Islam, on the other hand, was believed to have been preserved in its original form and was thus "simple" in the sense of being "pure" as well as "uncomplicated." "Islam," said Fauzuddin Ahmad Overing, "is the only pure religion, not a religion marred by Mythology, like Christianity and other religions."

Closely connected with this characteristic was the perception of Islam as a supremely *rational* faith. Some 21 percent of the converts claimed that the reasonableness of Islamic teachings was a major factor in their decision. Mohammed Webb noted that "Islam is the only system known to man which is strictly in harmony with reason and science." Through living among Muslims and discussing religious problems with them, Heidi Walser became acquainted with "the rationality and truth of the Islamic doctrines." And Harry Henkel found that "Islam appeals to one's reason; I found that it invites and encourages the pursuit of knowledge." Contrariwise, Christianity was perceived as being opposed to learning and science and replete with irrational beliefs such as the doctrines of the Trinity, the incarnation, the resurrection, and transubstantiation. In Islam one was not required to commit oneself to such unreasonable tenets; it was a natural religion that did not conflict with but rather accommodated the findings of modern science and was therefore the only viable option for the enlightened man or woman.

The preceding perceptions concern Islamic teachings in general. Specific precepts that were attractive to Westerners included first the emphasis upon Tawhīd (the Oneness of God) and its humanistic corollary the *universal brotherhood of man*. Some 19 percent of the converts mentioned this as being significant. Rolf Baron von Ehrenfels of Vienna listed as one of the primary reasons he adopted Islam the fact that "the concept of human brotherhood under all-encompassing divine fatherhood is much stressed in Islam." Sir Archibald Hamilton felt that he did not need "to say much about the Universal Brotherhood of man in Islam," for it was "a recognized fact [that] lord and vassal, rich and poor, are all alike." And H. S. Lewin stated that far from being only a theoretical formulation, "the brotherhood of men in Islam is very real." All but two of those who mentioned this aspect were European males, many of whom had served in the military during or following World War II. Concepts of brotherhood and unity were particularly appealing to these individuals. Contrast this with the fact that not a single American male mentioned this factor as important in his decision, which may be due to the fact that in his geographical, cultural, and historical environment the idea of unity was not significant. Among younger Americans, however, the idea of brotherhood may be more influential than the survey would indicate. John Renard observed that student converts to the Muslim faith are attracted by "Islam's positive stand on social justice and racial equality" and "the sense of belonging to a larger community."

Among the converts, 19 percent were attracted by what may be termed the *"this-worldly" focus of Islam* as opposed to the "other-worldly" orientation of Christianity. Christians were criticized for being too abstract and too impractical in their beliefs and for failing to provide a solution to the needs of human society. Hussain Rofe remarked that "both Christianity and Buddhism, if understood as the teaching of their founders, evaded social problems, for they had no interest in them."

Islam, on the other hand, was perceived as being a holistic faith which contained answers to every problem of mankind. Maryam Jameelah wrote that "Islam provided its adherents with a complete, comprehensive way of life in which the relation of the individual to society and the material to the spiritual were balanced in perfect harmony." And Wieslaw Zejierski believed "that mankind could be guided only by a religion which presented a perfect and complete code of individual and social life" and that he had "found in Islam [such] ... a code ... which is able to guide the individual and community towards the Kingdom of God on earth."

A somewhat smaller proportion (10 percent) of the converts to Islam indicated that the *lack of a priesthood or other medial agents* was appealing to them. Muhammad Asad was impressed by the fact that Islam contained "neither priest nor clergy." Michael Hames listed as one of the characteristics that most attracted him to Islam "the absence of priesthood," and R. L. Mellema was similarly struck by the fact that "in Islam contact with God depends on man himself" and that therefore "the believer does not need any mediation; Islam does not need priesthood." This aspect of Muslim theology appealed strongly to the individualism of Western men; women, however,

TABLE 3. Aspects of Islamic Teachings Significant in Conversion

Factor	American Males	american Females	European Males	European Females	Total (%)
Simplicity	1	4	9	1	15(21%)
Reasonableness and rationality	5		7	3	15(21%)
Brotherhood of man		1	12	1	14(19%)
"This-worldliness"	2	2	10		14(19%)
Lack of mediation	2		5		7(10%)

were apparently not concerned with this concept, for none mentioned it as a motivating force.

In contrast, then, to the "typical" Western religious convert described previously, the profile of the convert to Islam is as follows: an individual in his or her late twenties or early thirties whose integrative process, insofar as the metaphysical aspects are concerned, is prolonged beyond the normal time span due to a conscious and deliberate rejection of the parental or culturally dominant religion at age sixteen or seventeen. The integration process is eventually completed after an average of fourteen years, approximately six of which are devoted to active pursuit of a religious alternative. The final commitment to Islam is not made spontaneously but is rather the end result of considerable thought. The decision is therefore characterized as being intellectual rather than emotional. Only two of the motivational factors observed by Starbuck and others to be characteristic of Western converts to Christianity are applicable to Muslim converts: first, in almost every case conversion is attributable to the influence of a Muslim friend or acquaintance; second, certain aspects of Islamic doctrine are appealing and thus become significant in the decision-making process.

Only one of the seventy-two converts mentioned the influence of a "Muslim missionary," and very few attributed their decision to teachers or other formal leaders. The majority saw Islam in the daily lives of individuals like themselves and learned the precepts of the religion from the lips of friends and acquaintances who took the initiative upon seeing the interest of a fellow seeker. One searches the testimonies in vain for evidence of an external-institutional missiological approach, but the internal-personal emphasis upon the witness of the layman is everywhere present. Clearly the adoption of an Islamic form of Pietism is the key to spreading the religion throughout the Western world. But what is the prognosis for such an expansion in the future?

CONCLUSION: THE FUTURE OF
DA'WAH IN THE WEST

Muhammad Abdul-Rauf claimed in 1977 during a speech given at the Muslim World League's First Islamic Conference in North America that Islam is "spreading like a mighty torrent, sweeping through the doors of colleges and universities and even penetrating the thick walls of prisons." At this time, however, the total number of Muslims residing in the United States is not even 2 percent of the total population, and those who are converts to the faith are only a fraction of this number. Activism on the part of Muslims is increasing, but the growth is slow, and the majority continue to be assimilated into their secularized environments rather than functioning as missionary agents. Offensive-activist organizations are multiplying and increasing in size but for the most part they are small, disorganized, poorly staffed, and poorly funded. In addition they work in isolation from, and occasionally in opposition to, each other. Many are struggling with the difficulties involved in adopting non-Quranic and nontraditional strategies of Islamization; the internal-personal approach to missiology is a recent innovation for most adherents of the Islamic faith. The Muslim feels himself compelled by Quranic injunctions not to compel others to adopt his faith and yet in pluralistic America it is often the case that the one who is most forceful in his presentation gains the most publicity and, hence, the greatest number of converts. But the Muslim is repulsed by the idea that he must join the carnival atmosphere of American evangelicalism if he is to compete successfully for the souls of men. What, then, is the likelihood of Islam becoming a powerful religious force in America?

Jacob Needleman, an authority on contemporary religious movements in America, has analyzed the features deemed by Westerners to be the most attractive aspects of Zen Buddhism, Subud, Transcendental Meditation, and similar sects. In a book entitled *The New Religions* he stated that young Americans are searching primarily for religious faiths that are *self-centered* in the sense that they supply solutions to individual as opposed to societal difficulties. Buddhism, for instance, "provides release from *my* suffering," and herein lies its appeal. Second, the new religions accentuate the *mind* as opposed to the emotions, and since traditional Christianity and Judaism early on abandoned reason to the secularists, they have lost their appeal. Closely associated with this idea is the fact that today's young people are seeking a faith that involves ritual, discipline, and method. They are attracted to the rigor of meditation exercises and willingly submit themselves to the commands of a guru. Needleman notes that traditional Western religious forms have to a large extent abandoned such emphases.

The third source of appeal lies in the fact that while Christianity and Judaism are perceived as being religions which underestimate or denigrate human potential, the new religions emphasize the possibility of individuals to attain tremendously *advanced states of being* in the here and now. Among the beliefs imported from the Far East there are no pessimistic doctrines involving such theological concepts as original sin, and Needleman contends that this was to the liking of the Woodstock generation, who sang of a return to "the Garden."[1]

Measuring Islam by these three characteristics would lead one to conclude that this religion has great potential for expansion in the Western context. The Muslim faith is indeed self-centered in the sense that it acknowledges no mediators between the individual and God; one is responsible for his or her own spiritual development. Islam's emphasis upon reason has also been noted, and this accords well with Needleman's observations regarding the new religions' preoccupation with the mind as opposed to the emotions. Finally, Islam stresses the ritual of prayer and the disciplines of fasting and almsgiving, and it deems important the memorization of Quranic verses and traditions of the Prophet. Thus it would seem that this religion contains all of the characteristics found to be most appealing to Western young people.

A possible problem, however, is that Needleman's observations were made in 1970 during what was the culmination of the wave of spiritual experimentation begun in the 1960s. Jackson Carroll observed in his study of religion in America that "in the 1970s there has been a marked change. The upheaval and turmoil of the 1960s have given way to what appear to be disillusionment, cynicism, and a groping for direction."[2] And Martin Marty wrote in 1976 that "the New Religions now have their cultic place under the sun and they will continue to influence and suffuse other religious groups. But even as I write they draw less attention than they did. Their most effervescent period may well be past."[3]

The observations of Needleman, Carroll, and Marty taken together imply that had Muslims been mobilized in force, displayed a united front, and espoused a specific strategy during the 1960s and early 1970s, they might well have attracted large numbers of followers due to the social and spiritual dynamics present during that time. Certainly the Muslim Student Association realized significant gains during those years, but this organization appears to be exceptional. For the most part, Muslims in America were unprepared for this situation, the majority of them being assimilated into their surrounding culture and unmindful of any personal responsibility with regard to da'wah activity. Ethnic concerns were given priority rather than matters which involved the umma as a whole. Today, when awareness of the importance of da'wah is increasing, the culture of America has changed in a way that makes what would previously have been attractive elements of Islam less relevant or not relevant at all.

During the Reagan administration, however, a new emphasis upon conservative ethics and moral issues was seen on the part of a sizable element of American society. Reagan's outspokenness with regard to issues of abortion, homosexuality, chemical dependency, and the like, were both due to and accompanied by an increase in conservative religious values. Here is an area in which Islam has a distinct advantage over traditional Christian and Jewish denominations, which during the 1960s and 1970s adopted relatively liberal moral values. Some have recognized the possibilities inherent in an appeal to the Muslim Shari'a; Kerry Lovering, the publications secretary of the Sudan Interior Mission, wrote in 1979 that "Christianity ... has failed miserably ... it is now Islam that offers salvation from the drunkeness, sexual license, political corruption, violence, blasphemy and corrupt lifestyles that afflict 'Christian' nations."[4] The Reagan era has now drawn to a close, and the direction which American society will take is unclear. The Muslims of America find themselves still faced with the problem of a moving target. In order to become or to remain appealing they must adapt the precepts of their faith to the constantly changing trends of thought in America. And not only are these constantly changing; they are changing with an unaccustomed rapidity as well. Such transformations require planning and strategies that are consistently updated and allow Islam to maintain its supracultural aspects while simultaneously emphasizing various facets of the religion in accordance with contemporary culture. Capable, creative, and brilliant leadership is essential for the coming years.

Although the elements discussed by Needleman may no longer exercise a significant appeal and the conservatism of the Reagan era may be on the wane, there yet remain certain traits within the American ethos which Martin Marty believes have become so ingrained in the people as a whole that there is no danger of them disappearing in the foreseeable future. These traits include *pluralism*, *experimentalism* (the willingness of Americans to both seek and practice spiritual alternatives), *scripturalism* (adherence to a written revelation), a *positive view of Enlightenment thinking* with regard to reason, and *"voluntaryism"* ("the principle or tenet that the Church and educational institutions should be supported by voluntary contributions instead of by the State").[5] Each of these characteristics is favorable to the growth and expansion of Islam in America. Pluralism and experimentalism are generic traits, assuring Islam of a hearing as a religious alternative if it but proclaims its distinctive elements. Its emphasis upon and adherence to the Qur'ān as the revelation of God accords well with scripturalism, its emphasis upon reason makes it a viable alternative for those who are repulsed by the emotional emphases of contemporary Christianity, and its lay orientation endows it with characteristics of "voluntaryism." It may thus be concluded that the Muslim faith has potential for exercising a profound influence upon American society still today. But these advantages will avail Muslims nothing unless certain changes are effected within the ethos of American Islam.

First, unless Muslims develop an indigenous American leadership, Islam will retain a distinctly foreign character which is not likely to be advantageous for its growth and expansion. In the 1960s and early 1970s the *guru* from the Indian subcontinent or Sri Lanka was appealing due to the exoticness of his identification with things foreign to America. But this preoccupation with the exotic is, for the most part, a thing of the past, and one sees a renewed emphasis in the spiritual sphere (as in the area of economics) upon indigenous or "home-grown" ideas and personages. This fact, in combination with the essentially negative image of Islam conveyed by the American mass media, means that unless American converts are trained for positions of leadership Islam will continue to be categorized as an essentially alien cult.

A related item which has apparently received little (if any) consideration is the practice of adopting an Arabic name upon conversion. Although this may have merit within the community itself, it serves to maintain and even increase the aura of foreignness that characterizes Islam. As long as converts continue to use Arabic names publicly, their credibility will suffer.

Second, Muslims will have to transform the stereotypical image of Islam as consisting mainly of Iranian and Libyan terrorists, African-American activists, male chauvinists, and the like. Third, if the anti-Christian polemic does not cease, Muslims may create a situation precisely the opposite of that which they wish to produce. The Christian missionary movement of the nineteenth century sparked the renewed vigor seen among the major religions today with its inflammatory rhetoric. The potential exists for Islam to duplicate this phenomenon in the reverse. Direct attacks upon Christian teachings such as the divinity, crucifixion, and resurrection of Christ may cause some persons to forsake them (just as Christianity was able to attract a number of converts from Islam), but such attacks may also serve to increase the interest of nominal Christians in the precepts of their faith and in so doing solidify their commitment to the Christian religion.

Finally, the internal-personal missiological approach espoused by such thinkers as Khurram Murad will have to be expanded and developed. The ambivalence regarding the Quranic and traditional advocacy of an external-institutional strategy must be resolved once and for all and the mass of Muslim laymen must be mobilized through instruction regarding the responsibility of each individual to be involved in da'wah and through training in the principles and techniques of evangelical outreach. Unless a concept similar or analogous to this is promoted, Muslims in America will continue to become assimilated into and secularized by the surrounding culture.

The dream of a Muslim America is deeply rooted in the thinking of many Muslims. On a tour of the United States in 1977, Dr. Abdel-

Halim Mahmoud of al-Azhar University was asked if American Muslims might one day try to replace the Constitution with Shari'a Law. His reply: "We cannot deny such a possibility." Isma'il al-Faruqi wrote just prior to his assassination that

> the Islamic vision endows North America with a new destiny worthy of it. For this renovation of itself, of its spirit, for its rediscovery of a God-given mission and self-dedication to its pursuit, the continent cannot but be grateful to the immigrant with Islamic vision. It cannot but interpret his advent on its shores except as a God-given gift, a timely divine favor and mercy.[6]

Musa Qutub of the Islamic Information Center is fond of quoting an ancient tradition that in the latter days Islam will spread from the West to the East, and he intends to prepare workers for this task. And Sulayman Nyang concurs with this idea when he surmises that "American Muslims could one day be one of World Islam's major pillars of support," and that "U.S. Muslim Centres ... will play an important role in the cultural development of their brethren elsewhere in the Muslim world." But unless the changes described here occur within the very near future, the dream of an Islamic America will remain only a dream.

NOTES

Introduction

1. Unless otherwise indicated, all passages from the Qur'an are taken from *The Glorious Qur'ān*, trans. Muhammad Marmaduke Pickthall (Chicago: Global Publishing Co., n.d.).
2. Muhammad Khurshid, *Da'wah in Islam* (Houston: Islamic Education Council, n.d.), p. 1.
3. Isma'il Raji al-Faruqi, "On the Nature of Islamic Da'wah," in *Christian Mission and Islamic Da'wah*: *Proceedings of the Chambesy Dialogue Consultation* (London: The Islamic Foundation, 1976), p. 33.
4. Ahmad Sakr, "Islamic Da'wa: Some Problems," *Muslim World League Journal* 8 (1979): 14.
5. Robert D. Crane, personal letter, 25 August 1987.
6. Compare Suras 5:51, 57 and 9:29 with 2:62 and 5:48.
7. al-Faruqi, "Islamic Da'wah," p. 35.

Chapter 1

1. Sakr, "Islamic Da'wa," p. 14.
2. Maulana Muhammad Imran, *The Importance of Da'wa (Tabligh) in Islam* (Lahore: M. Siraj-ud-Din and Sons, 1976), p. 17.
3. Ānwar al-Jindī, *Āfāq Jadīda lil-Da'wah al-Islāmmiya fī 'Ālām al-Gharb* (Beirut: Mu'assasa al-Risāla, 1984), p. 335.
4. See Suras 19:97, 26:192, 39:28–29, 41:44, 42:5, and 43:2.
5. Compare Suras 29:45–47, 10:94, 3:113–115, and 3:199 with 9:29, 3:19, 5:57, and 3:85.
6. See W. Montgomery Watt, *Islamic Political Thought* (Edinburgh: University Press, 1968), p. 19. See also Majid Khadduri, *The Law of War and Peace in Islam* (London: Luzac and Co., 1941), in which it is claimed that Suras 68:51–52 and 21:107 are indicative of universal objectives.
7. Fred Donner considers these forays to be the outworking of a specific plan of expansion rather than strictly fortuitous, claiming that "the decision to launch the invasion was certainly not reached without careful deliberation and consultation with prominent members of the ruling elite in Medina, and we may accept the numerous descriptions of these consultations as

efforts to flesh out the vague recollections of the actual discussions that must have taken place." (Fred McGraw Donner, *The Early Islamic Conquests* [Princeton, N.J.: Princeton University Press, 1981], p. 113.)

8. Ali Issa Othman, cited in Charis Waddy, *The Muslim Mind* (New York: Longman, 1976), p. 100.

9. Rudolph Peters, *Islam and Colonialism: The Doctrine of Jihād in Modern History* (New York: Mouton, 1979), p. 18.

10. Nehemia Levtzion, "Toward a Comparative Study of Islamization," in *Conversion to Islam*, ed. Nehemia Levtzion (New York: Holmes and Meier Publishers, 1979), p. 11.

11. Mervin Hiskett, cited by Levtzion in ibid., p. 11.

12. Nehemia Levtzion, "Conversion Under Muslim Domination: A Comparative Study," in *Religious Change and Cultural Domination*, ed. David N. Lorenzen (Mexico City, Mexico: El Colegio de Mexico, 1981), p. 26.

13. Marshall G. S. Hodgson, *The Venture of Islam*, 3 vols. (Chicago: University of Chicago Press, 1974), I: 209 (emphasis added).

14. Levtzion, "Comparative Study," p. 15.

15. Ibid., p. 17.

16. J. O. Hunwick, *Islam in Africa: Friend or Foe?* (Accra: Ghana Universities Press, 1976), pp. 15, 25.

17. Fazlur Rahman comments that "the Sufistic impulse undoubtedly fed on that isolationism which set in as a tremendous reaction to Kharijism and the political controversies that it raised. This isolationism, which is preached side by side in Hadith literature with ijmā', teaches that men should desist not only from politics but even from administration and public affairs, and much Hadith seeks, indeed, to preach that a person should retire to a cave and live alone." (Fazlur Rahman, *Islam* [Chicago: University of Chicago Press, 1966], p. 129.)

18. Reynold Nicholson, "Sufis: The Mystics of Islam," in *Understanding Mysticism*, ed. Richard Woods (New York: Image Books, 1980), p. 180.

19. Hodgson, *Venture*, II: 206.

20. Richard Bulliet, *Conversion to Islam in the Medieval Period* (Cambridge, Mass.: Harvard University Press, 1979), p. 2.

21. Fathi Osman, "Islam: The Status of Non-Muslims." *Arabia: The Islamic World Review*, January 1987, p. 41.

22. Hodgson, *Venture*, II: 425.

23. Levtzion, "Comparative Study," p. 18.

24. Hodgson. *Venture*, II: 426.

25. Ibid., III: 71.

26. Ibid., p. 80.

Chapter 2

1. Beverlee Turner Mehdi, *The Arabs in America 1492–1977* (New York: Oceana Publications, 1978), pp. 1–2. See also Allen D. Austin, ed., *African Muslims in Ante-Bellum America: A Sourcebook* (New York: Garland, 1984).

2. Mahmoud Youssef Shawarbi, *Al-Islām w'al-Muslimūn fi'l-Qāra al-Amrīkiyya* (Cairo: Dar al-Qalam, 1963), p. 7.

3. Isma'il Raji al-Faruqi, "Islamic Ideals in North America," in *The Muslim Community in North America*, ed. Earle Waugh, Baha Abu-Laban, and Regula B. Qureshi (Edmonton: University of Alberta Press, 1983), p. 260.

4. Isma'il al-Faruqi, "How the U.S. and Islam Can Work Together," *Arabia: The Islamic World Review*, June 1982, p. 36.

5. Yvonne Yazbeck Haddad and Adair T. Lummis, *Islamic Values in the United States: A Comparative Study* (New York: Oxford University Press, 1987), p. 14.

6. Alixa Naff, "Arabs in America: A Historical Overview," in *Arabs in the New World*, ed. Sameer Y. Abraham and Nabeel Abraham (Detroit: Wayne State University Press, 1983), p. 9.

7. Lois Gottesman, "Islam in America: An Old Religion Seeks a New Place in American Society." *USA Today*, May 1980, p. 27.

8. Haddad and Lummis, *Islamic Values*, p. 18.

9. Sulayman S. Nyang and Mumtaz Ahmad, "The Muslim Intellectual Emigre in the United States," *Islamic Culture*, July 1985, pp. 277–278.

10. Muzammil H. Siddiqui, "Muslims in a Non-Muslim Society," *Islamic Horizons*, May–June 1986, p. 22.

11. From Nikki R. Keddie, ed. and trans., *An Islamic Response to Imperialism: Political and Religious Writings of Sayyid Jamāl al-Dīn al-Afghānī* (Berkeley: University of California Press, 1968), p. 87. Cited in John J. Donohue and John L. Esposito, eds., *Islam in Transition: Muslim Perspectives* (New York: Oxford University Press, 1982), p. 16.

12. Beshir Adam Rehma, "How to Establish an Islamic Center: A Step-by-Step Approach," in *Let Us Learn: Issues of Your Concern*, ed. Abdel-Hadi Omer (Beloit, Wisc.: Published by the Editor, 1987), p. 55.

13. Yvonne Yazbeck Haddad, "Muslims in the U.S.," in *Islam: The Religious and Political Life of a World Community*, ed. Marjorie Kelley (New York: Praeger, 1984), p. 261.

14. Yvonne Yazbeck Haddad, "Arab Muslims and Islamic Institutions in America: Adaptation and Reform," in *Arabs in the New World*, ed. Sameer Y. Abraham and Nabeel Abraham (Detroit: Wayne State University Press, 1983), p. 67.

15. Sameer Y. Abraham and Nabeel Abraham, eds., *Arabs in the New World* (Detroit: Wayne State University Press, 1983), p. 1.

16. See Yahya Aossey, Jr., *Fifty Years of Islam in Iowa 1925–1975* (Cedar Rapids, Iowa: Unity Publishing Co., 1975).

17. Shawarbi, *Al-Muslimūn*, pp. 9–10.

18. See Mehdi, *The Arabs in America*, p. 104.

19. Ibid. (Emphasis added).

20. E. Allen Richardson, *Islamic Cultures in North America* (New York: The Pilgrim Press, 1981), pp. 52–53.

21. Ibid., p. 50 (emphasis added).

22. Muhammad Abdul-Rauf, *History of the Islamic Center* (Washington, D.C.: The Islamic Center, 1978), p. 41.

23. Charles S. Braden, "Islam in America," *International Review of Mission* 48 (July 1959): 317.

24. *Manual of Da'wah for Islamic Workers* (Montreal: Islamic Circle of North America, 1983), p. 29.

25. Haddad and Lummis, *Islamic Values*, p. 11.

26. Harold B. Barclay, "The Perpetuation of Muslim Tradition in the Canadian North," *The Muslim World* 59 (January 1969): 65.

27. Harold B. Barclay, "Muslim Experience in Canada," in *Religion and Ethnicity*, ed. Harold Coward and Leslie Kawamura (Waterloo, Ont.: Wilfred Laurier University Press, 1978), p. 110.

28. Barclay, "Perpetuation," p. 70.

29. Barclay, "Experience," p. 112.

30. Gulzar Haider, "Canadian Saturdays, Pakistani Sundays," *Whole Earth Review*, Winter 1985, p. 38.

31. Haddad and Lummis, *Islamic Values*, p. 22.

32. Ibid., p. 171.

33. Ibid., p. 47.

34. al-Faruqi, "Islamic Ideals," p. 268.

35. Ilyas Yunus, *Muslims in North America: Problems and Prospects* (Indianapolis: Muslim Student Association, 1974), p. 18.

Chapter 3

1. J. Herbert Kane, *A Global View of Christian Missions* (Grand Rapids, Mich.: Baker Book House, 1971), p. 58.

2. It is told, for instance, that when asked concerning the efficacy of the five daily prayers, the Prophet in turn asked of the inquirer, "If you were to bathe five times a day, how much dirt would remain upon your body?"

The inquirer replied, "No significant amount." The Prophet then said, "So it is with the sins of one who prays five times daily."

3. Frank Whaling, "A Comparative Religious Study of Missionary Transplantation in Buddhism, Christianity and Islam," *International Review of Mission* 70 (October 1981): 331.

4. Bausani, cited in Whaling, "Missionary Transplantation," p. 331.

5. Isma'il Raji al-Faruqi, "Islam and Other Faiths," in *The Challenge of Islam*, ed. Altaf Gauhar (London: The Islamic Council of Europe, 1978), pp. 88–89.

6. Peters notes that this idea is not new. There is extant the concept of *jihād al-tarbiyah* (educational jihād) as recorded in Muhammad Shadid, *Al-Jihād fi'l-Islām* (Cairo: Mu'assasat at-Matbū'āt al-Hadithah, n.d.), pp. 7, 90; and Ni'mat Sidqī, *Al-Jihād fī Sabīl Allāh* (Cairo: Dār al-I'tisān, 1975), pp. 22–31. (see Peters, *Islam and Colonialism*, pp. 118–119.)

7. See Isma'il Raji al-Faruqi, *The Islamization of Knowledge: General Principles and Workplan* (Washington, D.C.: International Institute of Islamic Thought, 1982), p. 14. See also Robert D. Crane, ed., *Preparing to Islamize America: A Research Proposal* (Reston, Va.: International Institute of Islamic Thought, 1987).

It perhaps appears contradictory that al-Faruqi has been cited in so many contexts. In actuality this is only indicative of the complexity of this individual. He was an ecumenicist with regard to the *devout* adherents of other faiths, but an activist dā'ī par excellence to those whom he considered secularized, be they nominally Muslim or blatantly non-Muslim. His approach to persons in these latter categories was one of Islamization, hence his involvement in the foundation of the International Institute.

8. K. S. Latourette, *A History of Christianity*, 2 vol. (New York: Harper and Row, 1953), II: 895.

9. K. James Stein, *Philipp Jakob Spener: Pietist Patriarch* (Chicago: Covenant Press, 1986), p. 241.

10. Stephen Neill, *A History of Christian Missions* (New York: Penguin Books, 1964), p. 228.

11. See, for instance, Rahman, *Islam*, p. 129, and Hodgson, *Venture*, I: 393.

12. Rahman, *Islam*, p. 129.

13. Ibid., p. 130.

14. Al-Hasan al-Basrī, as recorded by Abū Nuaim, *Hilya*, II: 134–140. Cited by A. J. Arberry in *Sufism* (London: George Allen & Unwin, 1950; Unwin Paperbacks, 1979), p. 33.

15. William C. Chittick, *The Sufi Path of Love: The Spiritual Teachings of Rumi* (Albany: State University of New York Press, 1983), p. 154. Rūmī

is alluding to a hadīth in which the Prophet distinguishes between the Greater and Lesser Jihāds, the former being the internal struggles of the believer to master himself, and the latter involving physical combat.

16. B. G. Martin, *Muslim Brotherhoods in 19th Century Africa* (New York: Cambridge University Press, 1976), p. 6. In 1785–1786 occurred the Fulani jihād of Usuman dan Fodio in Northern Nigeria, and in 1881–1882 came the movements of the Sudanese Mahdī Muhammad Ahmad ibn ʿAbdallah and the Cyrenaican Muhammad al-Sanusī.

Chapter 4

1. *Five Tracts of Hasan al-Bannāʾ (1906–1949): A Selection from the Majmūʿat Rasāʾil al-Imām al-Shahīd Hasan al-Bannāʾ*, trans. and ed. Charles Wendell (Berkeley: University of California Press, 1978), pp. 1–2.

2. *Memoirs of Hasan al-Banna Shaheed*, trans. M. N. Shaikh (Karachi: International Islamic Publishers, 1981), p. 40.

3. *Ibid.*, p. 41.

4. Ibid.

5. Richard P. Mitchell, *The Society of the Muslim Brothers* (London: Oxford University Press, 1969), p. 234 (emphasis added).

6. John Obert Voll, *Islam: Continuity and Change in the Modern World* (Boulder, Colo.: Westview Press, 1982), p. 176.

7. Wendell, *Five Tracts*, p. 55 (emphasis added).

8. Cited by Mitchell in *Society*, p. 15.

9. Wendell, *Five Tracts*, p. 73.

10. Charles J. Adams, "Mawdudi and the Islamic State," in *Voices of Resurgent Islam*, ed. John L. Esposito (New York: Oxford University Press, 1983), p. 100.

11. Charles J. Adams, "The Ideology of Mawlana Mawdudi," in *South Asian Politics and Religion*, ed. Donald E. Smith (Princeton: Princeton University Press, 1966), p. 375.

12. Abul Aʾlā al-Mawdūdī, *Tadhkira Duʿāh al-Islām* (Cairo: Dar al-Ansar, 1977), pp. 7–8.

13. Abul Aʾlā Mawdūdī, *Witnesses unto Mankind: The Purpose and Duty of the Muslim Ummah*, ed. and trans. Khurram Murad (Leicester: The Islamic Foundation, 1986), p. 27.

14. Mawdūdī, *Tadhkira*, pp. 22–23.

15. Abul Aʾlā Maudūdī, *Guideline for Workers*, trans. Nawli Ali (Lahore: Islamic Publications, 1981), p. 29.

16. Ibid., pp. 16–17.

17. Abul A'lā Mawdūdī, *The Islamic Movement: Dynamics of Values, Power and Change*, trans. Khurram Murad (Leicester: The Islamic Foundation, 1984), p. 71.

18. Adams, "Ideology," p. 376.

19. Mawdūdī, *Tadhkira*, p. 16.

20. Edward Mortimer, *Faith and Power* (New York: Vintage Books, 1982), p. 204.

21. Adams, "Ideology," p. 394.

22. Adams, "Islamic State," p. 128.

23. Mawdūdī, *Witnesses*, p. 48.

24. Rehma, "Islamic Center," p. 54.

25. Ihsan Bagby, "Is ISNA an Islamic Movement?," *Islamic Horizons*, March 1986, p. 4.

26. Haddad and Lummis, *Islamic Values*, p. 124.

27. Yasin T. al-Jibouri, *A Brief History of the Islamic Society of Georgia, Inc.* (Atlanta: Islamic Society of Georgia, n.d.), pp. 3–4.

Chapter 5

1. Khurram Jah Murad, *Islamic Movement in the West* (London: The Islamic Foundation, 1981), p. 3.

2. Murad, in Mawdūdī, *Islamic Movement*, p. 36.

3. Mawdūdī, *Witnesses*, pp. 10, 18, 20, 21.

4. Khurram Jah Murad, "Third Opportunity to Keep Islam in the West," *Islamic Horizons*, November 1986, p. 10.

5. Murad, *Movement*, p. 14.

6. With respect to this latter category, Murad has himself contributed *Love Your Brother, Love Your Neighbor, Love Your God, The Brave Boy, Stories of the Caliphs, Love at Home, The Kingdom of Justice, The Persecutor Comes Home: The Story of Umar, The Singing Heart: Story of Abu Dhar, The Long Search: Story of Salman the Persian, The Desert Chief: Story of Thumama Ibn Uthal, The Broken Idol and the Jewish Rabbi and the Wise Poet: Story of al-Tufayl Bin Amr*. All are available from the Islamic Book Service, a division of the Muslim Student Association.

7. Murad, in Mawdūdī, *Islamic Movement*, p. 38.

8. Ibid., p. 49.

9. Khurram Jah Murad, *Da'wah Among Non-Muslims in the West* (London: The Islamic Foundation, 1986), pp. 19–20.

10. Ibid., p. 22.

11. Ibid., p. 28.

12. Murad, *Movement*, p. 11.

Chapter 6

1. Haddad and Lummis, *Islamic Values*, p. 59.
2. Mawdūdī, *Witnesses*, pp. 73–74.
3. Shawarbi, *Al-Muslimūn*, p. 14.
4. Sulayman Nyang and Mumtaz Ahmad mention the International Muslim Union, founded in New York City in 1895, Mohammed Webb's American Islamic Propaganda Society, formed in New Jersey also in the 1890s, and the Islamic Mission of America, established in the 1920s by Shaykh Daoud Faisal and his wife, Sister Khadija. See Sulayman S. Nyang, "The Stuff That Dreams Are Made Of," *Arabia: The Islamic World Review*, November 1982, p. 24. For further information see Akbar Muhammad, "Muslims in the United States," in *The Islamic Impact*, ed. Yvonne Haddad et al. (Syracuse: Syracuse University Press, 1984), pp. 198–201.
5. "Muslim Organizations in the West: An Overview," *Arabia: The Islamic World Review*, December 1986, p. 24.
6. Haddad, "Arab Muslims," p. 70.
7. Ibid, p. 71.
8. John Renard, "Understanding the World of Islam," *America*, October 20, 1979, p. 208.
9. "Know Your MSA," brochure (Plainfield, Ind.: The Muslim Student Association of the United States and Canada, n.d.).
10. Ibid.
11. Nyang and Ahmad, "Intellectual Emigre," p. 284.
12. Al-Jibouri, *Islamic Society of Georgia*, p. 2.
13. Ibid.
14. Ibid.

Chapter 7

1. Amin Ahsan Islahi, *Call to Islam and How the Holy Prophets Preached* (Safat, Kuwait: Islamic Book Publishers, 1978), p. 73.
2. Ibid., p. 13.
3. Ibid., pp. 151–153.
4. Imran, *Daʿwa*, p. 15.
5. Fathi Yakan, *Al-Istīʿāb fī Hayāh al-Daʿwah w'al-Daʿiyah* (Beirut: Mu'assasa al-Risāla, 1983), pp. 45, 64.
6. Akbar Muhammad, "Some Factors Which Promote and Restrict Islamization in America," *American Journal of Islamic Studies*, August 1984, p. 43.
7. Robert D. Crane, "Premise and Process in the Islamization of Knowledge: A Contribution Toward Unity in Diversity," in *Preparing to*

Islamize America: A Research Proposal, ed. Robert D. Crane (Reston, Va.: International Institute of Islamic Thought, 1987), p. 10.

8. Kamal Ali, "Islamic Education in the U.S.: An Overview of Issues, Problems and Possible Approaches," *The American Journal of Islamic Studies* 1 (August 1984): 130.

9. Islahi, *Call to Islam*, p. 89.

10. *Manual of Da'wah*, p. 84.

11. Tony Poon-Chiang Chi, "A Case Study of the Missionary Stance of the Ahmadiyya Movement in North America," Ph.D. diss. (Northwestern University, 1973), p. 92.

12. "Maryam Jameelah Answers Questions About Women," *Al-Ummah*, September 1985, p. 6.

13. Islahi, *Call to Islam*, p. 75.

14. *Manual of Da'wah*, pp. iii–iv.

15. Hadhrat Saeed Ahmad Khan, "Future Role of the Ahmadiyya as a Missionary Movement," *Islamic Review*, March–April 1983, p. 13.

16. Osman, "Better Presentation," p. 34.

Chapter 8

1. Ahmad Deedat, *Is the Bible God's Word?* (Durban, S.A.: Islamic Propagation Centre, 1980), p. 62.

2. Ahmad Deedat, *Crucifixion or Cruci-fiction?* (Durban, S.A.: Islamic Propagation Centre, 1984), p. 59.

3. Maryam Jameelah, *Islam Versus Ahl al-Kitāb: Past and Present* (Lahore: Mohammad Yusuf Khan and Sons, 1978), pp. 398–399.

Chapter 9

1. Erik H. Erikson, *Young Man Luther: A Study in Psychoanalysis and History* (New York: W. W. Norton and Co., 1958), p. 43.

Chapter 10

1. Haddad and Lummis, *Islamic Values*, pp. 9–10.

2. Such was the case with a young mother interviewed at the 1987 convention of the Islamic Society of North America. She expressed her frustration with the pressures brought to bear upon her by the "women's liberation movement" and said that her conversion to Islam and subsequent marriage to a Muslim involved a change in lifestyle which she felt was more

conducive to her perception of herself as a female. This phenomenon was also observed among British women by Mrs. Harfiyah Ball in her study *Why British Women Embrace Islam* (Leicester: Muslim Youth Education Council, 1987), p. 8.

3. Al-Jindī, *Āfāqjadīda*, p. 26.

4. Flo Conway and Jim Siegelman, *Snapping: America's Epidemic of Sudden Personality Change* (New York: J. B. Lippincott Company, 1978), p. 40.

5. Al-Jindī, *Āfāqjadīda*, pp. 349–350.

6. Ibid., pp. 347–349.

7. John Renard, "Understanding the World of Islam," *America*, October 20, 1979, p. 207.

Conclusion

1. See Jacob Needleman, *The New Religions* (New York): E. P. Dutton and Co., 1977).

2. Jackson W. Carroll et al., *Religion in America: 1950 to the Present* (New York: Harper and Row, 1979), p. 7.

3. Martin E. Marty, *A Nation of Behavers* (Chicago: University of Chicago Press, 1976), p. 206.

4. Kerry Lovering, "Though at Home, Aggressive Abroad: Islam on the March," *Muslim World Pulse*, August 1979, p. 6.

5. See Martin E. Marty, *Religion and Republic* (Boston: Beacon Press, 1987), pp. 36–48.

6. Al-Faruqi, "Islamic Ideals in North America," p. 270.

BIBLIOGRAPHY

General Works

Abdullah, A. "Khurram Murad: Worker and Thinker." *Arabia: The Islamic World Review*, December 1986, p. 63.

Abdullah, Ahmad. "Ten Unique Features of Islam." Brochure published by the Islamic Teaching Center, Plainfield, Ind., n.d.

Abdul-Rauf, Muhammad. *History of the Islamic Center*. Washington, D.C.: The Islamic Center, 1978.

Abraham, Sameer Y., and Abraham, Nabeel, eds. *Arabs in the New World*. Detroit: Wayne State University Press, 1983.

Adams, Charles J. "The Ideology of Mawlana Mawdudi." In *South Asian Politics and Religion*. Edited by Donald E. Smith. Princeton: Princeton University Press, 1966.

————. "Mawdudi and the Islamic State." In *Voices of Resurgent Islam*. Edited by John L. Esposito. New York: Oxford University Press, 1983, pp. 99–133.

"Ahmad Deedat: A Scholar for the People." *Arabia: The Islamic World Review*, March 1986.

Ahmad, Khurshid, ed. *Islam: Its Meaning and Message*. Leicester: The Islamic Foundation, 1975.

Aijian, M. M. "The Mohammedans in the United States." *The Moslem World* 10 (1920).

Ali, Kamal. "Islamic Education in the United States: An Overview of Issues, Problems and Possible Approaches." *The American Journal of Islamic Studies* 1 (August 1984): 127.

Allison, Joel. "Religious Conversion: Regression and Progression in an Adolescent Experience." *Journal of the Scientific Study of Religion* 8 (Spring 1969): 23.

Amīn, Sādiq. *Al-Daʿwah al-Islamiyya: Faridah Shariʿiyya wa Darūra Bashariyya*. Amman: Jamʿiyya Amman al-Matabiʿ al-Taʿawuniyya, 1987.

Andrew, M. K. "How Moslems Approach Christians." *Moslem World* 15 (1925): 289–296.

Aossey, Yahya, Jr. *Fifty Years of Islam in Iowa 1925–1975*. Cedar Rapids, Iowa: Unity Publishing Co., 1975.

Arberry, A. J. *Sufism*. London: George Allen & Unwin, 1950; Unwin Paperbacks, 1979.

197

Arnold, T. W. *The Preaching of Islam*. London: Constable and Co., 1913.

"The Association of Muslim Social Scientists." Brochure, n.d.

Austin, Allen D., ed. *African Muslims in Ante-Bellum America: A Sourcebook*. New York: Garland, 1984.

Bagby, Ihsan. "Is ISNA an Islamic Movement?" *Islamic Horizons*, March 1986, p. 4.

———. "Islamic Worker Training Program Held." *Islamic Horizons*, October 1986, p. 14.

Bagby, Ihsan, and Johnson, Steve. *Al-Daʿwah Bain al-Amrīkān*. Plainfield, Ind.: Muslim Student Association, 1987.

Ball, Mrs. Harfiyah. *Why British Women Embrace Islam*. Leicester: Muslim Youth Education Council, 1987.

Al-Bannāʾ, Hasan. *Five Tracts of Hasan al-Bannāʾ (1906–1949): A Selection from the Majmūʿat Rasāʾil al-Imām al-Shahīd Hasan al-Bannāʾ*. Translated and annotated by Charles Wendell. Berkeley: University of California Press, 1978.

———. *Memoirs of Hasan al-Bannāʾ Shaheed*. Translated by M. N. Shaikh. Karachi: International Islamic Publishers, 1981.

———. "The New Renaissance." In *Islam in Transition: Muslim Perspectives*. Edited by John J. Donohue and John L. Esposito. New York: Oxford Univesity Press, 1982.

Barclay, Harold B. "Muslim Experience in Canada." In *Religion and Ethnicity*. Edited by Harold Coward and Leslie Kawamura. Waterloo, Ont.: Wilfred Laurier University Press, 1978.

———. "The Perpetuation of Muslim Tradition in the Canadian North." *The Muslim World* 59 (January 1969): 64.

Boase, Abdelwahab. "The People of the Books." *Arabia: The Islamic World Review*, March 1987, p. 56.

Bousquet, G. H. "Moslem Religious Influences in the United States." *Moslem World* 25 (1935).

Braden, Charles S. "Islam in America." *International Review of Mission* 48 (July 1959): 309.

Bragan, K. "The Psychological Gains and Losses of Religious Conversion." *British Journal of Medical Psychology* (1977): 177–180.

Bulliet, Richard. *Conversion to Islam in the Medieval Period*. Cambridge. Mass.: Harvard University Press, 1979.

Carroll, Jackson W., Douglas, Johnson W. and Martin, Marty E. *Religion in America: 1950 to the Present*. New York: Harper and Row, 1979.

Chi, Tony Poon-Chiang. "A Case Study of the Missionary Stance of the Ahmadiyya Movement in North America." Ph.D. diss. Northwestern University, 1973.

"Chicago's Muslim Community Center." *Islamic Horizons*, July 1987. p. 42.

Christian Mission and Islamic Da'wah: Proceedings of the Chambesy Dialogue Consultation. London: The Islamic Foundation, 1976.

"Constitution of the Islamic Society of North America." Plainfield. Ind.: Islamic Society of North America, 1987.

Conway, Flo, and Siegelman, Jim. *Snapping: America's Epidemic of Sudden Personality Change*. New York: J. B. Lippincott Company, 1978.

"The Council of Muslim Communities of Canada." Brochure, n.d.

Crane, Robert D. "Premise and Process in the Islamization of Knowledge: A Contribution Toward Unity in Diversity." In *Preparing to Islamic America: A Research Proposal*. Edited by Robert D. Crane. Reston, Va.: International Institute of Islamic Thought, 1987.

De Planhol, Xavier. *Les Fondements Géographiques de l'Histoire de l'Islam*. Paris: Flammarion, 1968.

Deedat, Ahmad. *Christ in Islam*. Durban, S.A.: Islamic Propagation Centre, 1983.

————. *Crucifixion or Cruci-fiction?* Durban, S.A.: Islamic Propagation Centre, 1984.

————. *Is the Bible God's Word?* Durban, S.A.: Islamic Propagation Centre, 1980.

————. *Resurrection or Resuscitation?* Durban, S.A.: Islamic Propagation Centre, 1978.

————. *What the Bible Says About Muhummed*. Durban, S.A.: Islamic Propagation Centre, 1976.

————. *What Is His Name?* Durban, S.A.: Islamic Propagation Centre, 1981.

————. *What Was the Sign of Jonah?* Durban, S.A.: Islamic Propagation Centre, 1976.

Dhaouadi, Zouhaier. "La Da'wa: Les Mots du Ciel pour Les Annees de Braise." *Peuples Mediterraneens* 25 (October–December 1983): 157.

Donner, Fred McGraw. *The Early Islamic Conquests*. Princeton, N.J.: Princeton University Press, 1981.

Donohue, John J., and Esposito, John L., eds. *Islam in Transition: Muslim Perspectives*. New York: Oxford University Press, 1982.

Dorman, Harry Gaylord, Jr. *Toward Understanding Islam*. New York: Bureau of Publications, Columbia University Teachers College, 1948.

Elkholy, Abdo. *The Arab Moslems in the United States*. New Haven: College and University Press, 1966.

Engineer, Asghar Ali. *The Islamic State*. New Delhi: Vikas Publishing House, 1980.

Erikson, Erik H. *Identity, Youth and Crisis.* New York: W.W. Norton, and Co., 1968.

————. *Young Man Luther: A Study in Psychoanalysis and History.* New York: W. W. Norton and Co., 1958.

Al-Faruqi, Isma'il Raji. "First Principles in the Islamization of Knowledge." In *Preparing to Islamize America.* Edited by Robert D. Crane. Reston, Va.: International Institute of Islamic Thought, 1987.

————. "How the U.S. and Islam Can Work Together." *Arabia: The Islamic World Review,* June 1982, p. 36.

————. "Islam and Other Faiths." In *The Challenge of Islam.* Edited by Altaf Gauhar. London: The Islamic Council of Europe, 1978.

————. "Islamic Ideals in North America." In *The Muslim Community in North America.* Edited by Earle Waugh, Baha Abu-Laban, and Regula B. Qureshi. Edmonton: University of Alberta Press, 1983.

————. *The Islamization of Knowledge: General Principles and Workplan.* Washington, D.C.: International Institute of Islamic Thought, 1982.

————. "On the Nature of Islamic Da'wah." In *Christian Mission and Islamic Da'wah: Proceedings of the Chambesy Dialogue Consultation.* London: The Islamic Foundation, 1976.

Al-Fāsī, 'Allāl. "The Need of the Day in the World of Islam Is the Organizing of Missionary Work." *The Islamic Review,* December 1967, pp. 3–4.

Fowler, James. *Stages of Faith.* New York: Harper and Row, 1981.

Gabrieli, Francesco. *Muhammad and the Conquests of Islam.* New York: McGraw-Hill, 1968.

Al-Ghanoushi, Rashid. "What We Need Is a Realistic Fundamentalism." *Arabia: The Islamic World Review,* October 1986, pp. 13–15.

Ghayur, Arif. "Ethnic Distribution of American Muslims and Selected Socio-Economic Characteristics." *Journal Institute of Muslim Minority Affairs* 5 (January 1984): 47.

Gillespie, V. Bailey. *Religious Conversion and Personal Identity: How and Why People Change.* Birmingham, Ala.: Religious Education Press, 1979.

Gottesman, Lois. "Islam in America." *Islamic Review,* June–July 1983, p. 8.

————. "Islam in America: An Old Religion Seeks a New Place in American Society." *USA Today,* May 1980, p. 27.

Haddad, Abdul-Majid. "A Sitting with Fathi Yakan." *Islamic Horizons,* May 1983, p. 7.

Haddad, Yvonne Yazbeck. "Arab Muslims and Islamic Institutions in America: Adaptation and Reform." In *Arabs in the New World.* Edited by Sameer Y. Abraham and Nabeel Abraham. Detroit:

Wayne State University Press, 1983.

————. "Islam in America." *The Muslim World League Journal*, July 1982, pp. 30–34.

————. "Muslims in America: A Select Bibliography." *The Muslim World*, April 1986, p. 93.

————. "Muslims in Canada: A Preliminary Study." In *Religion and Ethnicity*. Edited by Harold Coward and Leslie Kawamura. Waterloo, Ont.: Wilfred Laurier University Press, 1978, pp. 71–100.

———— "Muslims in the United States." In *Islam: The Religious and Political Life of a World Community*. Edited by Marjorie Kelley. New York: Praeger, 1984.

Haddad, Yvonne Yazbeck, and Lummis, Adair T. *Islamic Values in the United States: A Comparative Study*. New York: Oxford University Press, 1987.

Haddad, Yvonne, Haines, Byron, and Findly, Ellison. *The Islamic Impact*. Syracuse: Syracuse University Press, 1984.

Haider, Gulzar. "Canadian Saturdays, Pakistani Sundays." *Whole Earth Review*, Winter 1985, p. 38.

Hamdani, Daood Hassan. "Muslims and Christian Life in Canada." *Journal Institute of Muslim Minority Affairs* 1 (May 1979): 51.

————. "Muslims in the Canadian Mosaic." *Journal Institute of Muslim Minority Affairs* 5 (January 1984): 7.

Hathout, Maher, "Muslim Americans' Dilemma: A Response." *Arabia: The Islamic World Review*, July 1987, p. 47.

Hayes, Herbert E. E. "Sufism in the West." *The Moslem World* 7 (1917).

Heirich, Max. "Change of Heart: A Test of Some Widely Held Theories About Religious Conversion." *American Journal of Sociology*, November 1977, pp. 653ff.

Henningsson, Jan. "Att Utbreda Guds Rike—Ett Uppdrag för Både Kristna och Muslimer?" *Svensk Missionstidskrift* 3 (1983): 1ff.

Hobohm, Mohummed Aman. *Islam's Answer to the Racial Problem*. Durban, S.A.: Islamic Propagation Centre, 1983.

————. "Why Do Westerners Embrace Islam?" In *Islam Our Choice*. Woking, England, 1961, pp. 161–162.

Hodgson, Marshall G. S. *The Venture of Islam*, 3 vols. Chicago: University of Chicago Press, 1974.

Holmes, Mary Caroline. "Islam in America." *Moslem World* 16 (July 1926): 262ff.

Hunwick, J. O. *Islam in Africa: Friend or Foe?* Accra: Ghana Universities Press, 1976.

Hussain, S. Mazhar, ed. *Proceedings of the First Islamic Conference of North America*. New York: Muslim World League, 1977.

Idris, Gaafar Sheikh. *The Process of Islamization.* Indianapolis: Muslim Student's Association, 1977.

Imran, Maulana Muhammad. *The Importance of Da'wah (Tabligh) in Islam.* Lahore: M. Siraj-ud-Din and Sons, 1976.

Inniger, Merlin W. "The Ahmadiya Movement: Islamic Renewal?" In *Dynamic Religious Movements.* Edited by David J. Hesselgrave. Grand Rapids, Mich.: Baker Book House, 1978.

"The International Institute of Islamic and Arabic Studies." Bloomington, Ind.: International Institute of Islamic and Arabic Studies, n.d.

"The International Institute of Islamic Thought." Washington, D.C.: International Institute of Islamic Thought, n.d.

"Introducing the Institute of Islamic Information and Education." Chicago, Il.: Institute of Islamic Information and Education, n.d.

"Islam and the Kingdom of God." In *The MacDonald Presentation Volume.* Princeton, N.J.: Princeton University Press, 1933.

"The Islamic Center of New England." Quincy, Mass.: The Islamic Center of New England, n.d.

"The Islamic Information Center of America." Des Plaines, Il.: Islamic Information Center of America, n.d.

"The Islamic Society of North America." Plainfield, Ind.: Islamic Society of North America, n.d.

Iqbal, Sheikh Muhammad. *The Mission of Islam.* New Delhi: Vikas Publishing House, 1977.

Irving, Thomas B. "Islam and Social Responsibility." In *Islam: Its Meaning and Message.* Edited by Khurshid Ahmad. Leicester: The Islamic Foundation, 1975.

Islahi, Amin Ahsan. *Call to Islam and How the Holy Prophets Preached.* Safat, Kuwait: Islamic Book Publishers, 1978.

"Islam at a Glance." *Arabia: The Islamic World Review,* July 1987, p. 19.

"Islam at a Glance." Brochure. Plainfield, Ind.: Islamic Teaching Center, n.d.

"Islam in Its Clearest Simplicity." *Pyam-E-Aman,* April–June 1985, pp. 13–15.

"Islam on the March!" Brochure. Durban, S.A.: Islamic Propagation Center, n.d.

Islamic Correspondence Course. Indianapolis: Muslim Student Association, 1982.

"The Islamic Foundation at a Glance." Brochure. Leicester: The Islamic Foundation, 1985.

Jafarey, N. Hassan. "Muslim Americans' Dilemma." *Arabia: The Islamic World Review,* April 1987, p. 46.

Jameelah, Maryam. *Correspondence Between Maulana Maudoodi and*

Maryam Jameelah. Lahore: Mohammad Yusuf Khan and Sons, 1969.

———. *Islam Versus Ahl al-Kitāb: Past and Present*. Lahore: Mohammad Yusuf Khan and Sons, 1978.

James, William. *The Varieties of Religious Experience*. New York: New American Library, 1958.

Al-Jibouri, Yasin T. *A Brief History of the International Islamic Society of Virginia, Inc*. Falls Church, Va.: International Islamic Society of Virginia, n.d.

———. *A Brief History of the Islamic Society of Georgia, Inc*. Atlanta: Islamic Society of Georgia, n.d.

Al-Jindī, Ānwar. *Āfāq Jadīda lil-Daʿwah al-Islamiyya fī ʿĀlam al-Gharb*. Beirut: Muʾassasa al-Risāla, 1984.

Johnson, Steve A. *Daʿwah to Americans: Theory and Practice*. Plainfield, Ind.: Islamic Society of North America, 1984.

———. "Effectively Advertising a Daʿwah Activity: A Step-by-Step Approach." In *Let Us Learn: Issues of Your Concern*. Edited by Abdel-Hadi Omer. Beloit, Wisc.: By the Editor, 1987, pp. 9–13.

Kasule, Omer, "Communications." In *Let Us Learn: Issues of Your Concern*. Edited by Abdel-Hadi Omer. Beloit, Wisc.: By the Editor, 1987, pp. 2–8.

Kateregga, Badru, and Shenk, David W. *Islam and Christianity*. Grand Rapids, Mich.: William B. Eerdmans Publishing Co., 1980.

Kerr, Malcolm. *Islamic Reform: The Political and Legal Theories of Muhammad ʿAbduh and Rashīd Rīdā*. Berkeley: University of California Press, 1966.

Khan, Hadhrat Saeed Ahmad. "Future Role of the Ahmadiyya as a Missionary Movement." *Islamic Review*, March–April 1983.

Khan, Mrs. Nafees-El-Batool. "A Study on Conversion." *Al-Ittihad*, July–October 1977, pp. 37–48.

Khurshid, Muhammad. *Daʿwah in Islam*. Houston: Islamic Education Council, n.d.

"Know Your MSA." Brochure. Plainfield, Ind.: The Muslim Student Association of the United States and Canada, n.d.

Latourette, K. S. *A History of Christianity*, 2 vols. New York: Harper and Row, 1953, 1975.

———. *A History of the Expansion of Christianity*, 7 vols. Grand Rapids, Mich.: Zondervan Publishing House, 1970.

Levtzion, Nehemia. *Conversion to Islam*. New York: Holmes and Meier Publishers, 1979.

———. "Conversion Under Muslim Domination: A Comparative Study." In *Religious Change and Cultural Domination*. Edited by David N.

Lorenzen. Mexico City, Mexico: El Colegio de Mexico, 1981.

―――. "Toward a Comparative Study of Islamization." In *Conversion to Islam*. Edited by Nehemia Levtzion. New York: Holmes and Meier Publishers, 1979, pp. 1–23.

Lewis, Bernard. *Islam from the Prophet Muhammad to the Capture of Constantinople*, 2 vols. New York: Harper Torchbooks, 1974.

Lincoln, C. Erik. *The Black Muslims in America*. Boston: Beacon Press, 1961.

Lofland, John, and Stark, Rodney. "Becoming a World-Saver: A Theory of Conversion to a Deviant Perspective." *American Sociological Review*, December 1965, pp. 862ff.

Lovell, Emily Kalled. "A Survey of the Arab Muslims in the United States and Canada." *Muslim World* 63 (April 1973): 139ff.

Lovering, Kerry. "Tough at Home, Aggressive Abroad: Islam on the March." *Muslim World Pulse*, August 1979.

A Manual for Islamic Weekend and Summer Schools. Indianapolis: Muslim Student Association, 1981.

Manual of Da'wah for Islamic Workers. Montreal: Islamic Circle of North America, 1983.

Al-Maqdissi, Nadim. "The Muslims of America." *The Islamic Review*, June 1985, pp. 28ff.

Martin, B. G. *Muslim Brotherhoods in Nineteenth Century Africa*. New York: Cambridge University Press, 1976.

Marty, Martin E. *A Nation of Behavers*. Chicago: University of Chicago Press, 1976.

―――. *Religion and Republic*. Boston: Beacon Press, 1987. "Maryam Jameelah Answers Questions About Women." *Al-Ummah*, September 1985, pp. 6–7.

Mawdūdī, Abul A'lā. *Guideline for Workers*. Translated by Nawli Ali. Lahore: Islamic Publications, 1981.

―――. *Islam: An Historical Perspective*. Translated by Khurram Murad. Leicester: The Islamic Foundation, 1974.

―――. *The Islamic Movement: Dynamics of Values, Power and Change*. Translated by Khurram Murad. Leicester: The Islamic Foundation, 1984.

―――. *Tadhkira Du'āh al-Islām*. Cairo: Dar al-Ansar, 1397 H. (1976–77).

―――. *Towards Understanding Islam*. Leicester: The Islamic Foundation, 1980.

―――. *What Islam Stands For*. Plainfield, Ind.: Muslim Students Association of the U.S. and Canada, 1981.

―――. *Witnesses unto Mankind: The Purpose and Duty of the Muslim Ummah*. Translated by Khurram Murad. Leicester: The Islamic Foundation, 1986.

McGavran, Donald. *Understanding Church Growth*. Grand Rapids, Mich.: William B. Eerdmans Publishing Co., 1970.

Mehdi, Beverlee Turner. *The Arabs in America 1492–1977*. New York: Oceana Publications, 1978.

Mitchell, Richard P. *The Society of the Muslim Brothers*. London: Oxford University Press, 1969.

Mohran, Khadiga. "Not by the Sword." *Arabia: The Islamic World Review*, December 1986, p. 68.

Mortimer, Edward. *Faith and Power*. New York: Vintage Books, 1982.

"MSA and Family Builds in the U.S." *Arabia: The Islamic World Review*, May 1983, p. 63.

Muhammad, Akbar. "Muslims in the United States." In *The Islamic Impact*. Edited by Yvonne Hadded et al. Syracuse: Syracuse University Press, 1984.

———. "Some Factors Which Promote and Restrict Islamization in America." *American Journal of Islamic Studies*, August 1984, pp. 41–50.

Muhammad, Maulana Hafiz Sher. "Who Is a Muslim?" *Islamic Review*, August–September 1982, pp. 3ff.

Muhammad, Mian Tufail. "The Islamic Agenda in North America." *Impact International*, October–November 1974, pp. 9–10.

Murad, Khurram Jah. *Da'wah Among Non-Muslims in the West*. London: The Islamic Foundation, 1986.

———. *Islamic Movement in the West*. London: The Islamic Foundation, 1981.

———. "Third Opportunity to Keep Islam in the West." *Islamic Horizons*, November 1986, p. 10.

Murghani, Sheikh Sharafuddin. "When in Rome. ..." *Arabia: The Islamic World Review*, May 1987, p. 46.

"Muslim Organizations in the West: An Overview." *Arabia: The Islamic World Review*, December 1986, pp. 24–25.

Nadwi, Syed Abu'l-Hasan Ali. *Muslims in the West: The Message and Mission*. Leicester: The Islamic Foundation, 1983.

Naff, Alixa. "Arabs in America: A Historical Overview." In *Arabs in the New World*. Edited by Sameer Y. Abraham and Nabeel Abraham. Detroit: Wayne State University Press, 1983.

Nasr, Seyyed Hossein. "Present Tendencies, Future Trends." In *Islam: The Religious and Political Life of a World Community*. Edited by Marjorie Kelley. New York: Praeger, 1984.

Needleman, Jacob. *The New Religions*. New York: E. P. Dutton and Co., 1977.

Neill, Stephen. *A History of Christian Missions*. New York: Penguin Books, 1964.

Nicholson, Reynold. "Sufis: The Mystics of Islam." In *Understanding Mysticism*. Edited by Richard Woods. New York: Image Books, 1980, pp. 179–191.

Nyang, Sulayman S. "Islam in the United States of America: A Review of the Sources." *Islamic Culture*, April 1981, pp. 93–109.

————. "The Stuff That Dreams Are Made Of." *Arabia: The Islamic World Review*, November 1982, p. 24.

Nyang, Sulayman S., and Ahmad, Mumtaz. "The Muslim Intellectual Emigre in the United States." *Islamic Culture*, July 1985, pp. 277–290.

Omer, Abdel-Hadi, ed. *Let Us Learn: Issues of Your Concern*. Beloit, Wisc.: By the Editor, 1987.

"An Open Letter to the President." Letter distributed at the 24th Annual Convention of the Islamic Society of North America, Peoria, Illinois, September 4–7, 1987.

Osman, Fathi. "Islam: The Status of Non-Muslims." *Arabia: The Islamic World Review*, January 1987, p. 40.

————. "Towards a Better Presentation of Islam." *Arabia: The Islamic World Review*, July 1987, p. 33.

Parrucci, Dennis J. "Religious Conversion: A Theory of Deviant Behavior." *Sociological Analysis* 29 (Fall 1968): 144ff.

Peters, Rudolph. *Islam and Colonialism: The Doctrine of Jihād in Modern History*. New York: Mouton, 1979.

Plowman, Edward E. "The Muslims in Our Midst." *Christianity Today*, May 2, 1980, p. 30.

Rahman, Fazlur. *Islam*. Chicago: University of Chicago Press, 1966.

————. *Major Themes of the Qur'ān*. Chicago: Bibliotheca Islamica, 1980.

Rao, K. S. Ramakrishma. *Muhummed: The Prophet of Islam*. Durban, S.A.: Islamic Propagation Centre, 1985.

Rehma, Beshir Adam. "How to Establish an Islamic Center: A Step-by-Step Approach." In *Let Us Learn: Issues of Your Concern*. Edited by Abdel-Hadi Omer. Beloit, Wisc.: By the Editor, 1987, pp. 52–74.

Renard, John. "Understanding the World of Islam." *America*, October 20, 1979, p. 207.

Renoux, Jean-Andre. *L'Islam et la Conquēte du Monde*. Carpentras, France: Cercidium, 1981.

Richardson, E. Allen. *Islamic Cultures in North America*. New York: The Pilgrim Press, 1981.

Rizvi, S. A. A. "Islamic Proselytization." In *Religion in South Asia*. Edited by G. A. Oddie. New Delhi: Manobar, 1977.

Roberts, F. J. "Some Psychological Factors in Religious Conversion." *British Journal of Social and Clinical Psychology*, 1965, pp. 185–87.

Said, Edward. *Covering Islam*. London: Routledge and Kegan Paul, 1981.

Sakr, Ahmad. "Islamic Da'wa: Some Problems." *Muslim World League Journal* 8 (1979): 14–16.

Salzman, Leon. "The Psychology of Religious and Ideological Conversion." *Psychiatry* 16 (May 1953): 177–87.

Al-Samad, Mrs. Ulfat Azīz. *Islam and Christianity*. Riyadh: Presidency of Islamic Research, IFTA, and Propagation, 1984.

Saqr, 'Abd al-Badī'. *Kayfa Nad'u al-Nās?* Cairo, Egypt: Maktaba Wahba, 1980.

Saunders, J. E. *A History of Medieval Islam*. London: Routledge and Kegan Paul, 1965.

Seggar, J., and Kunz, P. "Conversion: Evaluation of a Step-Like Process for Problem-Solving." *Review of Religious Research*, 1972, pp. 178–184.

Shaban, M. "Conversion to Early Islam." In *Conversion to Islam*. Edited by Nehemia Levtzion. New York: Holmes and Meier Publishers, 1979, pp. 24–29.

Shadid, Muhammad. *Al-Jihād fi 'l-Islām*. Cairo: Mu'assasat al-Matbū'āt al-Hadithah, n.d.

Shafaat, Ahmad. *The Gospel According to Islam*. New York: Vantage Press, 1979.

———. *Islam and Its Prophet: A Fulfillment of Biblical Prophecies*. Ville St. Laurent, Canada: Nur al-Islam Foundation. 1984.

———. *Missionary Christianity and Islam*, 2 vols. Montreal: NUR Media Services, 1982.

Shafaat, Ahmad, and Ansari, Irshad. *The Sign of Jonas: Is It Applicable to Jesus?* Ville St. Laurent, Canada: Nur al-Islam Foundation, n.d.

Sharafeldin, Ibnomer. "Motivation in Islamic Work." In *Let Us Learn: Issues of Your Concern*. Edited by Abdel-Hadi Omer. Beloit, Wisc.: By the Editor, 1987, pp. 157–164.

Sharpe, Eric J. "The Goals of Inter-Religious Dialogue." In *Truth and Dialogue in World Religions: Conflicting Truth Claims*. Edited by John Hick. Philadelphia: Westminster Press, 1974, pp. 77–95.

Shawarbi, Mahmoud Youssef. "The Federation of Islamic Associations in the United States of America and Canada." *Islamic Review*, October 1964, p. 37.

———. *Al-Islām w'al-Muslimūn fi 'l-Qāra al-Amrīkyya*. Cairo: Dar al-Qalam, 1963.

Siddiqui, A. "Islam and Missions: Mohammed or Christ?" *Arabia: The Islamic World Review*, July 1987, p. 30.

Siddiqi, M. Ahmadullah. "Strategy for an Islamic Movement in the U.S.: Why? Where? Who? How?" *Islamic Horizons*, January 1985, pp. 5ff.

Siddiqui, Muzammil H. "Muslims in a Non-Muslim Society." *Islamic Horizons*, May–June 1986, pp. 22ff.

Sidqī, Ni'mat. *Al-Jihād fī Sabīl Allāh*. Cairo: Dār al-I'tisān, 1975.

Spellman, Charles, Baskett, Glen, and Byrne, Donn. "Manifest Anxiety as a Contributing Factor in Religious Conversion." *Journal of Consulting and Clinical Psychology*, 1971, pp. 245–247.

Spener, Philip Jacob. *Pia Desideria*. Translated and edited by Theodore G. Tappert. Philadelphia: Fortress Press, 1964.

Spilka, Bernard, Hood, Ralph W., Jr., and Gorsuch, Richard L. *The Psychology of Religion: An Empirical Approach*. Englewood Cliffs, N.J.: Prentice-Hall, 1985.

Starbuck, Edwin D. *The Psychology of Religion*. New York: Charles Scribner's Sons, 1900.

Stein, K. James. *Philipp Jacob Spener: Pietist Patriarch*. Chicago: Covenant Press, 1986.

Suleiman, Michael W. "Arab-Americans: A Community Profile." *Journal Institute of Muslim Minority Affairs* 5 (January 1984): 29ff.

Sultan, Talat. "Needs and Requirements of Muslim Students in Public Schools." Letter distributed at the 24th Annual Convention of the Islamic Society of North America, Peoria, Illinois, September 4–7, 1987.

Tisdall, W. St. Clair. "Islam as a Missionary Religion." *The Moslem World* 4 (1914).

Trimingham, J. S. *The Sufi Orders in Islam*. Oxford: Clarendon Press, 1971.

Voll, John Obert. *Islam: Continuity and Change in the Modern World*. Boulder, Colo.: Westview Press, 1982.

Von Denffer, Ahmad. *Key Issues for Islamic Da'wah*. Delhi: Hindustan Publications, 1983.

Von Sicard, S. "Contemporary Islam and Its World Mission." *Missiology: An International Review*, July 1976.

Waddy, Charis. *The Muslim Mind*. New York: Longman, 1976.

Watt, W. Montgomery. *Islamic Political Thought*. Edinburgh: University Press, 1968.

Waugh, Earle H., Abu-Laban, Baha, and Qureshi, Regula B., eds. *The Muslim Community in North America*. Edmonton: University of Alberta Press, 1983.

Webb, Mohammed Alexander Russell. *Islam in America*. New York: The Oriental Publishing Co., 1893.

Whaling, Frank. "A Comparative Religious Study of Missionary Transplantation in Buddhism, Christianity and Islam." *International Review of Mission* 70 (October 1981): 314ff.

Wolf, C. Umhau. "Muslims in the American Midwest." *Muslim World* 50 (January 1960): 39ff.

Yacoob, May Mirza. "The Ahmadiyya: Urban Adaptation in the Ivory Coast." Ph.D. diss. Boston University Graduate School, 1980.

Yakan, Fathi. *Islamic Movement: Problems and Perspectives.* Indianapolis: American Trust Publications, 1984.'

———. *Al-Istī'āb fī Hayāh al-Da'wah w'al-Dā'iyah.* Beirut: Mu'assasa al-Risāla, 1983.

———. *Kayfa Nad'u ila'l-Islām?* Beirut: Mu'assasa al-Risāla, 1980.

———. *Qawārib al-Najah fī Hayah al-Du'āh.* Beirut: Mu'assasa al-Risāla, 1983.

Younis, Adele L. "The First Muslims in America: Impressions and Reminiscences." *Journal Institute of Muslim Minority Affairs* 5 (January 1984): 17ff.

Yunus, Ilyas. *Muslims in North America: Problems and Prospects.* Indianapolis: Muslim Student Association, 1974.

Testimonies of Converts to Islam

Abu-Ghosh, Ann. "Why I Became A Muslim." *The Invitation* 3 (December 1986): 3.

Ahmad, Selim. "Islam My Choice." *Islamic Review*, August–September 1983.

Aitken, Luzita Fatima. "Why I Accepted Islam." *Muslim News International*, October 1969, pp. 14–15.

Ali, Nancy. "Testimony." *Newsletter of the Islamic Information Center of America*, May 1984, p. 1.

Al-Amin, Wadiah. "Islam Gave Me a Sense of Dignity." *Islamic Horizons*, September 1979, pp. 8–9.

Asad, Muhammad. *The Road to Mecca.* London: Max Reinhardt, 1954.

Benjelloun, Amina. "Why I Am a Muslim." *Islamic Horizons*, September 1984, p. 6.

Chattopadhyaya, Nishikanta. *Why Have I Embraced Islam?* Chicago: Kazi Publications, n.d.

Chipperfield, P. E. Sa'eed. "Why I Joined the World Brotherhood of Islam." *Islamic Review*, December 1952, pp. 14–15.

Clark, Peter. *Marmaduke Pickthall: British Muslim.* New York: Quartet Books, 1986.

Clayton, Thomas Muhammad. "Why I Embraced Islam." *Islamic Review*, September 1949, pp. 20–21.

Cohen, Sylvia E. Salma. "At the Threshold of Islam." *Islamic Review*, September 1953, p. 19.

Connolly, Cecilia Mahmuda. "Islam My Choice." *Islamic Review*, June–July 1983, pp. 15–16.

Davis, B. "Why Islam Satisfies Me." *Islamic Review*, November 1949, p. 35.

Dickenson, R. C. "My Approach to Islam." *Islamic Review*, January 1950, p. 40.

Al-Farooq, Al-Hajj Lord Headley. "Islam My Choice." *Islamic Review*, May 1983, pp. 14–19.

Fellowes, H. F. "Why I Accepted Islam." *Muslim News International*, June 1968, pp. 17–18.

Flowers, Reverend R. J. "Why I Accepted Islam." *Islamic Review*, August 1961, p. 20.

Germanus, Abd al-Karim. "Why I Accepted Islam." *Muslim News International*, July 1968, pp. 31–32.

Hames, Michael. "What Attracts Me in Islam." *Islamic Review*, February 1959, pp. 17–18.

Hamilton, Archibald. "Islam My Choice." *Islamic Review*, June–July 1983, p. 15.

Henkel, Harry E. "Islam My Choice." *Islamic Review*, June–July 1983, p. 16.

Hienekamp, Ahmad M. "Impressions of a Convert." *Muslim News International*, March 1969, pp. 35–36.

Hill, Jeanette D. Salma. "The Story of My Becoming a Muslim." *Islamic Review*, March 1954, pp. 25–28.

Howard-Smith, Abd al-Rashid Derek. "How I Came to Embrace Islam." *Islamic Review*, January 1952, pp. 42–43.

Howe, Jalal-ud-Din. "At the Threshold of Islam." *Islamic Review*, June 1953, pp. 32–33.

Irving, T. B. "An Old Convert Recalls His Story and Experiences." *Islamic Order* 3 (1981): 50–57.

Jameelah, Maryam. *Why I Embraced Islam*. Lahore: Mohammad Yusuf Khan and Sons, 1978.

Johnson, Steve. "Seed, Flower, Fruit: The Search That Ended in Islam." *Islamic Horizons*, October 1985, pp. 5–6.

Jolly, Mavis B. "Why I Accepted Islam." *Muslim News International*, November 1968, pp. 38–39.

Leon, H. M. "Islam My Choice." *Islamic Review*, August–September 1983, pp. 18–19.

Lewin, H. S. "Why I Joined the World Brotherhood of Islam." *Islamic Review*, July–August 1958, p. 47.

Marcus, Hamid. "Islam My Choice." *Islamic Review*, October–November 1983, p. 13.

Marcus, Margaret [Maryam Jameelah]. "How I Became Interested in Islam." *The Islamic Review*, April 1961, pp. 8–9.

Mellema, R. L. "What Has Attracted Me to Islam." *Islamic Review*, July 1960, pp. 24–25.

Moore, Abd al-Hayy Daniel. "Choosing Islam: One Man's Tale." *Whole Earth Review*, Winter 1985, p. 16.

Al-Nasir, Muhammad. "How I Came to Islam." *Islamic Review*, June 1954, p. 19.

Overing, Fauzuddin Ahmad. "How and Why I Encountered the Religion of Islam." *Islamic Review*, August 1950, p. 40.

————. "Islam My Choice." *Islamic Review*, December 1983, p. 8.

Pickard, William Burchell Bashyr. "Why I Accepted Islam." *Muslim News International*, October 1968, p. 39.

Plant, Jamil Abd al-Shukoor. "At the Threshold of Islam." *Islamic Review*, April 1953, p. 22.

Priestley, Hussain R. L. "Why I Became a Muslim." *Islamic Review*, September 1957, pp. 32–33.

Robinson, Percy. "Islam My Choice." *Islamic Review*, December 1983, p. 8.

Rofe, Hussain."Why I Accepted Islam." *Muslim News International*, August 1968, p. 34.

Ruxton, J. F. "Why I Embraced Islam." *Islamic Review*, June 1959, pp. 30–31.

Saleem, Sara. "These Were Happy People." *Arabia: The Islamic World Review*, December 1986, pp. 65–66.

Shah, Samia. "Testimony." *Newsletter of the Islamic Information Center of America*, October 1984, p. 3.

Sims, Harold A. "On Becoming a Muslim." *Islamic Review*, April 1949, p. 49.

Smith, Cheryl. "Testimony." *Islamic Affairs*, October–November 1977, p. 4.

Smith, Russell. "The Former Cat Steven's Peace Training." *Chicago Tribune*, October 28, 1987, sec. 4, p. 3.

Steinmann, Masʻudah. "Why I Accepted Islam." *Muslim News International*, January 1969, p. 39.

————. "Why I Am Impressed by Islam." *Islamic Review*, September–October 1959, pp. 23–24.

Tunison, Emory H. "Mohammed Alexander Russell Webb: First American Muslim." *The Arab World* 3 (1945): 13–18.

Van der Grijn, Fatimah J. B. "Why I Accepted Islam." *Islamic Review*, March–April 1960, p. 29.

Von Ehrenfels, Umar Rolf. "The How and Why of Conversion to Islam." *Islamic Review*, June 1961, pp. 23–24.

Wagener, Feysal W. "Islam My Choice." *Islamic Review*, October–November 1983, p. 13.

————. "Why I Joined Islam." *Islamic Review*, December 1952, p. 22.

Walser, Hediye-Heidi. "My Choice of Islam." *Islamic Review*, October 1964, pp. 36–37.

Warrington-Fry, Denis. "Why I Have Accepted Islam as My Faith." *Islamic Review*, October 1951, p. 44.

Zejierski, Ismail Wieslaw. "Why I Accepted Islam." *Muslim News International*, February 1969, p. 39.

INDEX